Anya Mali, Ph.D. (1991) in Comparative Religion, Hebrew University of Jerusalem, has published several articles on Church history and Christian mysticism. She is currently a Research Fellow at the Franz Rosenzweig Center, Hebrew University.

MYSTIC IN
THE NEW WORLD

STUDIES IN THE HISTORY
OF
CHRISTIAN THOUGHT

EDITED BY

HEIKO A. OBERMAN, Tucson, Arizona

IN COOPERATION WITH

HENRY CHADWICK, Cambridge
JAROSLAV PELIKAN, New Haven, Connecticut
BRIAN TIERNEY, Ithaca, New York
ARJO VANDERJAGT, Groningen

VOLUME LXXII

ANYA MALI

MYSTIC IN
THE NEW WORLD

TUTA SUB AEGIDE PALLAS
· 1683 ·

MYSTIC IN THE NEW WORLD

MARIE DE L'INCARNATION
(1599–1672)

BY

ANYA MALI

E.J. BRILL
LEIDEN · NEW YORK · KÖLN
1996

The paper in this book meets the guidelines for permanence and durability of the Committee on Production Guidelines for Book Longevity of the Council on Library Resources.

Library of Congress Cataloging-in-Publication Data

Mali, Anya.
    Mystic in the new world : Marie de l'Incarnation (1599-1672) / by Anya Mali.
        p.   cm. — (Studies in the history of Christian thought, ISSN 0081–8607 ; v. 72)
    Includes bibliographical references and indexes.
    ISBN 9004106065 (cloth : alk. paper)
    1. Marie de l'Incarnation, mère, 1599-1672. 2. Ursulines—Québec (Province)—Biography. 3. Missionaries—Québec (Province)–
–Biography. 4. Mystics—Québec (Province)—Biography.   I. Title.
II. Series.
BX4705.M3564M35   1996
271'.97402—dc20
[B]

                                       96–32576
                                       CIP

Die Deutsche Bibliothek - CIP-Einheitsaufnahme

Mali, Anya:
Mystic in the new world : Marie de l'Incarnation (1599 - 1672) / by Anya Mali. – Leiden ; New York ; Köln : Brill, 1996
  (Studies in the history of Christian thought ; Vol. 72)
  ISBN 90–04–10606–5
NE: GT

ISSN 0081-8607
ISBN 90 04 10606 5

PRINTED IN THE NETHERLANDS

For my parents — with love and thanks

CONTENTS

Acknowledgements ix
Abbreviations xi
Preface xiii

I.   The Meanings of Tradition:
     Marie's Religious Formation 1

II. The Dynamics of Conversion:
     Marie's Mystical Transformation 32

III. Sublime States and Divine Duties:
     Marie's Spiritual Autobiography 56

IV. New France: Frozen Earth, Heavenly Splendour 90

V.   The Harvest of Souls:
     Marie's Missionary Activity 108

VI. The Ascent of Souls:
     Marie's Spiritual Teaching 134

Epilogue: Images of the Other
and Mysticism in the New World 164

Bibliography 174

Index of Names 183

Index of Subjects 187

ACKNOWLEDGEMENTS

Over the years in which the present study was written, I received assistance from many sources and was fortunate to meet with several people whose interest in mystical literature and traditions has spurred my own. In one way or another this book owes much to those encounters, though responsibility for its contents is my own.

I would like first to thank Heiko Oberman for his careful reading of the manuscript and for accepting this study for the HISTORY OF CHRISTIAN THOUGHT series. I owe a special debt of gratitude to R.J. Zwi Werblowsky, an inspiring teacher and amiable thesis supervisor, who has shown great faith in my work over the years, offering wise counsel and prompt assistance from near and far whenever it was needed. Warm thanks are also due to Andrew Louth and to Dom Guy Oury for being so generous with their time, comments and encouragement over the years.

Michael Heyd and Bernard McGinn read the first version of this study, and their detailed critical comments were extremely useful. I am also grateful to Ghislaine Boucher, Elfrieda Dubois, Marcel Dubois, Cornelius Jaenen, Guy Stroumsa, Avihu Zakai and the late Amos Funkenstein, all of whom read parts of the manuscript at various stages and were most helpful with their comments. Thanks also to Arie Shahar for supporting this project and to Josef Schmidt who first introduced me to Marie de l'Incarnation. I am indebted to all the friends who helped me to get the task done, and in particular to Yohanan Elihai (Jerusalem) and Sister Seraphina (Oxford) for illuminating some basic issues.

This book evolved out of my doctoral thesis, submitted to the Hebrew University of Jerusalem in 1990. I would like to express my thanks to the F.C.A.R. (Québec), the S.S.H.R.C.C. (Canada), the Lady Davis Fellowship Trust, the Rothschild Foundation, and the Israel Association for Canadian Studies for research funds which made this work possible. A grant from Yad Avi Hayishuv helped fund preparation of the final manuscript.

Finally, I must extend my fondest thanks to my husband Josi, whose unshakeable common sense was an indispensable aid at all stages of the work, and to my children Maya, Daniella and Tom, whose exuberance knows no bounds — for which I am very grateful.

I have drawn on material from *History of European Ideas*, 22/2, A. Mali, "Strange Encounters: Missionary Activity and Mystical Thought in Seventeenth-Century New France," pp. 67–92, Copyright 1996 with kind permission of Elsevier Science; and from *Studies in Spirituality* 2, A. Mali, "Patterns of Conversion in Christianity," pp. 209–222, Copyright 1992 with kind permission of the editors. I am also grateful to Loyola University Press for permission to quote from J. Sullivan, trans. *The Autobiography of Venerable Marie of the Incarnation*, Copyright 1964.

ABBREVIATIONS*

A = *The Autobiography of Venerable Marie of the Incarnation, O.S.U. Mystic and Missionary.* Trans. John Sullivan, Chicago: Loyola University Press, 1964.

E = *Marie de l'Incarnation, Ursuline de Tours: Fondatrice des Ursulines de la Nouvelle-France, Écrits spirituels et historiques* (Tours & Québec) 2 vols. Ed. Dom A. Jamet. (1929) Québec: Les Ursulines de Québec, 1985.

C = *Marie de l'Incarnation, Ursuline (1599–1672), Corréspondance.* Ed. Dom G.-M. Oury, Solesmes: Abbaye Saint-Pierre, 1971.

Unless otherwise indicated, all translations of quotations into English are my own.

PREFACE

A century before the scientific revolution upset the European view of the world and nature of things, the discovery of the New World played an important role in breaking political, religious and also epistemological boundaries. Like other travellers to the New World and like other European thinkers of the period, Christian missionaries were faced with previously unknown places, peoples, and the very idea of "newness." The "discovery" widened not only their knowledge of the world, but also their horizons of understanding, as they realized that traditional or preconceived categories could no longer account adequately for the new reality confronting them. They had to be respectful of the past, but at the same time flexible in their pursuit of knowledge. To use Anthony Pagden's words, "modern man had no choice but to be a rational experimentalist, true to the word of God, ... but experimental in his own inquiries."[1]

The activity of missionaries in New France in the seventeenth century illustrates just such a mixture of reverence for the old and attentiveness to the new. For the missionaries brought their traditional notions and religious training to bear on their encounter with the Amerindians, but were soon compelled to adjust their approach to the natives and to the very idea of conversion. In 1632 the Jesuit missionary Paul Le Jeune, newly arrived in the wilderness of New France and faced with the foreignness of the tribes he encountered there, wrote these words:

> When a person first visits a country, he writes a great many things upon the words of others, believing them to be true; [but] time reveals the truth. I have been told many different things about the customs of these tribes; we shall have time enough to learn how true they are.[2]

The Jesuits' first encounter with the natives of the New World had of course been in the Old World where, having read earlier missionary accounts and travel literature, they formed their initial image of the

[1] A. Pagden, "'The Impact of the New World on the Old': The History of an Idea," *Renaissance and Modern Studies* 30 (1986), p. 3.

[2] R.G. Thwaites, ed., *The Jesuit Relations and Allied Documents*, 73 vols., Cleveland 1876–1901, vol. 5, p. 115.

Amerindians as simple, pagan beings, devoid of reason, religion and culture.[3] Once they settled in the new colony, however, the Jesuits had "time enough to learn" that contrary to what "the words of others" had led them to believe, these natives did in fact have a culture of their own, and it was only by reckoning with it that the missionaries could hope to make any progress. The New World experience, however, had an impact not only on the cultural attitudes of the missionaries, but also on their spiritual development (and by extension, on what is loosely known as seventeenth-century mysticism in general). At the same time that Jesuit missionaries in the New World were describing the flora, fauna and native folk surrounding them (a meticulous undertaking which later earned them recognition as the fathers of modern-day ethnography), Jesuit theologians in Europe were engaged in the close scrutiny and systematic description of the minutiae of mystical experience — in effect making a science of mysticism — to help the Church bolster, and at the same time monitor, the spiritual life of its adherents. And yet the spiritual thought of the New World missionaries, though compatible with the traditional schemes of mystical ascent that were being hammered out by contemporary theologians, in fact added its own distinctive dimensions to this mystical tradition. Reduced to primitive living conditions and aspiring to spiritual heights, the missionaries strove to fulfil their personal spiritual goals while hacking out their active mission in the wilderness. And the result was novel forms of spiritual expression.

The life and writings of the Ursuline missionary Marie de l'Incarnation attest to the impact of this cultural encounter on the formation of spiritual identity in the colony and indeed indicate that in New France — as in Puritan New England — spiritual life and self-image were by no means a mere extension of what they had been in Europe, for new circumstances led to a shift in conventional religious notions, and in some cases to a radically new relationship with God.[4] As one of the first female missionaries to the New World and the author of a mystical autobiography which ranks among the finest in the spiritual literature of the day, Marie de l'Incarnation has long been seen as an exemplary type, reflecting the mood and aims of the Catholic Reformation. Renowned both as one of the

---

[3] O. Dickason, *The Myth of the Savage and the Beginnings of French Colonialism in the Americas*, Edmonton 1984, p. 205.

[4] D. Lovejoy, *Religious Enthusiasm in the New World: Heresy to Revolution*, Cambridge 1985, p. 5. See also C. Cohen, *God's Caress. The Psychology of Puritan Religious Experience*, Oxford 1986; and Avihu Zakai, *Exile and Kingdom: History and Apocalypse in the Puritan Migration to America*, Cambridge 1992.

founders of the Church in New France and as a major representative of seventeenth-century mysticism, she has been labelled the "Teresa of the New World," because like Teresa of Avila, she achieved a fine balance of action and contemplation in her religious life. Such portrayals, however, are misleading. For one thing they obscure the fact that this balancing act was in fact a source of pain and bewilderment for Marie, who overcame institutional obstacles and the seeming dissonance of her inner callings to achieve religious goals which were not in keeping with her sex and situation. For another, they perpetuate the popular but imprecise notion that mystical writing inevitably conforms to and recycles the standard, predictable images and patterns of the literary tradition in which it is embedded.

It has become a commonplace in the history of spirituality that mystical writing must be examined against the backdrop of the mystic's specific religious tradition, for as Gershom Scholem noted, "there is no such thing as mysticism in the abstract, that is to say, a phenomenon or experience which has no particular relation to other religious phenomena. There is no mysticism as such, there is only the mysticism of a particular religious system."[5] And tradition, it is argued, not only shapes the literary expression given to the experience after the fact, but also shapes *a priori* the experience itself.[6] However, this recognition of the conservative element in mystical experience — though a necessary corrective to those who would see mysticism in isolation from, or even in opposition to, an institutional framework or theological tradition — can lead to a certain methodological conservatism, and overdependence on existing classifications of mystics.

In studies on Christian mysticism, the general emphasis on tradition has strengthened the tendency to assess the mystic's experience according to "typical" patterns of mystical ascent, and the specific focus on a mystic's literary predecessors has encouraged scholars to enrol mystics in this or that "school" of mysticism, often without due attention being paid to the personal concerns reflected in spiritual texts.[7] The result is that particulars of spiritual thought are often passed over, and some interesting questions

[5] G. Scholem, *Major Trends in Jewish Mysticism*, New York 1941, pp. 5–6.

[6] S. Katz, "The 'Conservative' Character of Mysticism," in *Mysticism and Religious Traditions*, ed. S. Katz, Oxford 1983, pp. 3–60; see especially pp. 4–13.

[7] Evelyn Underhill considers the use of this threefold sequence "by different schools of contemplatives" to be "one of the many indirect testimonies to the objective reality of mysticism, and states in sweeping fashion that "the school for saints has never found it necessary to bring its curriculum up to date." See *Mysticism. A Study in the Nature and Development of Man's Spiritual Consciousness*, New York new ed. 1974, pp. 198f., 232f., 413f., and pp. 91–2.

are left unasked, such as what were the specific religious concerns in light of which the individuals in question interpreted their experience?

The following case-study of a missionary in seventeenth-century New France provides a good illustration of this problem. Marie de l'Incarnation's mysticism, with its unique emphasis on victimhood rather than spiritual marriage as the summit of mystical experience, was certainly informed by the images and schemes of her tradition, but also gave new and concrete meaning to old concepts, a meaning which can best be understood in light of the New World context in which it took shape. Because she has been seen primarily as a typical representative of Catholic Reformation spirituality, however, her mystical self-understanding — and specific contribution to the Christian mystical tradition — have not been adequately treated.

In this study I shall argue that Marie de l'Incarnation's life and works should not be examined exclusively in reference to broad trends in Catholic Reformation society, but more specifically against the backdrop of the new religious milieu in which her spiritual identity found its fulfilment and literary expression. For in the wake of her encounter with the natives of New France, she conferred new meaning on her perceived encounter with God and developed a spiritual identity quite distinct from that considered characteristic of the French school of mysticism.

Two major contributions in the first half of this century paved the way for critical research on Marie de l'Incarnation's life and writings. The first was Henri Bremond's presentation of her works in volume six of his *Histoire littéraire du sentiment religieux* in 1922.[8] In contrast to the handful of biographical and hagiographical works published in the nineteenth century, Bremond's major critical study of the Ursuline mystic aroused widespread interest among the significantly wider audience it reached. Another propitious event was the undertaking of the Benedictine scholar Dom Albert Jamet to publish a six-volume critical edition of Marie's spiritual writings and correspondence. A seventh volume was foreseen to meet the need for a critical biography of the renowned mystic. Jamet managed to complete only four of the planned volumes, two of which contain her "spiritual and historical writings," and the remaining two of which include many of her letters.[9] Dom Guy Oury, the foremost

---

[8] H. Bremond, *Histoire littéraire du sentiment religieux en France depuis la fin des guerres jusqu'à nos jours*, 12 vols., Paris 1923–1936, vol. 6, "La Conquête mystique, Marie de l'Incarnation," pp. 3–176.

[9] A. Jamet, ed., *Marie de l'Incarnation, Ursuline de Tours: Fondatrice des Ursulines de la*

scholar on Marie de l'Incarnation, published her existing correspondence
in its entirety in a new critical edition in 1971.[10] His critical biography of
Marie, published in 1973, and his numerous studies on her spiritual
thought have become indispensable aids for subsequent scholars in their
scrutiny of various aspects of her life and writings.

Research to date has tended, in general, to focus either on Marie de
l'Incarnation's mysticism or her missionary work, and although some
works do highlight the link between her apostolic and mystical experiences,
none deals specifically with "conversion" as the crux of the reciprocal
relationship between the two. I shall argue that both her missionary
activity and her spiritual life were marked by the experience of conversion,
which she herself underwent and came to understand more fully through
her contact with the Amerindians in the colony of New France. Though
she considered her conversion of 1620 to be a specific event and turning-
point in her life, she also perceived conversion as an ongoing process of
mystical growth. Her spiritual growth was influenced by her experience
among the natives, and so a certain dynamics of conversion can be
discerned, for her mystical experience was directed to, and fulfilled in, her
missionary activity, which in turn enriched her own ongoing spiritual
conversion.

The idea of conversion, then, is the key to understanding how Marie de
l'Incarnation perceived and worked out her calling to an active spirituality.
She referred to her own spiritual conversion at the age of twenty as the
turning-point in her life, an event which transformed her into a "new
creature" and initiated her into mystical life. Within the framework of her
mystical development, the conversion experience ultimately found expression in conversion activity. Both in her attempts to convert Indians to
Catholicism, as well as in her spiritual instruction of the nuns in her order,
she developed modes of conversion which reckoned with the emotions and
imagination of the individuals involved. When writing about the extraordinary and ineffable aspects of mystical transformation, she was also able
to manipulate images — even when negating their role — in order to hint
at the sublime nature of the divine reality which she had experienced.

In her own mystical writing, as well as in her conversion activity among
Indian girls and contemplative women, Marie de l'Incarnation's experience

---

Nouvelle-France, Écrits spirituels et historiques, (Tours & Québec), 2 vols., (1929) Québec,
1985.

[10] Guy-Marie Oury, ed., *Marie de l'Incarnation, Ursuline (1599–1672), Corréspondance*,
Solesmes 1971.

not only represents the broad trends underlying the Catholic reform movement in her day, but also serves as a good illustration of the cultural and psychological dynamics which affected individuals and their spiritual world in the seventeenth century. Far from being simply another cog in the spiritual machinery of the Catholic Reformation Church, she was a dynamic and determined individual, whose attempt to resolve her interior malaise led her from the cloister in Tours to the wilderness of Québec, where she composed a mystical work which injected novel nuances into the tried and true patterns of the Christian spiritual tradition.

CHAPTER ONE

THE MEANINGS OF TRADITION:
MARIE'S RELIGIOUS FORMATION

It is a commonplace in studies on mysticism that while spiritual experience — be it an interior conversion or mystical vision — is something highly personal which can radically transform the individual's identity, it is also a phenomenon which can only be understood in relation to the tradition in which the individual is rooted. And while this tradition provides the individual with the basic terms of reference and mental constructs for his or her experience of faith, its impact can be hindered or enhanced by a myriad of social and psychological factors.[1] Seen as a willed turning to God, spiritual conversion for example presupposes a certain emotional maturity on the part of the individual, who must attain a strong awareness of self before that self can radically change. This process of emotional and mental development, or growing sense of identity, is affected by various incidents and influences, by personal crises, by attachments to others, or even by stray impressions gleaned from one's surroundings.

The following sketch of the formative stage of Marie's religious life provides an overview of her social setting, religious milieu, and family life insofar as these shaped her character and contributed to the events — particularly her conversion experience at the age of twenty — that were to give her life a new direction. Her religious identity developed within the traditional Catholic framework, whose teachings she accepted without question; her personal experience was always verified within the theological confines and expressed in the religious language and imagery of the tradition which shaped her faith from the outset. Of particular import

---

[1] Recent studies on the concept of the individual make a distinction between the individual and the person, that is, between the self's awareness of a unique identity and society's assessment of the role and significance of that identity in a wider context. See M. Carrithers, S. Collins, and S. Lukes, eds., *The Category of the Person. Anthropology, Philosophy, History*, Cambridge 1985, esp. the essays by C. Taylor, pp. 257–281, and J.S. Lafontaine, pp. 123–140; and K. Weintraub, *The Value of the Individual. Self and Circumstance in Autobiography*, Chicago 1978.

were the agents and forms that mediated between Marie and the religious institution with which she identified. The Catholic tradition which informed her and to which she conformed in her younger years without much reflection or understanding, was an essential ingredient of her spiritual turning at the age of twenty; but this radical transformation, which marked the first step of her unique mystical journey, could only come about once Marie had reached a certain emotional and mental maturity, attained a better grasp of the teachings of her faith and developed a heightened sense of self in relation to God.[2] In a sense this was the crux of her spiritual life: the crossing of a strong personality with a rich religious tradition, the combination of an individual's direct experience of God and the context of mediated religious experience which, in Catholic terms, is the only proper framework for personal faith.

It may be useful here to say a few words about the idea of formation, which is the key to understanding Marie's mystical life in its incipient stage. The word "formation" is useful because it not only evokes the idea of organised learning and the inculcation of values, but also suggests the fact that religious training could be facilitated and enhanced by the *forms* used to confer religious knowledge and convey its moral or spiritual message more effectively. Apart from its importance with regard to Marie's religious development, this dual sense of formation is significant in the general context of the study since both of these concerns — the "ethos" of education *per se*, as well as the controversy over acceptable "forms" of religious faith — played a central role in the Protestant and Catholic reform movements, and bulked large in the religious consciousness of the seventeenth century.[3]

Religious formation, which pertains to the personality and spiritual life of the individual, can be seen as a gradual shaping as well as a formal

---

[2] Charles-André Bernard notes that both religious self-consciousness and a certain "reflective consciousness of one's religious acts" are necessary prerequisites for conversion. See his *Traité de théologie spirituelle*, Paris 1986, pp. 402–403. C. Taylor also writes "it is having a mind and self-consciousness that makes us a person." See "The person" in Carrithers et al., *The Category of the Person*, p. 280.

[3] See R. Chartier, D. Julia, and M.-M. Compère, *L'éducation en France du XVIe au XVIIe siècle*, Paris 1976. This work shows to what extent the school was one of the fundamental vehicles of diffusion for the Catholic and Protestant reforms, both of which recognized that literacy, and hence some form of schooling, were necessary for the work of "christianising" the masses. See also Jean de Viguerie, *L'institution des enfants. L'éducation en France. 16e–18e siècle*, Paris 1978. See also Leibniz's comment regarding the controversy over appropriate forms of faith in P. Hazard, *The European Mind 1680–1715*, trans. J. Lewis May, New York 1973, p. 261.

educative process. This sense of formation, which has early roots in the history of Christian thought, is best captured in the concept of *paideia* which was appropriated from classical culture and refitted in Christian garb to combine the idea of character moulding with the "idea of man's dignity and of his reformation and rebirth through the spirit."[4] As Werner Jaeger writes:

> What in Greek paideia had been the formation or morphosis of the human personality now becomes for the Christian the metamorphosis which Paul had spoken of when he wrote to the Romans asking them to undergo a process of radical metamorphosis through a renewal of their spirit.[5]

Formation in this Christian sense, then, connotes or promotes moral betterment or a process of spiritual perfection, and aims at an increase in personal virtue. The process is governed both by external influences and by the innate qualities of the individual on the receiving end. For, as Jaeger explains, "the spiritual process called education is not spontaneous in nature but requires constant care. The virtues, be they moral or intellectual, are the fruit of both a man's nature and his training."[6]

For the Christian it is of course understood that God guides this process of religious growth and ultimately determines both the shaping of an individual's personality and the efficacy of his training.[7] In fact it is the role attributed to divine assistance in determining religious formation that marks the pointed difference between the Christian and classical notions of *paideia* as the path to perfection.[8] Rather than broaching the broad theological issue of the cooperation of human effort and divine grace in

---

[4] W. Jaeger, *Early Christianity and Greek Paideia*, London 1962, p. 99. For Jaeger the concept of *paideia* represents a form of ancient Christian humanism, one that is akin to the Renaissance idea of spiritual rebirth.

[5] Ibid., pp. 97–98.

[6] Ibid., p. 87.

[7] In theological terms, especially in the writings of the Greek fathers, formation is seen in terms of personal spiritual reformation or the restoration of the image of God in the human soul. The individual's willed and intentional return to this perfect norm is distinct from the spiritual renewal effected by divine grace. See L.W. Spitz, "Reformation," *Dictionary of the History of Ideas*, vol. IV, New York 1973, pp. 60–69.

[8] The Christian doctrine of *creatio ex nihilo* rejected the Platonic idea of the soul's kinship with the divine. On the Christian view, the ontological divide between God and created man — both body and soul — means that the process of the soul's ascent necessarily requires God's help. See A. Louth, *The Origins of the Christian Mystical Tradition. From Plato to Denys*, Oxford 1983, pp. 26, 76–77; and Jaeger, *Early Christianity and Greek Paideia*, pp. 60–67.

shaping and transforming an individual's religious life, I shall concentrate here on the other two aspects mentioned: the character and training of the individual.

Paideia or 'formation' has been referred to as:

> what one has to undergo in order to grow up, and also what it is that one grows up into. Paideia suggests etymologically the rearing of a child (pais), and in its use it means education and what this makes available to us: broadly, culture.[9]

Formation is thus a process of cultural initiation. As Jaeger notes, "if we regard education as a process of shaping or forming, the object of learning plays the part of the mould by which the subject is shaped."[10] In the context of early patristic writing, Scripture was the prime formative instrument, seen to "educate" not only because it contains Christian teaching, but because it also transmits a pneumatic message. For Marie de l'Incarnation, who grew up in the age of post-Tridentine Catholicism, the formative mould was much broader. It comprised not just the scriptural, but also the liturgical and devotional traditions of the Church. The particular way in which Marie absorbed that cultural heritage and fashioned herself in its mould depended on both her social context and temperament.

In order to gain access to what Peter Brown refers to as "that crucial area where external and internal changes touch each other" and shape a person's identity, I shall first discuss Marie's religious setting and then highlight those details of her Catholic upbringing which nurtured her spiritual leanings in her formative years.[11] For as Jean Leclercq has written, "spirituality is never something purely individual: a person receives the grace of God only within a given group or society and partly by its mediation."[12] A spirit of change permeated Marie's world, a world still basking in the heritage of the medieval Church, while at the same time beginning to feel the impact of preachers and "active contemplatives" who were beginning the work of reform and renewal.

The Catholic Reformation sought to mend and revitalize both the

[9] A. Louth, *Discerning the Mystery. An Essay on the Nature of Theology*, Oxford 1983, p. 42; and G.B. Ladner, *The Idea of Reform: its Impact on Christian Thought and Action in the Age of the Fathers*, Cambridge, Mass. 1959.

[10] Jaeger, *Early Christianity and Greek Paideia*, p. 91.

[11] Peter Brown, *Augustine of Hippo. A Biography*. London 1967, p. 9.

[12] J. Leclercq, introduction to *The Roots of the Modern Christian Tradition*, ed. E.R. Elder, Kalamazoo 1984, pp. x–xi.

institutional life of the Church and the flawed or failing faith of its individual members; it was a complex movement which had roots in the late Middle Ages and was to have far-reaching implications for the face of Catholicism in the modern era.[13] The Protestant challenge of the sixteenth century — in particular its attack on the authority of the Catholic Church — lent urgency to the latter's reforming endeavours and prompted a concerted counter-offensive and vociferous reassertion of the Catholic claim to the keys of tradition and truth. It is this aspect of the Catholic reform which has led to the use of the term "counter-reformation" as a blanket label for the movement. The desire for internal reform and spiritual renewal, however, had in fact arisen already in the fifteenth century and was the result of dissatisfaction with a Church at best grown stagnant and at worst, corrupt in its administrative and moral life. The attempts to give the medieval Western Church a face-lift led to a religious revival, both organizational and personal, aimed at the restoration of order, values and a living Christian faith. The Catholic movement for reform — especially in its later stages — was also a response to innovations, not just in religious society, but in the spheres of science, politics, and exploration as well. It reflected the Catholic Church's awareness that, in this age of religious upheaval and shifting boundaries of knowledge, Christianity, indeed the Catholic faith itself, could no longer be considered a monolith, and that the very ideas of religious authority and tradition were no longer uniform and unassailable.[14]

It is now generally agreed that the term "counter-reformation" does not do justice to the complex reality of the Catholic reform movement as a whole, and is even misleading inasmuch as it focuses our attention primarily on those efforts aimed at controverting the Protestant reformers.[15] It

[13] For a general account of the medieval sources of Catholic revival see A.G. Dickens, *The Counter-Reformation*, pp. 19–28; and H. Oberman, *The Dawn of the Reformation. Essays in Late Medieval and Early Reformation Thought*, Edinburgh 1986, which elucidates many issues in Reformation studies by discussing their medieval origins. J. Bossy sees the Catholic Reformation as a "silent revolution" which contributed much to altering the social climate of Catholic Europe, and even laid many foundations of the modern state. See "The Counter-Reformation and the people of Catholic Europe," *Past and Present* 47 (1970), pp. 51–70.

[14] For a brief discussion of the change in the nature and availability of knowledge in the seventeenth century see R. Briggs, *Early Modern France 1560–1715*, Oxford 1984, p. 166; and C. Ginzburg, "High and Low: The Theme of Forbidden Knowledge in the Sixteenth and Seventeenth Centuries," *Past and Present* 73 (1970), pp. 28–41, which discusses the dissolution of traditional limits on human knowledge and the implications of the new intellectual drive for the spheres of religious and political authority.

[15] On the use and sense of the term "counter-reformation" in modern historiography see

seems, however, that the ghost of this period-label still haunts much of the writing on Reformation topics and reinforces the equally common yet imprecise view that the Catholic reform endeavours were, on the whole, backward-looking and anti-individual. There has long been a tendency to draw a sharp contrast between Protestantism as "a personal, interior religion, engaging the deepest level of the soul," and Catholicism as a religion of conformity which views "salvation as a matter of uniform practices, common rites, beliefs accepted en-bloc," and which effectively leaves "the individual not directly involved, as such, by religion."[16] Hence the prevailing view of Catholic reform as a quest for uniformity and the assumption — only recently contested in convincing fashion by social historians — that Protestantism offered more scope for personal religion.[17]

Although recent trends in French historiography towards detailed studies of society and culture in this period have provided a more balanced picture of the nature and aims of the Catholic reform, the polarized view of the two reform movements has not entirely faded. Even more nuanced assessments of modern scholars seem to leave room for an implicit equation of "Catholic reform" with a quest for "parochial conformity"[18] or an attempt to impose "on all of society ... norms that distinguished true beliefs from illicit superstitions and reverential acts from reprehensible excesses."[19] This has perhaps contributed to the general idea that the Catholic reformers, in contrast to their Protestant counterparts, were intent on upholding authority and imposing order at the expense of personal religious freedom.

At first glance, the initial charge of seeking uniform faith seems to be borne out by what we know of the debates waged and decisions taken at the Council of Trent, which effectively ruled out the possibility of com-

---

M. Mullet, *The Counter-Reformation and the Catholic Reformation in Early Modern Europe*, London 1984, pp. 2–6.

[16] L. Bouyer, *The Spirit and Forms of Protestantism*, trans. A.V. Littledale, London 1956, pp. 98–99.

[17] N.Z. Davis, for example, challenges the view that the Protestant framework generally facilitated more rapid and creative changes in sex roles than did the pluralistic structure found in Catholicism of the sixteenth and seventeenth centuries. See *Society and Change in Early Modern France*, Stanford 1975, pp. 81–85.

[18] J. Bossy claims that the Tridentine Church's principle of parochial conformity was unable to accommodate certain channels of autonomous participation in religious life — such as kinship patterns and the family's role in organizing religious activity — which the medieval Church had fostered. See "The Counter-Reformation...", pp. 59 and 69.

[19] R. Chartier, *The Cultural Uses of Print in Early Modern France*, trans. L. Cochrane, Princeton 1987, p. 344.

promise with the Protestants and sought recognition for the Catholic Church as the sole repository of truth; and there was indeed a well-orchestrated project for getting the faithful to conform to the moral and doctrinal teaching laid down by Rome. But the real picture is more complex and the Church's approach to the internal failings and external challenges which the new age had forced them to face was fraught with ambiguities, and even contradictions.

What remains of the lingering notion that the Catholic Reformation pitted religious tradition against personal religion is rooted, at least in part, in a failure to distinguish between two distinct and, in some respects, conflicting concerns of the Church in its attempt to reform the masses. As Robin Briggs has explained, the Church officials of the day were indeed intent on the "imposition of a new style of religion on the community as a whole," but they were equally concerned to turn "the ordinary practitioner of religion into a heartfelt Christian believer."[20] Often the first of these two concerns is emphasised to the neglect of the latter, adding to the impression that the Church was more interested in uniformity of religious practice than the transformation of individuals into genuine believers.

Briggs' work on religious culture and change in Early Modern France has amply demonstrated the need to make distinctions between the theories propounded and actual activities implemented in the Catholic reform movement; between broad-based social trends and the minutiae of religious life; and between ideas represented by educated society and the mental world of the unlettered or popular masses.[21] With regard to Catholic reform strategies, for example, he makes the important point that even where wide-scale conformity of beliefs and habits was advocated in theory, its practical application was often neglected or adjusted to suit individual needs and particular situations.[22] Local priests often used their own discretion in deciding how strictly to enforce the official Church directives regarding reform of moral and ritual matters. Thus on many fronts there was a large gap between the theory and practice of reform, as both conservative and experimental approaches characterized a situation

---

[20] R. Briggs, "*Idées* and *Mentalités*; the case of the Catholic reform movement in France," *History of European Ideas* 7 (1986), p. 13.

[21] R. Briggs, *Communities of Belief. Cultural and Social Tensions in Early Modern France*, Oxford 1989.

[22] Briggs notes: "in practice the Catholic Reform was prevented from alienating the mass of the faithful only because the village proved an easy victor in the battle with higher authority for the soul of the priest." Ibid., p. 256, See also pp. 392–398, 406.

in which the Church had the rather paradoxical task of "trying to promote individual Christianity by compulsory legislation."[23]

In its reaction to the sweeping iconoclasm of Luther's followers the Church did uphold Catholic tradition *per se* in a seemingly uncritical and belligerent manner, but, as I shall suggest below, the traditionalism which characterized the movement was itself a complex matter and, far from trampling on either innovation or individuality in religious life, could be seen to promote both. It is important to touch on these broad issues of Catholic Reformation historiography because Marie de l'Incarnation is usually seen as a stellar representative of post-Tridentine Catholicism — i.e., as a perfect embodiment of the spirit of the Catholic reform, which in turn is usually depicted in monochrome fashion with a few sweeping strokes of the brush. In order to better see Marie as an individual and to better understand the mechanics of her conversion at a time when the nature and features of conversion were shifting in so many ways; it is important to break down or at least qualify some of the preconceptions one usually encounters when broaching the subject of the Catholic attitude to tradition and the individual in the reform context.

After a few comments on Protestant and Catholic notions of tradition, I shall focus on the aesthetic element in religious tradition, which was a particular source of controversy between the two camps, in what was essentially a debate over the legitimate path to salvation and whether religious objects and images should be seen as aids or obstacles to personal conversion. At the risk of simplifying the issue one could say that Protestant and Catholic were of one voice in their call for conversion and of one mind in their view that man can do nothing for his own salvation without God, but they parted company when it came to the role of tradition in mediating between God and the individual convert.[24] Strictly speaking, the controversy over tradition in Reformation thought pitted the Protestant recognition of Scripture alone (*sola scriptura*) as a divinely revealed source of authority against the Catholic contention that tradition comprised both Scripture and Church teaching throughout the ages.[25] Whereas

---

[23] Bossy, "The Counter-Reformation...", p. 66.

[24] For the Protestants the Catholic emphasis on the sacerdotal aspect of tradition signified that human efforts or material means could be involved in the process of mediating or receiving God's grace. In contrast, the Reformers saw the Church as a priesthood of believers, whose sole inspiration should be God's Word as revealed in and received from the Bible. See B. Reardon, *Religious Thought in the Reformation*, London 1981, pp. xii and 10–14.

[25] See "*Quo Vadis, Petre?* Tradition from Irenaeus to *Humani Generis*," in Oberman, *The*

the Reformers rejected the role of the Church in mediating the grace whereby the believer could be justified, the Catholic view insisted on the importance of the priest in administering the sacraments and channelling the grace necessary for conversion and faith.

Apart from its sense as received teaching or its association with the principle of supreme authority in matters of faith, the term "tradition" also signifies a cultural inheritance, a body of stories, beliefs and customs which, through history and social use, have become synonymous with religious faith for a given group or individual. The Catholic reaffirmation of the value of icons, relics and various devotional practices, which was codified at Trent and put into practice at the community level by encouraging pilgrimages, the use of religious images, and the invocation of saints, reflected an awareness that these could play an important role in the individual's apprehension of tradition and in his or her personal expression of faith.[26]

With regard to this more general idea of tradition or Church "traditions," the Protestant reformers also took a negative stance. They rejected not only the sacerdotalist-sacramental conception of tradition, but also the Catholic adherence to certain traditional ceremonies and devotions which they considered to be not only obstacles to the pure experience of true faith, but also an infringement of the individual's religious freedom. The Protestants objected to elaborate rites and veneration of places and objects, not only on the grounds that they constituted an unnecessary and often commercial barrier between God and man, but also because their forms distracted the believer and undermined genuine, direct faith.

They found it particularly irksome that the sacraments were administered by the Church in an elaborate or stylized fashion. In his commentary on the Council of Trent, compiled between 1565–1573, the Lutheran theologian Martin Chemnitz attacked the "multitude, splendour, and pomp of these human rites," arguing that "there should be a distinction between divine actions, whose beauty and dignity is found in the Word, and the theatrical processions of the word which by their splendour commend themselves to the senses."[27] Chemnitz's contention that such

---

Dawn of the Reformation, pp. 269–296. This meticulous study of what is usually described as the clash between the Protestant principle of *sola scriptura* and the Catholic principle of Scripture-plus-tradition, sketches out the development and exact nature of what Oberman terms "a clash between two concepts of tradition."

[26] See A. Michel, *Les decrets du Concile du Trente*, Paris 1938, especially the decrees 888, 984–8, 998.

[27] Martin Chemnitz, *Examination of the Council of Trent* (1565), 2 vols., trans. F.

pomp "occupies the senses and the minds to such an extent that either no or only very little attention is given to those things which have the institution of God" is reflected in modern writing — both popular and scholarly — on the subject of Catholic devotion in the sixteenth and seventeenth centuries.[28] The claim that these religious ornaments or ceremonies and "every convulsed line of art that enshrines them, the grappling angels and the surging saints, the plethora of bosses and stars and roses and bows and garlands" effectively stifled the individual's prayer life, is one that recalls the sentiments of the Reformers themselves and one which surfaces also in more recent assessments of this period in Church history.[29] Owen Chadwick's comment that Catholics "cultivated a religion of externals and substituted a pilgrimage, an indulgence, a relic for a genuine change in heart and life" is another example of the view that the Catholic preoccupation with devotions or the "externals" of religion impeded personal religious change and was incompatible with true religious experience.[30]

The Protestant attack on religious imagery and on certain religious artefacts and devotions was rooted in a desire to purge tradition of the trammels and trinkets of the past and to purify religion for the individual in search of God, but there was a risk of uprooting the believer from his cultural ground and of severing conceptual, emotional and aesthetic ties with the past.[31] In their denial of the aesthetic component of religious tradition these modern-day iconoclasts failed, in a sense, to recognize a key element of religious expression. Lucien Febvre points out that generations before the Reformers were to call for a more heartfelt and personal form of faith, religious art had already become more emotional and human, and had contributed to a different spirit of religion; this art in fact

Kramer, St. Louis 1971, vol. 2, p. 114. Chemnitz did not reject the use of rites *per se*, but rather those which were "added by churchmen," and for which there was no scriptural justification. He criticized in particular the "secret mumbling" in Latin, and "the things that consist of ceremonies and gestures" which, in his eyes, represented ungodliness and superstition. See pp. 111, and 116–117.

[28] Ibid., p. 114.

[29] M. Warner, *Alone of All Her Sex. The Myth and the Cult of the Virgin Mary*, London 1978, p. 298.

[30] O. Chadwick, *The Reformation*, rev. ed., Harmondsworth 1973, p. 38.

[31] See B. Dompnier, "Le débat sur les images dans la France du XVIIe siècle," *History of European Ideas* 9 (1988), pp. 423–441. The debate over images surfaces much earlier in Church history, most notably in the Iconoclastic controversy in the eighth and ninth centuries. See P. Brown, "A Dark-Age Crisis: Aspects of the Iconoclastic Controversy," *English Historical Review* 88 (1973), pp. 1–34.

already conveyed the idea of "a religion stripped of priestly trappings, filled with compassion, making a direct and continual appeal to the heart."[32] Febvre suggests that in view of this, the Protestant iconoclasts can be seen not only as vandals but as "ingrates with respect to an art which had covertly prepared the way for them."[33]

The Catholic affirmation of the place of saints and ceremonies and the like in religious life and worship was perhaps rooted in a realization that these things were an inevitable part of the believer's mental world and religious fibre insofar as religion is a social practice which is culturally shaped and emotionally grounded in historical forms, language and customs passed on from one generation to the next. Stressing the role of traditional forms for sustaining religious beliefs, Natalie Zemon Davis has suggested in fact that one of the reasons that Calvinism never won massive support among French peasants was because it did not sufficiently accommodate the traditional and ritual culture of the countryside. As she notes, a Protestant *calendrier* stripped of saints could have little appeal for the common man.[34]

A valuable contribution to research on religious history is the methodology which has been developed for investigating the mentality of given groups of individuals. Michèle Ménard's meticulous and absorbing study of the *retables* or altar pieces in a rural parish in seventeenth-century France for example, not only demonstrates the importance of statues and figures as an expression of God's majesty and as a tool for the edification of the local parishioners, but also explores the interdependence of the scriptural word and mental images which both issued from, and in turn reinforced, biblical accounts and Church teaching. Apart from emphasising the general need to try and unpack the mental baggage of people living in a certain time, place, and culture, she also illustrates the import of visual forms of religious tradition for rooting and reinforcing the latter's teaching in the hearts and imagination of the believer. Her work provides an illustration of the fact that tradition — or the "Word" — is neither Scripture alone, as the Protestants would have it, nor is it simply the combination of Scripture and Church teaching as Catholic apologists argued in their theoretical quarrel with the Reformers; for in practice the "Word" — or God's revelation to man — could not be separated from the

---

[32] L. Febvre, *Life in Renaissance France*, ed. and trans. M. Rothstein, Cambridge, Mass. 1977, p. 83.

[33] Ibid., pp. 82–83.

[34] Davis, *Society and Change in Early Modern France*, p. 203.

imagery and devotional traditions which came to represent and evoke the Word in the minds of believers.[35] As Marie discovered in her childhood, and later on in life also in her activities among the natives of the New World, the aesthetic component of religious culture could both enhance religious life and spur growth on a personal level.

However historians may characterize the Catholic Reformation, and whether the Church is portrayed as having responded in a negative or positive fashion to the needs of the individual believer in the age of reform, our discussion ultimately hinges on how Marie herself received and perceived her tradition. In assessing the burdens and benefits which Catholicism presented for her, we shall see that she embraced the very things which the Protestant Reformers had vilified, and that far from obstructing her path to heightened spiritual experience, the pomp and splendour surrounding sacraments, sermons, saints and ceremonies were in fact instrumental in forming her religious sensibilities. Indeed, in the period leading up to her conversion the aesthetic element of Catholic life was perhaps the most dominant feature of Marie's attachment to her tradition and played an important part in the formative process which culminated in conversion or, to use Chadwick's phrase, "a genuine change of heart and life."

By the seventeenth century the Catholic reform was in full swing and its activities spanned several continents and all sectors of society. Although the changes and disciplinary reforms decided on by the Council of Trent were fully implemented in France only by about 1660, other reform features, such as the spread of the overseas missions and the flowering of spiritual movements and mystical literature were part of the religious reality into which Marie Guyart was born.[36] The reforming spirit which she was to encounter was characterized both by innovative trends and by the vestiges of medieval religiosity which had been carried over into the

---

[35] See Michèle Ménard, *Une histoire des mentalités religieuses au XVIIe siècle. Mille retables de l'ancien diocèse du Mans*, Paris 1980. See also A. Louth's discussion of the complementarity of Scripture and tradition in *Discerning the Mystery*, pp. 108–109.

[36] Although the king and the *parlements* refused to accept officially the decrees of the Council of Trent — primarily because the rulings on ecclesial justice impinged on the Gallican liberties enjoyed by the French Church — many of the disciplinary and moral demands of the Council were met by local bishops and clergy. In 1615 the cardinals, bishops, and general representatives of the French clergy declared their obligation to receive and observe the dictates of Trent regarding pastoral and spiritual matters in spite of the royal refusal to legalize the Council's decrees. See J. Delumeau, *Le catholicisme entre Luther et Voltaire*, Paris 1971, pp. 62–68; and A. Latreille, E. Delaruelle, and J.-R. Palanque, *Histoire du catholicisme en France sous les rois très chrétiens*, 3 vols., Paris 1957, vol. 2, pp. 289–291.

new age. The average Catholic felt a mixture of filial reverence for the old and an excitement at all that was new in Church life. Marie's religious growth must be seen against this hybrid backdrop of old and new, tradition and innovation. In her life the Catholicism of saints and relics was joined with the spirit of adventure and devotion which permeated this new chapter in Catholic history.

Marie Guyart was born on October 28, 1599 in Tours, a large bustling town stretching along the south bank of the Loire.[37] Tours had a thriving silk manufacturing industry which was the most important source of employment and revenue for its inhabitants. The Catholics of Tours could boast of an unbroken religious tradition dating back to Merovingian times, and at the turn of the century when Marie's story unfolds the city was considered a bastion of Catholic faith. In the same year that Marie was born the Reformers were allowed, in accordance with rights acquired through the Edict of Nantes, to set up a place of worship a few miles from the centre of town. Although the Protestants enjoyed some prestige among influential families of the bourgeoisie, from whom they drew most of their support, they were few in number and, on the whole, made little inroad into this essentially Catholic milieu which had proven itself to be true to king and Church in the turbulent years of the century now drawing to a close.[38]

Marie was the fourth of eight children born to Florent Guyart, a master baker, and Jeanne Michelet, who was descended from the Babous de la Bourdaisière, an established family ennobled in the previous century. The Guyart family lived in the parish of St. Saturnin — one of the most prosperous in the city — and the church they frequented was a massive edifice which had once housed Michel Colombe's masterful *Death of the Virgin* before the painting was damaged by Huguenot protesters. In keeping with the practice of the times Marie was baptized the day after she was born, and this ceremony, which took place in the Church of St. Saturnin, officially marked her entry into the Church and the beginning of her Christian life. She was to grow up with a strong religious identity and sense of rootedness nourished by a family life and social setting which were steeped in Catholic tradition.

For the Catholic in seventeenth-century France sacraments such as

---

[37] See G.-M. Oury, *Marie Guyart 1599–1672*, trans. M. Thompson, Cincinnati 1978. This exhaustive biography is the best available source of information on Marie's life and social setting. References are to the English translation.

[38] Ibid., pp. 4–6.

baptism, communion, matrimony, or holy orders were important rites of
passage which imparted special status to the individuals and the families
involved and enhanced the religious meaning of life in general. Baptism
was a particularly powerful social custom, signifying as it did both a
religious rite of initiation for the individual and a collective celebration of
kinship ties. Church officials were in fact at pains to tone down the kinship
aspect of the sacramental gathering and introduced measures designed to
ensure that the baptism signified the individual's entry not so much into
the family clan as into the larger community of the Church as represented
by the local parish.[39] The parish was seen as one's extended family and
served as the focal point of the liturgical and sacramental life of its
members. The significance of Marie's own baptism was drummed home to
her on the numerous occasions when she witnessed and helped to celebrate
this rite. She became a godmother for the first time at the age of eleven,
symbolically adopting a share of responsibility for the spiritual welfare of
the infant being baptized. This was a role which was to repeat itself often
as Marie had over fifteen godchildren during her lifetime.

Religious identity was linked with and reinforced by one's family roots,
parish activities, and membership within the longstanding institution and
spiritual community of the Catholic Church. The unfolding of the liturgical
year, which highlighted the holy seasons of Christmas and Easter and was
punctuated by a host of other feasts and saints' days, provided an intricate
religious framework which at one and the same time could be a unifying
force for Catholics and also allow them a degree of personal expression in
their choice of saints and forms of devotion. Families in Tours could be
seen at various times of the year making a pilgrimage to the tomb of their
patron St. Martin, who had been a soldier, bishop, missionary, and the
first monk of the Gauls in the fourth century. The Guyarts would have
been familiar with this custom and it can be assumed that they were among
the pilgrims who visited his tomb or the Abbey of Marmoutier which was
another place of devotion to the saint. According to her son's biographer,
Dom Martène, Marie went to the Abbey shortly before her son was born
to pray for him and to dedicate his life to St. Martin.[40]

But the Guyart family also had a personal saint of sorts, St. Francis de
Paola, who held a special place in their devotions. This Calabrian hermit
and founder of the Order of the Minims, who was renowned for his
prophecies and miraculous powers, was brought to France at the behest of

[39] Bossy, "The Counter-Reformation...", pp. 57–58.
[40] Oury, *Marie Guyart*, p. 13. See also G.-M. Oury, *Dom Claude Martin*, Solesmes 1983.

an ailing Louis XI in 1482. The Guyarts felt a particular reverence for Francis because one of their ancestors had been among the party sent by the king to bring the holy man to France.[41] Marie recounts the story and suggests its importance in strengthening the family's religious identity and sense of tradition:

> It is this recollection which has always given our family a great devotion to this great Saint. My grandfather used to tell us this story frequently, so that after his death we would continue to pass on the memory and devotion, just as he had received them from his grandfather. (C 661)

Dom Oury tells us that in Marie's day Tours was the "religious metropolis of the West" whose very boundaries were defined by the monasteries located outside the town walls.[42] In Tours, the imposing medieval cathedral of St. Gatien and the ancient Abbey of St. Martin were "the two rallying points for religion" and served as visual reminders of both the majesty and historical continuity of the heritage to which Catholics in all of Tours' sixteen parishes bore witness.[43] Besides the many time-worn churches and chapels which dotted the city, new buildings were beginning to spring up, for in the age of the cardinals, both secular and religious building increased and with it the demand for religious art with which to ornament all kinds of new edifices both within and without.[44] Another visible expression of the reforming spirit were the colourful religious processions which were as popular in the seventeenth century as they had been in medieval times and served to underscore the collective aspect of Catholic worship and the mingling of the latter with popular festive sentiment. For Marie the marching masses immediately conjured up the image of a devout army and evoked a desire to join up with such a *militia christi*:

> Whenever I saw the faithful following the cross and banner in processions my heart would leap with joy. I have seen a captain who was stationed in our district leading his troops carrying their banner. Hence on seeing the crucifix and the banner with its figures I would say to myself: "Ah, here is my Captain! See, He has His banner too. I wish to follow it just as the soldiers follow theirs." And so I would follow the procession in a spirit of great fervour, having my eyes fixed on the crucifix and saying to myself as I marched along, "Ah, here is my Captain! I wish to follow Him!" (A 10)[45]

---

[41] Oury, *Marie Guyart*, p. 13.

[42] Ibid., p. 5.

[43] Ibid., p. 5.

[44] R.H. Wilenski, *French Painting*, London 1931, p. 37.

[45] *La Relation de 1654* is the only complete work of Marie de l'Incarnation which exists in

In an age when the taking up of arms was associated not only with service to king and country but also with defense of the faith, religious and military banners could conjure up similar, even overlapping, notions of support for traditional bases of authority. It is not surprising that Marie connects the sight of a religious procession and raised cross with the image of marching troops and a hoisted flag. For her, both signified rallying round a noble cause and the call for a loyal following — even to the point of sacrifice. The connection between the cross and the crown and their absorption into the common mentality as symbols of authority, loyalty and tradition had a strong socio-cultural basis. In France the interests of Church and state were often one and the same, and their activities mutually reinforcing.[46] In fact both the king and Church officials exercised sweeping power over their subjects. Of the three estates in France, the Church enjoyed the most esteem and influence.

If the Church enjoyed special favour in the realm, the king's position was no less enhanced by the Church's support. And of course, the awe and allegiance inspired by the king was due largely to his status as a divinely appointed terrestrial ruler. When Marie was growing up, motifs and phrases related to royal power and splendour had already entered the spiritual vocabulary and were transmitted in the spiritual literature of the day.[47] The link between the celestial and mundane realms and their rulers thus existed both in the minds of the faithful and in concrete social terms.

It is easy to imagine the excitement of a girl such as Marie at the visit in Tours of the young Louis XIII in 1614. In preparation for the meeting of the Estates General the king and his entourage made a tour of cities in the West of France to arouse public sentiment and revive loyalty to the crown.[48] During the week he spent in Tours he visited many religious sites and groups. Apart from a pilgrimage to the tomb of St. Martin, he also met with the Carmelites, Dominicans, and Capuchins in the city. Marie

English translation: *The Autobiography of Venerable Marie of the Incarnation, O.S.U. Mystic and Missionary*, trans. John Sullivan, Chicago 1964.

[46] Briggs, *Communities of Belief*, pp. 229–234.

[47] See J. Leclercq, "La royauté du Christ dans la spiritualité française du XVIIe siècle," *La Vie Spirituelle Supplément* I (1947), pp. 216–229, 291–307.

[48] The Estates General of 1614 was the occasion of heated debate between the French clergy and those representing parliamentary gallicanism over the reception of the disciplinary decrees of Trent. See Latreille et al., *Histoire du catholicisme en France*, pp. 289–304. On the "royal entrances" in France during this period see V.E. Graham and W. McAllister Johnson, *The Paris Entrées of Charles IX and Elisabeth of Austria, 1571*, Toronto 1974; and Claude d'Acreigne, *Récit véritable de la deffaite des trouppes de Mr. le prince par Mr. le duc de Guise, le septiesme de ce mois. Ensemble le départ du roy pour venir à Tours*, Paris 1616.

could not fail to be impressed by the pomp and circumstance of the royal visit which threw the city into upheaval, engendered a sense of pride and excitement and strengthened bonds between regal and religious rule. The king came to Tours again in 1616 for a three-month stay, and during this time Marie, who was just a year older than the teenage monarch, probably saw him from a distance on one or more occasions. The king's position and pedigree earned him esteem as a matter of course, and the majesty and aura which surrounded him increased his popular appeal. In keeping with the spirit of the times Marie affirms that "the brilliance and pomp of the kings of the earth is the most beautiful image that our minds can form of God." (E I 433) This is significant, for her image of God developed in an interesting manner as her spiritual life progressed, becoming less concrete, less linked with analogies and examples from everyday life and language. In her formative years, however, she relished the external majesty and ceremony of both the Court and the Church.

In the years leading up to her conversion at the age of twenty, Marie's Catholicism was a patchy mixture of the formal and the informal. Her religious allegiance was firm but her imagination fertile. Her apprehension of both Catholic teaching and the sights, sounds, and aura of her religious milieu was by no means a systematic and ordered process and, initially at least, her understanding was fuelled by religious hear-say. In her account of her childhood, she frequently begins some comment on her views or practices by saying "I'd heard it said" or "I'd been told that ..." (A 7–9) During this formative period, Marie received her basic Catholic education, was influenced by her parents' religiosity, and began appropriating for herself the various teachings and practices of her faith, not always comprehending their significance, but ever ready to embrace both the concrete manifestations and the opaque mysteries of Catholicism. A few remarks on the kind of religious education she might have received should be made before discussing those features of religion which especially appealed to her.

Because Marie's writing reveals a solid grasp of theology, notable gift of expression, and command of language and religious imagery, one would assume that her formal training had been extensive. Unfortunately we know very little about what specific education she received. At the time it was quite common that large families with relatives in the clergy would have some instruction given to their children. Though there is no concrete evidence of this, it is possible that Marie attended one of the "little schools" which were set up throughout France during the years when she was growing up. This possibility is reinforced by her mention of a schoolyard as the place of her first spiritual vision at the age of seven. (A 7) Another hypothesis advanced by Dom Oury is that she was perhaps taught in one of the groups set up by religious women in the period dedicated to the teaching of girls.[49] It is worth mentioning a few points about the idea and substance of childhood education in Marie's day, not just to get an overview of what learning a young Catholic girl at the time would have been likely to receive, but also because the education of children was an important issue in seventeenth-century France and specifically linked with religious programs of reform.

In the seventeenth century both Protestant and Catholic leaders saw education *per se*, i.e., reading and writing, as a means to a most worthy end: namely, the inculcation and reinforcement of Christian values.[50] It was recognized that childhood education had the benefit of forming the child to a life of virtue before vice took its steely grip. And so the Protestant Reformers sought to provide the child with the ability to read Scripture, and Catholic educators prepared "little catechisms" so that youngsters could learn the basic tenets and moral rules of the faith. Despite the fact that an extensive network of schools and seminaries was created, and schooling for children was widely promoted by moralists and reformers of the age, the extension of schooling to girls was still not common. On the whole, girls' training in religious and domestic matters was mostly conducted in the family home, sometimes with the aid of a relative or neighbour. As Philip Ariès informs us, "if schooling in the seventeenth century was not yet the monopoly of one class, it remained the monopoly of one sex."[51]

In essence the Catholic and Protestant notion of education for girls did not differ. For both camps, a young girl was to be trained to be a good housekeeper and paragon of moral virtue in order to educate her children by example. Girls often learned at a young age the skills needed to help in family business and this instilled in them a sense of responsibility and a special role in family life, so that "by the age of ten, girls were already little women: a precocity due in part to an upbringing which taught girls to behave very early in life like grown-ups."[52] In like manner they absorbed the religious norms and rules which they would soon be called upon to impart to their own children.

---

[49] See Oury, *Marie Guyart*, p. 14.
[50] See Chartier et al., *L'éducation en France*, pp. 8–11, 293–295.
[51] P. Ariès, *Centuries of Childhood*, trans. R. Baldick, London 1962, p. 331.
[52] Ibid., p. 332.

In an age when elementary education was a growing concern, and the very concept of family was crystallizing — largely as a result of shifting views on the nature of childhood — the issue of religious formation must be addressed with special emphasis on the role of the family. For as Ariès points out, the family now "assumed a moral and spiritual function, it moulded bodies and souls."[53] The new emotional attitude of parents towards their children and the stress on parental responsibility and care was magnified by the literature of the Jesuits, Oratorians, and other pedagogues in the period, who "taught parents that they were spiritual guardians, that they were responsible before God for the soul, and indeed for the bodies too, of their children."[54]

Religious society in this period was to a large degree obsessed by the idea that the world was the devil's playground, that sin lurked in every corner and that man's eternal soul was threatened on many fronts and at every turn in his day-to-day life. The preoccupation with the possibility and means by which to save one's soul saturated religious thought not just at the higher level of theological rumination, but also on the basic, instinctive level of the common man's anxiety. In the given context it is clear why devout women like Jacqueline Pascal saw the moral training of children as the best means of keeping them from sin and ensuring their commitment to an ongoing conversion. A "holy childhood" was seen as the right way to make children increasingly "new creatures" and to lead them to salvation and immortality.[55] And Bossuet, writing towards the end of the century, even stated that one of the primary obligations of marriage is "to obtain salvation by the holy education given to one's children."[56]

Marie's upbringing was typical in that she acquired domestic as well as basic accounting skills at home. Her mother taught her cooking, sewing and many other household matters, and her father trained her in the rudimentary business affairs which would enable her to help him in his work. Marie's son, Claude Martin, and her most recent biographer, Dom

[53] Ibid., p. 412.

[54] Ibid., p. 412.

[55] Jacqueline Pascal exhorted the girl boarders at Port-Royal to be like new-born children and taught them the following prayer in honour of Christ's childhood: "Give us a holy childhood, which the course of the years may never take from us, and from which we may never pass into the old age of old Adam, or into the death that is sin; but which may make us increasingly new creatures in Jesus Christ and lead us to His glorious immortality." Quoted in Ariès, *Centuries of Childhood*, p. 122.

[56] Quoted in Briggs, *Communities of Belief*, p. 238.

Oury, extol Marie's talents for embroidery and painting and her handiness at all manner of mechanical chores. The family home not only provided the conditions for learning basic skills and values but also reinforced Marie's social and religious sense of belonging and her notions of authority and obedience. Despite official Church reluctance to encourage any organized family role in religious training and its emphasis instead on the parents' disciplinary function, the family, as Ariès and others have noted, remained nonetheless an important foyer for instilling and nurturing spiritual leanings.[57] Marie's religious growth was particularly enhanced by the family atmosphere and this fact reflected a widespread trend in family life in the seventeenth century, when both Catholic and Protestant families "felt the need for a piety which was neither public nor entirely individual: a family piety."[58]

As a child Marie was very much inspired by the charity and piety of her mother. She mentions in a letter to her sister that her mother's praying aloud while doing housework had made a strong impression on her when she was a child. She also shared her mother's desire to help the poor and claimed to be happiest when in their company. In the grand tradition of venerable figures like St. Brigid or St. Francis, Marie's compassion for the poor led her to give away things from the household without the knowledge of her parents. As a young girl she seems to have had an earnest yet cheerful attitude towards religion, fostered in large part by the family atmosphere. Dom Oury describes her as having a sensitive but fun-loving nature, chatty and eager to please, but also strong-willed and well-suited to leading others. It is clear that these character traits along with her intelligence, critical spirit and attention to detail, affected the way she responded to the religious environment in which she grew.[59]

Marie took what religious rules she knew seriously, but her theological understanding would have been limited to the basic doctrines which she imbibed from sermons or from one of the basic catechisms used in her day. Even if learned by heart, catechetical points would probably have made less impact on her than the powerful images of demons and angels, sinners and saints and holy figures like Christ and Mary — all of whom peopled

---

[57] J. Bossy suggests that the Church preferred to limit the family's involvement in the religious life of the children to a disciplinary role. See n. 18 above. Ariès suggests that the family nonetheless thrived as the centre of religious growth. See *Centuries of Childhood*, pp. 357–359, 412–413.

[58] Ariès, *Centuries of Childhood*, p. 362.

[59] G.-M. Oury, *Ce que croyait Marie de l'Incarnation et comment elle vivait de sa foi*, Paris 1972, p. 13.

the colourful sermons of the day and inhabited the average Catholic's mental world. It was only in her teen years that she began to think about Catholic teaching in a more sophisticated manner and started weighing up her behaviour according to moral principles.

Religion was both a routine which coloured day-to-day life and an intangible, awe-inspiring mystery which infused the Catholic mind with an other-worldly aura. Miracles were seen as extraordinary signs from above which cut through the divide between divine and human and brought the supernatural into the natural realm. Marie recounts an incident in which her dress got caught in the wheels of a cart which started up suddenly as she passed. That she was not killed or even seriously injured in the incident was a miracle in her view, that is, a reason-defying instance of divine intervention, and one which she attributed to the fact that she was engaged in an act of charity at the time: she had been on her way to give alms when the accident occurred. (E I 185)

The little we know about her Catholic girlhood is mostly gleaned from her own testimony — limited to a few pages in her *Relation de 1654* — but it is interesting to note those things which an older Marie singled out in describing her childhood. The importance of the family environment for her direction and formation cannot be overemphasised. She herself saw her parents as the primary instruments of religious growth and change in her life and states:

> The education I had received from my parents, who were good Christians and quite pious, laid a solid foundation in my soul for everything Christian and for good morals, so that when I reflect on this I bless God for the graces He has been pleased to give me in that regard, all the more so as such an education is an excellent disposition for the practice of virtue and for being truly prepared for a vocation to high sanctity. (A 6)

This passage immediately brings to mind the opening paragraph of St. Teresa's life of herself, in which she praises her parents for providing their children with holy books, encouraging devotions to the saints, and by themselves being examples of piety, charity, and virtue. Teresa opens her autobiography with the statement: "If I had not been so wicked, the possession of devout and God-fearing parents, together with the favour of God's grace, would have been enough to make me good."[60] Marie's comment differs from that of Teresa in that, instead of an expression of

---

[60] Teresa of Avila, *The Life of Saint Teresa*, trans. J.M. Cohen, Harmondsworth reissued 1987, p. 23.

her own worthlessness — which is a conventional ingredient of such spiritual writing — Marie implies that her life is not only characterized by good morals, but also disposed to the practice of virtue and a vocation to high sanctity. While both Marie and Teresa give credit to their parents for their religious upbringing, they take care to render unto God that which is God's alone, namely, praise and thanksgiving for the grace without which this parental guidance would have been as naught. God is considered by both to be the prime and ultimate mover behind their religious formation.

Dom J. Huijben, writing from within the monastic tradition, also points to the working of the Holy Spirit as the main formative agent in Marie's life. But Huijben, conceding that "God does not disdain the use of human means to accomplish his work," also examines three other major factors in her spiritual development: her parents and her education; the liturgy; and reading and sermons.[61] The influence of sermons is the main focus of Huijben's study for he claims that by way of oral instruction, i.e., through sermons, Marie was influenced in her youth by the christological thought of Bérulle, the founder of the Oratorians, a religious order who were active in Tours from 1615.[62] Dom Oury also suggests that Scripture and the liturgy form the foundations on which Marie's spiritual life was built. He emphasises the link between the two and says "for the Christian educated in the school of the Church, the Word of God is known first of all by means of the liturgy."[63] But he does not refer to liturgy only as a vehicle for the teaching and stories of Scripture, nor solely as "a collective expression of faith" as Huijben does, but rather notes its specific import for the individual believer. He grasps the personal significance of liturgy for Marie, who is enabled through the liturgy, to "celebrate Scripture lyrically, to surround it with symbols expressing her faith, respect and adoration."[64] Here he touches on something that was central to her faith, namely the emotive and creative element of religious expression, whether in private prayer or in a shared ceremony.

It is clear, then, that tradition is not just Scripture nor "that by which we

---

[61] J. Huijben, "La Thérèse de la Nouvelle-France", *Supplément à la Vie Spirituelle* 22 (1930), pp. 106–111.

[62] Ibid., pp. 125–128. Dom Oury suggests that the traces of Berullianism in her thought can be linked to the sermons of Père Metézeau (1583–1632), one of Bérulle's devoted disciples and the first superior of the Oratorians who were active in Tours from 1615. See *Marie Guyart*, p. 23.

[63] Oury, *Ce que croyait*, p. 75.

[64] Ibid., p. 75.

receive Scripture" but also "the context in which we interpret it."[65] Andrew Louth has made this point and, using the example of the Mass which is the *locus* for the celebration of Scripture and the Eucharist, suggests that the amalgam of language, custom and associations which has been drawn from and draws one back to the Eucharist is all part of tradition. Because the meaning of the Eucharist is absorbed by the individual "in what is potentially an infinity of ways," and since the gestures and movements, chanting and singing, images present in the words we hear, or in the paintings, statues and stained glass we see around us, all kindle our devotion, we must see these things as an integral part of the tradition in which God's Word has been passed on.[66] For Marie, tradition comprised Scripture, sacraments, sermons, ceremonies and devotions and not necessarily in that order of preference for they were all seen as mutually supportive means to enriching faith and attaining greater proximity to God. As Dom Oury suggests, though she loved the celebration of the Mass best of all, she was also very attached to processions, jubilee stations, the exposition of the Eucharist, the prayer of "forty hours", and the popular parades with crosses, banners and music which were all important in her religious life.[67] Tradition was embodied in the rites and teachings of the Church, mediated by its representatives, and lived out in the liturgy; and when we read Marie's account of how she responded in her youth to the impulses of her Catholic surroundings it is the details which command our attention.

For Marie the Church was an absolute authority and guiding force and her unequivocal devotion to it is expressed in the simple statement "so vivid was my faith in regard to all that the Church did that it seemed to me to be my life and my sustenance." (A 10) Religious faith was inseparable from the sacramental life and the latter was inconceivable without the sacerdotal ministry which was seen as the mediating force between God and the individual Catholic. As already mentioned, Scripture and the liturgy were the corner-stones of Marie's spiritual life. With regard to her acquaintance with Scripture Dom Oury remarks that her conscious Christian life began by hearing the word of God spoken in church and was expanded by her assiduous reading of the Bible later on.[68] Marie was inspired by Scripture throughout her life — in particular by the psalms

---

[65] Louth, *Discerning the Mystery*, p. 107.
[66] Ibid., p. 109.
[67] Oury, *Ce que croyait*, p. 77.
[68] Ibid., p. 69.

and the *Song of Songs* which she quotes frequently in her writings:

> I had heard it said that the Spirit of God dictated the Psalms, and since I
> read them in French they stirred up various thoughts and reflections in my
> mind. In making use of them I believed that everything said by the Spirit of
> God was true and infallible, and that all things would fall into nothingness
> sooner than the words of the Psalms would fail me. This it was that caused
> me to hope that He would grant me all that I might ask of Him — for I took
> Him at His word — and that consequently I would never be disappointed in
> my expectations. (A 8)

No less influential than the biblical stories and symbols were the priests
and preachers who transmitted them; who made the Gospels come alive
and rendered their moral and spiritual meaning more accessible to the
masses. In the first quarter of the century Tours saw the influx of new
religious orders and a new emphasis on preaching — even in established
orders such as the Feuillants. The work of the mendicant friars who
preached in various parishes was an important contribution to the
Church's reform initiative in that it was geared to evoking remorse, moral
betterment and a greater devotion on the part of the believers. The
sermons of the preachers in Tours, to which Marie had repeated exposure,
captured her imagination and had a lasting impact.[69] "While still a child,"
she writes, "I heard that God spoke through those who preach. This made
a deep impression on me and gave me a strong urge to listen to them, even
though I was so young that I understood very little of what they said
except the narrative parts, which I recounted on my return home." (A 8)
Marie illustrates the dramatic effect of such sermons and the strong
emotions which they could awaken in their auditors in another statement:

> One Lent, when a good Capuchin father preached a sermon on our Lord's
> passion, my spirit was so strongly plunged into this mystery that day and
> night I found it impossible to listen to anything else. (A 9)

It is noteworthy that although the content and message of the sermons
often made little sense to Marie as a young girl, the narrative form had
such an impact on her that she regarded preaching as an inspired act and
the preachers themselves as holy men. She tells us that as she grew older
hearing the word of God preached begot "an even greater desire to hear it
preached." In the same passage she continues:

> I had such a veneration for preachers that whenever I saw one in the streets I

---

[69] See Oury, *Marie Guyart*, p. 12.

felt drawn to run after him and kiss his footprints. Prudence restrained me from doing so, but I would follow him with my eyes until he was out of sight. I considered nothing greater than proclaiming the word of God, and this begot my esteem for those to whom our Lord had given the grace to preach His word. As often as I heard it preached it seemed to me that my heart was like a vase into which this divine word flowed like a liquid. (A 8)

Marie stresses that this image of flowing liquid was

not the work of my imagination but rather of the Spirit of God present in the divine word who, by an abundant communication of His graces, produced such a sense of fullness in my soul that I had to relieve it by having recourse to prayer. (A 8)

The sermons contributed to her intellectual grasp of religion as well as appealing to her spirit of devotion. The preachers' words provided food for thought as well as the seeds of prayer: "I spoke to God with great fervour, as well as to the people in our home, telling them what the preacher had said and then my own thoughts, a practice which gave me a certain eloquence." (A 8)

The sacraments provided perhaps the single most important source of nourishment for Marie's faith and she avows "the more I approached the sacraments the more I desired to approach them, for I found in them true life and every good, as well as an attraction for prayer." (A 7) The sacraments, then, had a self-perpetuating effect and afforded her "great courage and great peace of soul, as well as a very lively faith which begot in [her] a firm belief in the divine mysteries." (A 6) In particular, the tangible symbols of sacramental life were important. The bread and wine consecrated in the sacrament of the Eucharist were not just commemorative, but also effective symbols of grace. Even in the sacrament of penance there seemed to be material aids to grace at hand. She recounts that she used holy water as part of an act of penance "because I had been told that it had the effect of effacing venial sins." (A 7) Holy water, the crucifix, relics, rosary beads, the invocation of saints or prayers offered up before statues or holy images were all considered to be useful tools of the faith. Marie claims to have experienced many moral insights and spiritual visions while praying before images or kneeling before statues.

Her attraction to the symbols, activities, and material objects of religious life indicates that these were perhaps as important in her mind as the theological content of her faith. Forms and gestures in religious practice seemed to her to be an integral component of faith, not just ornamenting religious life, but effectively enhancing its inner core. She would have seen making the sign of the cross or genuflecting before the altar not as mere reflex actions, but as solemn religious gestures directed at God. In addressing God a sincere demeanour was as important as the content of the prayer itself. Marie explains that as a young girl she was "quite persuaded that He would not refuse anything one humbly asked of Him. That is why, if I saw anyone in church praying in a humble posture, I would say to myself, "Surely God will hear this person since his posture shows that he prays with humility." (A 4)

She recounts that on special holy days she "would be among the first to enter the churches in order [to] see the ceremonies and the solemn office which took place on such an occasion." (A 10) While the word "ceremony" often has negative connotations and brings to mind the idea of stiff or empty formalism, in Marie's case it was a vital and dynamic component of religious life.[70] She revelled in both the public religious displays and the private devotional acts which seemed to form the core of her religious experience as a young girl. Once, while watching a procession of the Blessed Sacrament, she felt herself to be literally caught up and intoxicated by the event:

> my mind and my heart were so ravished in God by this sacrament of love that I was carried along by the movement of the crowd without being aware of it. My eyes were closed so that I walked along haphazardly, like a person who has drunk too much. (A 10)

The aesthetic and the spiritual went hand in hand in Marie's religious consciousness. She explains for example:

> Among the things which have been a great help for my spirit of devotion are the ceremonies of the Church, which powerfully attracted me from the time of my childhood. I found them so beautiful and so holy that for me there was nothing like them. When I had grown older and could grasp their meaning, my love for them increased as a result of my admiration for the holiness and majesty of the Church. (A 10)

Holiness and majesty are closely linked and Marie's admiration for the ceremonies not only "increased her faith" but also bound her to the "Lord in a quite extraordinary way." (A 10)

When she was seven years old — the age of reason, when Catholics are deemed ready both to partake of the sacraments of communion and confession and to discern between right and wrong moral actions — Marie had a dream which gave her the first indication of the spiritual direction

[70] Oury, *Ce que croyait*, p. 77.

her life was to take later on. Her sense of certainty, innocence and confidence in God's love and the excitement inspired by the image of Christ as a tangible, human figure and personal friend is suggested in the account she gives of the vision on the opening page of her autobiography:

> When I was only about seven years old it seemed to me, one night during my sleep, that I was in a schoolyard with one of my companions engaged in some innocent activity. While my gaze was fixed upon the heavens I beheld them open and our Lord Jesus Christ come forth from them in human form and approach me. Upon seeing him I cried out to my companion, "Oh, look at our Lord! He is coming to me!" And it seemed to me that because this girl had committed some imperfection our Lord chose me rather than her, although she was a good child. But there was a secret involved in this, a secret which was not then known to me. As His adorable Majesty drew near to me my heart felt all on fire with His love. I began to reach out to embrace Him. Then this most beautiful of the sons of men, His face reflecting an unspeakable sweetness and attractiveness, said to me as He embraced me and lovingly kissed me, "Will you be Mine?" "Yes," I replied. When He had heard my consent we saw Him return to heaven. (A 3–4)

This passage illustrates her sense of chosenness vis-à-vis others, as well as the esoteric aspect of the special relationship with God that involved a secret which was yet to be revealed. This dream, which is considered to be a foretaste of the mystical experiences in later years, was a decisive event in the religious life of the young girl who henceforth "sighed only for holy commerce with Him" and did everything possible to effect a renewal of this encounter. (A 6)

The details of this incident seem to have remained very clearly etched in her memory. Though on the whole, Marie's christological visions often seem to dwell more on abstract notions of Christ's life in the Trinity than on his humanity, we shall see in the next chapters that her spiritual experience is nourished throughout by "a sure and simple but overwhelming consciousness of Christ's presence, not the thought of a deity, not worship and praise, but an awareness by the senses."[71] In the above passage her emphasis on Christ's human form, beauty and sweet demeanour suggest not only the visual impact of the dream, but also the aesthetic component of her religious sensibility. Indeed at this early point in her spiritual life her faith seemed to thrive on the sights and sounds, forms and figures which were part of her tradition. In the more advanced stages of

---

[71] J. Marshall, ed. and trans. *Word From New France. The Selected Letters of Marie de l'Incarnation*, Toronto 1967, p. 6.

her itinerary this same attachment to the form, or the beautiful, though not as prominent, does not disappear completely but rather functions on another plane and finds its expression in a new mode — the mode of mystical discourse and imagery.

Marie explains that this special dream or grace which she received at age seven was constantly in her mind and caused her to long for another "holy communication." This wish was directed also at the Virgin Mary, whom she fervently desired to see at least once before the end of her life, for she was convinced that the holy mother would protect her. The figure of Mary seems closely associated with her spiritual development at all stages and on many levels. In his article on Marie's devotion to the Virgin Mary, Henri De Lubac notes that it was natural for the figure of Mary to loom large in the prayer life of a Catholic living in the seventeenth century, but adds that in Marie Guyart's life, Mary was more than the object of common piety.[72] She played a special part in the flowering of Marie's faith into mystical experience. The small chain which Marie wore around her neck for more than thirty years not only expressed her strong devotion to Mary but also symbolized spiritual enslavement to this figure. (C 661)

It is interesting to note the central place that Mary holds in the early years of Marie's budding spirituality. At first the Virgin not only appealed to Marie on an emotional level, serving as a protective mother figure, but also figured largely in Marie's moral growth in the period leading up to her conversion. "Once when I was at the foot of the altar of our Lady," she tells us, "an interior light showed me so clearly the importance of making one's confessions well that I felt persuaded beyond the possibility of a doubt that I myself must do so." (A 7) For her, the Virgin Mary served as an intermediary through whom she could offer up her prayers, and through whom she received inspiration and understanding in moral and spiritual terms.

This illumination occurred when Marie was preparing for confession at a time when she was in the middle of a moral crisis. This episode is worthy of closer scrutiny, for the doubts and uncertainty which she experienced in the formative years prior to her conversion preoccupied her for some time. In contrast to her childhood when she seems to have enjoyed a sense of religious security and contentment, unmarred by any great qualms about sin or metaphysical anxiety about God, the adolescent years were accom-

---

[72] H. De Lubac, "Marie de l'Incarnation et la Sainte Vierge," in *Maria, Études sur la Sainte Vierge*, sous la direction d'H. Du Maunoir, vol. 3, Paris, 1954, pp. 181–204; and Ch. Moussé, *Le Culte de Notre Dame en Touraine*, Tours 1915.

panied by a growing self-consciousness, awareness of moral imperfection and mental reservations with regard to actions which had previously seemed harmless. As she grew older, questions of individual sin and morality no longer seemed as straightforward as they had in earlier years. While on the one hand, she tended to think of "true devotion" as consisting in nothing other than "praying to God, serving Him by frequenting the sacraments, and ... not knowingly committing sin," she began, on the other hand, to be troubled by actions which before had always seemed innocent but were now the cause of growing anxiety and guilt feelings. (A 10)

Although a bright and precocious girl, Marie was slow in shaking off some of her childhood habits related to religious practice.[73] She admits:

> As I was only a child and didn't know any better, I would mix recreation with prayer, for I made no distinction between them. I continued thus until, when I was about sixteen, remorse of conscience weighed upon me when I went to confession, and I distinctly felt that [God] wanted me to confess my childish pranks and puerilities and to regard nothing as negligible in this matter. But I didn't dare, as I was ashamed; and I said to myself that I didn't think I had ever offended God in these things, since there was no sin unless one believed something to be a sin when he did it. (A 4)

Marie is vague as to what puerile acts caused her such heartache, but her son tells us that as a child she enjoyed imitating those marching in processions, and acting out the rites of the Mass.[74] It is natural for impressionable children to mimic their elders both in earnest and in jest. St. Teresa recounts instances of such religious make-believe in her autobiography. Both she and her brother dreamed of sailing off to unknown lands to offer up their lives to God's greater glory, but when they realized that their parents would interfere with their plans for martyrdom, they set their sights on a more feasible goal and played at being hermits, retiring to a nearby orchard to build their "cells" among piles of stones.[75] As a young girl Teresa also imitated her mother whom she saw saying her rosary and "enjoyed playing at nunneries, and pretending to be nuns."[76] Learning by example and association was an important part of a child's religious formation, but what was deemed acceptable in children, whose enthusiasm

---

[73] Oury, *Marie Guyart*, p. 21.

[74] C. Martin, *La Vie de la Vénérable Mère Marie de l'Incarnation, première Supérieure des Ursulines de la Nouvelle-France, tirée de ses Lettres et de ses écrits*, Paris, 1697, p. 6.

[75] Teresa of Avila, *The Life*, p. 24.

[76] Ibid., p. 24.

outweighs their understanding, was seen as a mark of immaturity border-
ing on irreverence at a later age.

When she was about fifteen Marie began to regret having indulged in
these seemingly harmless religious games and her "failure to confess those
imperfections" weighed heavily upon her. (A 5) "During more than a
year," she tells us, "I judged that it was not necessary to confess my
childish pranks," but although she insists that she felt sure she "was acting
properly in the matter," she does admit that this was the only aspect of her
religious life about which she wondered whether or not she was acting
"under inspiration." (A 5) No longer cheerfully confident that she was
more or less a good Catholic who fulfilled all her duties, she experienced
repeated doubts which culminated in a crisis at the age of sixteen.

Marie's crisis or preoccupation with this rather trivial matter of childish
games reflects a broader trend in Catholic society, for in the context of the
"great repression" of sinful behaviour and beliefs and the general education
and reform of the Catholic masses, clergy and laymen alike were affected
by the increased emphasis on the use of the confessional and, by extension,
the emotional ramifications of the sacrament of penance which was now
seen as a reconciliation of the individual sinner with God. She was living in
an age which saw the world as the domain of Satan, and all believers, even
the most saintly among them, as sinners who must make every effort to
avoid damnation since despite Christ's meritorious death, those chosen
for salvation are few.[77] She also experienced this heightened awareness of
personal responsibility for sin and the profound *Angst* of a generation of
believers who increasingly felt themselves to be standing alone before
God.

Marie's deliberations about which actions were harmless and which
required confession reflect her growing self-awareness, personal dissatisfaction, and an independent assessment of her responsibility for her moral
life. Her shame, as Dom Oury tells us, was not due to the nature of the
games, but rather the result of not having the courage to confess a lack of
maturity, of which she was by now fully aware. She recounts that one day,
while praying before an altar of the Virgin Mary (in the incident mentioned
above) she suddenly saw the need to make a full confession, but was put
off in the confessional by the fact that the priest heard confessions in a
routine fashion and she felt unable to unburden her conscience in detail as
she had intended. She mentions that she felt no remorse over this missed

    [77] Delumeau, *Le catholicisme entre Luther et Voltaire*, pp. 87–92.

opportunity and after doing her penance she went to communion as if she had made a full confession.

The fact that the subject of this latent imperfection or moral sloppiness takes up so much space in a relatively brief account of the first twenty years of her life suggests that this *crise de conscience* stood out in her memory as a major problem in her religious life in the time before her conversion. In retrospect, Marie considers her youthful inability to discriminate between harmless child's play and immature actions and the hesitation to confess her puerile religious behaviour as having placed a major obstacle in the way of the spiritual experiences she was subsequently to enjoy. She tells us that this moral dalliance resulted in the delay of "a more abundant communication of God's gifts until such time as it pleased Him to gain me at a single stroke, as I shall narrate later on." (A 5) She is referring here to her conversion experience which was to resolve the conflict by making her see her sins in a sudden and unsettling vision which drove home the personal significance of the blood which Christ had shed for the redemption of sinners. It was an enlightening and humbling experience, and marked a decisive turn of events.

CHAPTER TWO

THE DYNAMICS OF CONVERSION:
MARIE'S MYSTICAL TRANSFORMATION

A.D. Nock, in his classic study of religious change in the ancient world, wrote:

> By conversion we mean the reorientation of the soul of an individual, his deliberate turning from indifference or from an earlier form of piety to another, a turning which implies a consciousness that a great change is involved, that the old was wrong and the new is right.[1]

In Nock's definition we see the mingling of objective and subjective elements of conversion. The change involved is external, the embracing of a new form of piety, but it is also internally determined for it is rooted in the subject's consciousness of a radical change having occurred. What is perhaps most striking in this definition — one which in itself is culturally bound — is Nock's implicit acknowledgement of conversion's intangible quality when he refers to it as the "reorientation of the soul of an individual." This phrase illustrates the difficulty in trying to account for conversion in purely objective terms, and suggests that conversion, by its very nature, invites the use of metaphysical language.

Because religious conversion is both an individual experience grounded in the personal conviction of a radical change, as well as an event which is assessed according to the norms or criteria of a given society or religious group, the attempt to categorize and describe conversions is problematic, not least of all for the historian of religious life in the seventeenth century, who is confronted by a myriad of social phenomena, church activities and literary testimonies — all of which fall under the heading of "conversion." But it is often the methods used in discussing conversion — and not just the multitude of categories which the topic encompasses — that hamper our understanding of the phenomenon. In fact, much of the research on

---

[1] A.D. Nock, *Conversion. The Old and the New in Religion from Alexander the Great to Augustine of Hippo*, Oxford 1960, p. 7.

conversion to date has been dominated by two basic approaches to conversion — that of the social scientist and that of the religious believer — which seem geared more towards explaining than understanding conversion.[2] The former often explains the nature and causes of conversion in terms of prior conditioning, social influences and psychological patterns. In particular, psychological and sociological methods often emphasise unconscious elements or functional features of the experience and seem intent on reducing conversion to "real," i.e., quantitatively describable causes; to strip away, as it were, the religious layer which is seen as a dispensable superstructure which only obscures what "really" happens in conversion.

The religious believer, on the other hand, sees conversion as a change on the ontological and not just personal-subjective level, and points to the intervention of a transcendental being as the ultimate cause of the transformation. Thus, while one approach is concerned primarily with the objective factors and external circumstances which govern conversion, the other posits God as the prime agent, root cause and ultimate object of the turning process. Whereas the social scientist has a positivistic bias, the religious believer has a supernatural frame of reference, and their discourse reflects their respective concerns; the former uses scientific, the latter metaphysical language. What both have in common, however, is the tendency to explain religious phenomena in absolute terms, reducing them in almost deterministic fashion to a final cause. Both the rationalist and the religious believer also have rules of discourse which enable them to understand and explain the fact of the other's faith or rational atheism.[3]

When discussing radical religious experiences such as conversion — or indeed, any spiritual claims — it is important to avoid the tone of "the village preacher" but equally imperative to eschew the stance of "the village atheist," for it is the antagonism between the two which can obscure valid perspectives on issues in religious culture.[4] The basic problem with both the village preacher and the village atheist approaches is that there is often little concern to get at the underlying moods and motivations which shape the individual's culture, personality, and also inevitably, his or her religious experience. Since the religious experience is explained according to preconceived notions, the individual's perception of the

[2] Max Heirich, "Change of Heart," *American Journal of Sociology* 83 (1977), p. 653.

[3] Leszek Kolakowski militates against the tendency to subordinate religious thought to rational ways of looking. See *Religion*, London 1982, p. 213.

[4] These terms are borrowed from Clifford Geertz's "Religion As a Cultural System" in *The Interpretation of Cultures. Selected Essays*, New York 1973, p. 123.

conversion is not always considered essential to the enquiry. In order to come to a close understanding of what actually happens in conversion, however, the individual must be placed in the centre of the assessment of the experience. Between scientific diagnoses of the psychological roots or social benefits of conversion and the self-contained theological assertion of a human soul being infused with divine grace there remains an impasse which can only be bridged by a rigorous appraisal of both sets of claims and how they relate to the convert's particular situation, character and self-understanding.

Fortunately, there is a tendency nowadays to nurture a less mechanical and more hermeneutical approach to religious phenomena and to see all social constructions as the result of the meanings we confer on experience. In cultural anthropology it is a commonplace that interpreting requires one to understand from the point of view of the agents themselves. This approach is rooted in the view that since human beings are "self-interpreting animals" it is important to understand what their cultural and social beliefs and practices mean for *them*.[5] This means that the thoughts and feelings, the emotional make-up and mental world of the convert must be investigated on their own terms and not dismissed in favour of external facts and factors whose appeal is often in the veneer of objectivity and rationality which they provide. This is not to say that subjectivity and irrationality must in themselves be lauded, but it must be recognized that there are phenomena which cannot be understood without recourse to viewpoints which the positivist of yore would have thrown out simply because they are not susceptible of rational analysis. With regard to the convert's understanding of his experience, then, today's cultural anthropologists would concur with the phenomenologists of half a century ago who argued that one "cannot describe the structure of conversion in itself without taking this divine influence into account as one factor in our comprehension."[6] Religious believers live in a world of meaning which is shared with others. Neither religious beliefs nor experiences can be seen as purely subjective inventions, rooted only in the individual's psyche. Nor is conversion imposed on the individual from without. Since religious experience is always real and ultimate for the religious individual, religious needs and beliefs are as real as material needs and social conditioning.

---

[5] Charles Taylor, "Self-Interpreting Animals," in *Human Agency and Language, Philosophical Papers*, vol. 1, Cambridge 1985, pp. 45–76.

[6] See G. van der Leeuw, *Religion in Essence & Manifestation. A study in Phenomenology...*, trans. J.E. Turner, London 1938, p. 534.

Beliefs do not develop in an individual alone, but in a collective system of values, practices and cultural forms. Any interpretative theory which seeks to reduce these to objective underlying realities such as social pressure or psychological crisis, is missing the point about religious life as a cultural reality.

The aim of this study, then, is neither to explain away conversion nor to unquestioningly accept its characterization as a divine gift, but rather to understand what religious conversion meant for Marie de l'Incarnation in her religious context. Instead of probing primarily the unconscious elements or external factors that might explain her conversion, we should focus on its conscious elements, i.e., those recounted by the convert herself. This is important in the case of Marie, not least of all because we are dealing with her written testimony, or her ordering and interpretation several decades after the fact, of an experience for which her autobiographical account is ultimately the only real source of information. Of course one need not and should not stop the investigation with an assessment of the agent's account of conversion for there are many elements which the agent may not mention, or even be aware of, which are nonetheless important to the picture as a whole. The hermeneutical approach requires us not to believe, but to take very seriously the meaning which the convert confers on his experience and the implications of this transformation for his self-understanding and subsequent religious life. However, this does not preclude consideration of unconscious motives, nor does it rule out the discussion of social influences and psychological factors in the conversion process. It merely suggests that these cannot be made exclusive foci in our attempt to come to terms with conversion as a historical phenomenon and cultural experience.

In our attempt to muddle through fact and fiction and understand the agent we must therefore also consider factors contributing to and consequences issuing from the conversion, which the convert may or may not have taken into account in describing its nature and effects. This is what is meant by the fusion of horizons which is sought after in a hermeneutical approach. Marie's vantage point when she writes about conversion includes her recollection of her spiritual turning some thirty-four years earlier, as well as her basic theological understanding of what happens in conversion, and her own involvement in the conversion of others. Her overall idea of conversion, then, comprises experiential, theoretical and practical dimensions, all of which must be kept in sight when bringing our own critical tools and modern understanding to bear on her testimony.

It is worth noting that A.D. Nock prefaces his characterization of

conversion with the words "By conversion we mean ...," and indeed his
own classic study of religious change in the ancient world is positive proof
that the attempt to penetrate the convert's world of meaning is a much
more interesting and rewarding enterprise than is the pursuit of definitions
and theories. To know what meaning a Catholic in the seventeenth century
would have attached to the term conversion we must consider both the
Catholic tradition of conversion and the social reality of religious change
in that period. It is not a definition or theory that we are after but rather a
cultural and contextual understanding of conversion. The seventeenth-
century context is particularly important not only because Marie's experience manifests several of the "types" of conversion prevalent in her day,
but also because the very idea of conversion was in the air and this
ambiance du mot pervaded her religious situation.[7]

Marie's conscious and subconscious notions concerning conversion
were culled from a long-standing tradition of Catholic conversion, of
which its manifestations in Reformation society were only the tip of the
iceberg. The idea of conversion in the Catholic tradition has a long
history, one with roots in the biblical and classical notions of spiritual
turning, and one which has been passed on in images, concepts and stories
in a host of different writings. This literary inheritance, which spans many
centuries, includes material on the theoretical, historical, and practical
aspects of conversion. For the Church, conversion had always been rooted
in theory — that is, in the theological description of what happens between
God and man. Since its earliest days the Church had also had to tackle the
practical question of how to achieve conversion of others or of oneself. In
the history of Christianity, however, it is not so much the what or the how
of conversion which immediately jumps to mind, but rather the individuals
who have shaped not only the idea of conversion but also the whole course
of Christianity. Indeed, it is the "history" of conversion — the repository
of examples of famous converts and their stories — which makes up the
core of our basic knowledge of conversion.[8]

At the beginning of the seventeenth century the Catholic reform was in
its prime and conversion was at the centre of theological debate, pastoral

---

[7] P. Aubin uses the term *ambiance du mot* in reference to the contexts in which the word
conversion is used, and the images it evokes in a given period. This *ambiance* is thus an
important component of the word's religious meaning. See *Le problème de la conversion*,
Paris 1963, p. 18.

[8] The notion of historical knowledge as a repository of examples is common to medieval
and renaissance historiography. See Denys Hay, *Annalists and Historians: Western Historiography from the Eighth to the Eighteenth Centuries*, London 1977.

activity, moral teaching, missionary work and spiritual life.[9] Both in its
drive for institutional reform (an initiative dating back to the late medieval
Church) and in its attempts to counter the reformation tide of its oppo-
nents, the Catholic Church showed a frenzied concern with and promotion
of conversion.[10] Conversion had by this period become a science, the
moral, psychological and social aspects of which were being more carefully
assessed, documented and applied in the Church's attempt to review and
reform the religious life of its adherents, and to convert those still dallying
outside the fold. Apart from the polemics aimed at subverting the Protestant reformers' message, the Catholic Church also channelled much energy
into the growing organization of the overseas missions which helped the
Church to expand in geographic terms and strengthen its claim to universal
truth. Parallel to the missionary campaign to win new members in far-flung
lands, Catholic Europe saw the launching of the Church's "inner mission"
which consisted of reforms and pastoral strategies at the basic level of
popular religion designed to turn the "nominally" Catholic in local communities — especially in rural areas — to a more pristine form of Catholic
faith and orthodox behaviour.[11] At the same time the monastic communities, traditionally the mainstay of Catholic belief and practice, were also
the object of wide-sweeping reforms; they witnessed changes in the rules
and running of their ordered life and harkened to the call to reform and
renew their spiritual life. In fact, much of the Church's reforming endeavour can be seen as conversion activity and much of the spiritual writing of
the period can be read as conversion literature.

Conversion as a turning or orientation of one's life to the way of
spiritual perfection was a central theme in the substantial body of spiritual
literature available to the reading public in the seventeenth century.
Throughout the sixteenth century, French spirituality had been nourished
by an abundant variety of devotional literature comprising for the most
part imported editions and translations of older spiritual classics. But by
the beginning of the new century a myriad of spiritual texts — from the

---

[9] An excellent collection of essays on various aspects of conversion in this period is *La Conversion au XVIIe Siècle. Actes du XIIe Colloque de Marseille*, C.M.R. 17, 1983.

[10] It has been suggested that both reform movements were essentially aimed at conversion and acculturation. See R. Chartier, D. Julia, and M.-M. Compère, *L'éducation en France du XVIe au XVIIe siècle*, Paris 1976, p. 294.

[11] See *XVIIe siècle* 41 (1958), a special issue devoted to the Catholic missions within France during this period. See also Jean Delumeau, "Missions de l'intérieur au XVIIe siècle" in *Un chemin d'histoire. Chrétienté et christianisation*, Paris 1981, pp. 154–187. *La Conversion au XVIIe Siècle* also contains several essays on the inner mission.

sixth-century mystical writings of Pseudo-Dionysius to modern spiritual classics such as the works of St. Teresa of Avila — were also available in French translation.[12] At the same time original works of contemporary French authors were also being published and disseminated to a wider reading audience. This writing reflected the Catholic Church's strategy for spiritual renewal, but was also a manifestation of the religious enthusiasm which reigned in devout circles and which by the beginning of the century had also filtered down to the ordinary Catholic. In this period mystics were to be found not only among the clergy and female religious but in all classes of society.[13] Partly as a result of the influx of preachers into towns and rural districts and the impact of their sermons, and partly as a result of the increased printing and circulation of religious books in the period, the desire for spiritual growth and proximity to God was now taking root in Catholic consciousness at all levels of society.

But it would be wrong to leave the impression that the stress on methods, images, and meditations as a course of action for devout souls was the essence of spirituality in the seventeenth century. Certainly, in texts which instructed the individual to order his prayers, habits and decisions to the end of greater spiritual perfection, particularly by meditating on the life and mysteries of Christ, conversion meant a turning to a devout life. But there were also spiritual texts which outlined in speculative or in descriptive personal terms the experience of special chosen souls who reached the extraordinary heights of spiritual life. In fact, it was in the seventeenth century that the noun mysticism as a formal term referring to this kind of literature, appeared for the first time.[14] These mystical, as opposed to ascetic, works described spiritual conversion not so much as the orientation of the soul to an imitation of Christ, but rather as the soul's total transformation through union with Christ. Obviously spiritual directors and church leaders were reluctant to highlight this heightened stage of spiritual life, which is characterized not by our efforts but by God's gift of extraordinary graces, by infused as opposed to acquired grace, for it could lead believers to seek these unusual experiences for their own sake; it could lead to delusions and excesses among those who convinced themselves that they had received this extraordinary gift of contemplation; and it

---

[12] L. Cognet, *Crépuscule des Mystiques. Le Conflit Fénelon-Bossuet*, Tournai 1958, p. 13. See also J. Dagens, *Bibliographie chronologique de la littérature de spiritualité et de ses sources, 1501–1610*, Paris 1953.

[13] Bremond, *Histoire littéraire du sentiment religieux*, vol. 1, p. xviii.

[14] M. De Certeau, *La Fable mystique. XVIe–XVIIe siècle*, Paris 1982, p. 47.

could encourage them to abandon the ordinary efforts or active way of contemplation.

Thus, for the average Frenchman the idea of conversion was still inextricably caught up in the teaching on sin and damnation, but the message was reinforced by the sermons, iconography and literature of the day;[15] famous converts such as St. Paul and St. Augustine still peopled the Christian imagination but a host of other saints and martyrs now joined the roster of exemplary figures as new critical editions of lives of saints and translations of classical devotional works became increasingly available;[16] and the practical problem of converting heretics and pagans was a concrete reality in the minds of a people just emerging from the bloody wars of religion and also beginning to hear reports of the mission to evangelize the inhabitants of the New World.

By the seventeenth century, then, the theory, practice and experience of conversion had taken on new dimensions and the idea of religious change in its various guises infiltrated the public imagination and was captured in a rapidly expanding body of Christian literature. The general theological, historical and practical notions of conversion mentioned above, that is, conversion as the crux of personal salvation, as a powerful literary motif or as a missionary activity, were part of the mental baggage which Church leaders and ordinary Catholics carried over into this new age. In France, as elsewhere in Catholic Europe, innovation and change were beginning to make their impact on what was still very much a traditional society, and while the idea of conversion retained much that was old it also acquired — not surprisingly — new dimensions.

The above overview suggests that while conversion is totally personal and interior, its causes and consequences are invariably linked to the religious tradition to which one has been exposed and to the community in which one's conversion is ratified and lived out. Marie de l'Incarnation's experience of conversion, both as an event and process in her own life and

[15] See M. Vovelle, "La conversion par l'image: Des vanités aux fins dernières en passant par le macabre dans l'iconographie du XVIIe siècle", in *La Conversion au XVIIe Siècle*, pp. 297–310. But not all conversion imagery was of the hell-fire and brimstone variety. From around 1300 onwards the *tolle, lege* scene of Augustine's *Confessions* appeared in Christian iconography and came to dominate pictorial representations of the saint's life. See P. Courcelle, *Les Confessions de Saint Augustin dans la tradition littéraire. Antécédents et Postérité*, Paris 1963.

[16] On the pursuit of secular knowledge and adoption of critical historical methods by the Jesuits, Benedictines, Trappists and Bollandists, and the special interest in France on critical work on hagiography and ecclesiastical history, see Hazard, *The European Mind 1680–1715*, pp. 67–69.

as an activity directed at others, must be seen against the backdrop of religious society in seventeenth-century France, a society which was permeated by the idea and spirit of conversion.

When Marie was fifteen years old, she felt a strong pull towards religious life and broached the subject with her mother. Her mother immediately thought of the Benedictine monastery at Beaumont-les-Tours as a possibility since the abbess there was a distant relative and could facilitate Marie's acceptance. But she didn't really take seriously the option of a cloistered life for Marie, whose cheerful and high-spirited temperament she thought much better suited to married than to monastic life. Her parents found a likely suitor: Claude Martin, a master worker in the silk industry, and Marie acquiesced to their wishes. She left home at the age of seventeen when, as she somewhat wistfully notes, "our Lord permitted that my parents should marry me off." (A 5) Psychologically, the months during which she was married must have brought many changes. It is clear that the experience and responsibilities of married life prepared her in many ways for the hardships and duties that were to follow.[17]

Marie tells us that marriage was liberating in the sense that she left the parental home and the constraints which filial obedience and respect for her parents had entailed. During this period, for example, she began reading novels and romances "purely for the sake of pleasure and recreation" and this undoubtedly influenced her own facility of expression and writing style later on. (A 5) During this first year of marriage, however, she soon abandoned "books treating of useless things" in favour of "books of piety" and developed a spirit of retirement, preferring solitude, prayer and the practice of virtue to the company and ordinary pastimes of her peers. (A 5) This increase in piety perhaps had something to do with the activities and sermons in the jubilee year of 1617. Unfortunately we don't know much about the books which Marie read during this period, although Dom Oury suggests that it is quite possible that she read translations of works by both Catherine of Siena and Gertrude of Helfta before 1620.[18]

This monastic bent which had surfaced in her teen years and was now a fixed disposition increased the burden posed by married life. Along with

[17] Oury, *Marie Guyart*, p. 66.

[18] Ibid., pp. 30–2. Dom Oury mentions both popular and devotional works which were available in Tours during Marie's youth. He also points to the books which Marie considered fundamental to the spiritual training of Ursuline novices as a good indication of works which probably had an impact on her own spiritual formation. See his "Marie de l'Incarnation et la bibliothèque du noviciat des Ursulines de Québec," *Revue d'Ascétique et de Mystique* 46 (1970), pp. 397–410.

what Dom Oury refers to as the "psychological and physical maturity that marriage called forth in her," Marie felt a deepening in her spiritual life.[19] It was during this time that she felt a strong attraction to the sacraments and a desire not only to avoid sin and pursue virtue but also to make progress in prayer. Although Marie informs us that her husband was a good man and even encouraged her in her devotions, marriage brought its crosses and she refers to her married state as "a condition ... which was a constant source of opposition to the realization of the desire of the Spirit to gain my heart and my affection for Himself." (A 9)

The distractions of domestic life were amplified by the fact that Marie found herself in charge of a rather full household. Since the silk workshop was actually in the family house many of her husband's workers lived with members of their family under the Martins' roof. Marriage was thus not only a commercial apprenticeship for Marie but an initiation into the worldly company of sometimes unruly men whose language, manners, and general lack of virtue often caused her great distress. Despite her basic repugnance towards a position which was at odds with her deep inclination to a totally religious life, Marie claims to have enjoyed "great courage and great peace of soul, as well as a very lively faith." (A 6) In retrospect she felt that from the time of her childhood dream, up to and including her married years, God had been gently disposing her soul.

The contentment and self-assurance reflected in Marie's account of God's workings in her soul and of the effects of the sacraments during this period, are striking. This faith, she writes, "led me to perform many good works and begot in my soul a spirit of prayer which perfected whatever good was mine as a result of the graces and favours previously given me." (A 7) When she writes in matter-of-fact fashion that she "no longer had either taste or thought for anything except for what was good" one has the impression — as in the case of her mystical dream at age seven — that she saw herself in a sense as having a moral upper hand over others who had not been singled out for special divine graces. She did not consider herself perfect but certainly seemed more concerned about the morality of others:

> I wished that all those with whom our Lord put me in contact would also love to frequent the sacraments. I feared for them because of a certain type of sin which I learned was mortal and which they failed properly to confess. For I knew that in the sacrament of penance one was washed by the blood of Jesus Christ, and also that it was necessary to fulfil very exactly the penance

---

[19] Oury, *Marie Guyart*, p. 37.

enjoined. All of this caused me to exhort these persons to do what was
necessary in this matter. (A 7)

Marie seems to have no doubt that the persons in question — presumably
her husband's workers — had not confessed their sins properly, and gives
the impression that she considered herself to be conducting her own
sacramental life in impeccable fashion.

Despite the joy derived from her deepening spiritual life, Marie found
her second year of marriage demanding in both practical and emotional
terms. Among the trials she faced during the two years she was married
was an incident involving a female client of Claude Martin which ended in
disaster for the Martins. The incident is shrouded in mystery and seems to
have centred around the misplaced affections of a woman, who, when
rebuffed by Marie's husband, reacted in a nasty manner and caused the
financial downfall of the factory.[20] In April 1619 Marie gave birth to a son,
Claude, but this happy event was soon clouded over by the anxiety of the
summer months when her husband fell ill and the factory was teetering on
the brink of financial ruin. When Claude Martin died in the autumn, the
twenty-year old Marie was left to support a baby son and to take charge of
her husband's business, which had been suffering production loss for some
months and was beset with financial problems. Marie's practical sense and
the domestic skills she had acquired over the years served her well during
the fall and winter months. Despite her efficiency in overseeing the faltering
workshop production and in obtaining funds from the officers of the silk
guild in order to face lawsuits and reimburse creditors, the pressure and
uncertainty engendered by the situation were immense.

As evidenced in many conversion cases in the history of Christianity,
the convert is usually primed for conversion by a variety of factors,
intellectual, emotional, psychological, and especially by exposure to, or
immersion in, a defined religious context. Thus "even when the convert
may in all good faith profess that the beliefs which have won his sudden
assent are new to him, there is a background of concepts to which a
stimulus can give new life."[21] There is often a religious inclination on the
side of the subject which is shaped and intensified by factors which make
the object of the desire seem more attractive or feasible. But a catalyst is
usually required to bring religious inclination, mental or emotional needs,
and personal understanding together in a conversion experience.

There were many factors in Marie's case which helped set the stage for

---

[20] Ibid., p. 28. See Martin, *La Vie de la Vénérable Mère Marie de l'Incarnation*, p. 638.
[21] Nock, *Conversion*, p. 8.

her spiritual conversion in the spring of 1620. The exposure to a rich tradition had left an impact on her since earliest childhood, as had the authority and piety of her parents. But we must also take into account the thwarted desire for religious life and the protracted and simmering quandary over the niggling matter of the failure to confess childhood imperfections, both of which preoccupied her in her adolescence; and the conflict between the demands of married life and her deepening spiritual life, and finally, the shock and stress unleashed by her husband's death and the legal responsibilities which were thrown on her shoulders thereafter. It is significant that she ends her first chapter by mentioning her husband's death and the ensuing "crosses" which she had to carry, "crosses which naturally speaking were greater than a person of my sex, my age, and my capacity could have borne," were it not for the power and courage provided by God. (A 11) It is a commonplace that conversion often occurs at a time of emotional upheaval and although Marie hastens to add that God gave her such faith, hope and confidence "that neither the loss of temporal goods, nor the lawsuit, nor our poverty, nor the fact that my six-month-old son was as despoiled as I was of all possessions, made me in any way anxious," it is fair to assume that, her faith notwithstanding, she was under great strain at the time. (A 11)

In the months following her husband's death, Marie went to the factory every day and had to contend with the overwhelming administrative tasks and complications involved in closing down her late husband's business. She claims that her unwavering religious faith stood her in good stead as always and sustained her during this period. On her daily walk to work, which took her through the parish of St. Pierre-des-Corps and past the massive edifice of the medieval cathedral, she prepared herself for the day's tasks and troubles by offering up a prayer of confidence in God's help. It was on such a walk, one cool spring morning, that Marie stopped suddenly, losing all sense of time and place as she experienced a startling vision. The date was March 24, 1620 and this is how she describes the event:

> It happened that morning as I was on my way to begin my duties, duties which I earnestly recommended to God with my usual aspiration, *In Te Domine speravi, non confundar in aeternum*. This aspiration was so deeply rooted in my mind that I believed with the certitude of faith that He would infallibly assist me. Suddenly I was stopped in my tracks, both interiorly and exteriorly. This sudden arresting blotted out of my mind all thoughts about my duties. In a flash the eyes of my mind were opened and all the faults, sins, imperfections I had ever committed were represented to me

both in general and in particular, with a distinction and clarity more certain than any certitude that human effort could produce. At the same moment I saw myself completely immersed in blood, and I was convinced that ... this precious blood had been shed for my salvation.

If the goodness of God had not sustained me, I believe I would have died of fright, so horrible and shocking is the sight of sin, however small it may be. No human tongue can express it. Rather, to see a God of infinite goodness and purity offended by a worm of the earth surpasses horror itself, and especially to see a God-made-man die to expiate sin and shed all His precious blood to appease His Father and in this way reconcile sinners to Him! ...

These insights and operations are so penetrating that in one moment they express everything and produce their effects. In this same moment my heart felt snatched from itself and transformed into His love who had done it this signal mercy; and the experience of this love begot in me the most intense sorrow and regret for having offended Him. It would be impossible to imagine its intensity. This shaft of love is so penetrating and so inexorable ... that I would have cast myself into flames to satisfy it. But what is most incomprehensible is that its very severity seems sweet. This shaft of love possesses charms and chains which so bind the soul as to lead it whither it will, and the soul esteems itself fortunate to be thus captivated.

But in all of these extraordinary experiences I didn't at all lose the impression that I was plunged into the precious blood and that I was responsible for its having been shed. And it was this that caused my extreme sorrow at the very time that the arrow of love was ravishing my soul and also gave me an urge to go to confession. Coming to myself, I found myself standing in front of the little chapel of the Feuillant Fathers, who were just beginning to establish themselves at Tours. I was happy to find my remedy so close at hand. (A 13–14)

This dramatic experience, perceived as a sudden, direct and personal religious illumination, marked a radical change in the identity of Marie who writes "I returned to our home changed into another creature, but so powerfully changed that I didn't know myself any more." (A 15) She suddenly became aware of all her imperfections and was immediately overwhelmed by the thought that her sins were responsible for Christ's expiatory suffering and death. She writes "I saw unmasked my ignorance which had caused me to believe that I was quite perfect, that my actions were innocent, and finally that all was well with me; but I now humbly confessed that my justices were but iniquities."(A 15) The horror and fear which she felt at this insight into the personal nature of sin and her responsibility for Christ's suffering was accentuated by the impression of being immersed in his blood.

This inner conversion was not just a matter of acquisition of knowledge, for apart from the clear conviction of her sinfulness and the simultaneous and equally rivetting certainty of God's mercy, the experience sparked a powerful turn-around on an emotional and moral plane. Along with the intellectual — in this instance specifically theological — flash of under-standing with regard to the individual believer's role in Christ's death and redemption of sinners, and the feelings of fear and remorse which resulted from the attendant vivid vision, there was a moral change: a turn to a more devout life, marked by the urge to make a more thorough confession than ever before. As for new converts to Christianity, the sacraments were important for Marie in her new spiritual state, as they provided her with a continuous cycle of renewal in emotional and spiritual terms.[22]

Her experience has the classic markings of Christian conversion: it is a dramatic and total change, labelled as such by Marie herself; it occurs during a period of stress and pressure in her personal and professional life; it brings changes in emotional, intellectual, and moral terms; it not only illuminates her past but gives her a new spiritual identity in relation to Christ; and though a very personal experience, it is one which is clearly rooted in her Catholic upbringing and in the context of spiritual revival. By the time of her conversion Marie had amassed a wealth of religious knowledge and imagery, and some months before her conversion was already preoccupied with the image of Jesus' blood washing away sins.[23] Thus, the cultural, intellectual and emotional ingredients for conversion were present, and the primed material, as it were, needed only a catalyst in order to come to the fore as a conversion experience.

The conversion brought to her religious life a certain harmony or balance between personal spiritual leanings and a shared traditional framework. The relation between personality and religious structures, and the balance between passive absorption and active, conscious practice of faith began to shift. It was around this time that a sense of personal conviction or autonomous experience of faith emerged which established her religious identity and gave her strength to face future obstacles which clashed with her religious aspirations, be they as simple as the desire to enter a convent or as problematic as the unprecedented project of crossing the ocean as a woman missionary. Her habitual faith, love for the rites, forms and tenets of her Catholic faith were not in the least weakened or

[22] A.J. Krailsheimer, *Conversion*, London 1980, pp. 4–5.
[23] Huijben, "La Thérèse de la Nouvelle-France," pp. 110–111.

undermined by this conversion, but rather carried over and deepened in
the subsequent stages of religious life.

Conversion often brings little by way of a dramatic, perceptible change
in the external behaviour of the convert who, to the average observer,
seems to be behaving in the same way as always.[24] However, the significance of the event for the convert is overwhelming in personal terms. In
Marie's case it was the apprehension, in personal terms, of divine love and
mercy which constituted the radical change in her religious life and
identity. Indeed, perhaps most significant in her conversion was the
change from received faith to a living personal sense of God, from the
certitude afforded by habitual faith (as evidenced in her confident morning
prayer) to certitude of a different order — one acquired by a sudden
transforming experience.

The difference between the two stages of faith is reflected in the language
which Marie uses in her account of the event. The psalm which she offered
up on the way to work suggests the traditional mode of religious expression; following her conversion, she emphasises the intensity of the experience and tries to convey something of its ineffable nature through the use
of conflicting images. Though God's transforming love is harsh and
unrelenting it leaves Marie content, for "its very severity seems sweet ...
[It] possesses charms and chains which so bind the soul as to lead it
whither it will, and the soul deems itself fortunate to be thus captivated."

Conversion, as already noted, is not just a self-contained event but an
ongoing process, and this is implicit in Marie's own account of her
spiritual life. She understood this interior illumination not just as an
isolated incident which occurred on a given day in a certain place, but
rather as the beginning of her spiritual transformation. She experienced
this process in increasingly passive fashion, but Dom Jamet's claim that in
1620 she entered a state of "infused contemplation" seems inappropriate
since it underplays the active aspects of Marie's spiritual experience in the
initial stages of her journey.[25] In linking the notions of "second conversion"
and "infused contemplation" so closely, Jamet is using the term "second
conversion" in its narrower sense — that usually associated with the Jesuit
Louis Lallemant, who saw it as the entrance into a passive state characterized by total dependence on God. Marie's spiritual turning, however, is
closer to the general Jesuit notion of second conversion "through which
a soul good and regular passes on to a life completely interior and

---

[24] Krailsheimer, *Conversion*, p. 1.
[25] Jamet, *Écrits*, vol. I, p. 157.

detached, but not necessarily characterized by passive or infused prayer."[26]

It is significant that in ordering the various stages of her life, Marie allots only one of the thirteen chapters to the period of nineteen years leading up to her conversion. She is indicating that it was only after the spiritual conversion which she underwent at the age of twenty that her real life began, or took on meaning. Unlike a convert such as Augustine, who chronicled in detail his lengthy pursuit for truth and his sinful life prior to conversion, thereby highlighting the unsatisfactory past which he abandoned in favour of God, Marie was more interested in describing the years following, than the years preceding her conversion. This is because for her, the conversion meant something different. While she also indicates that this experience brought an end to a moral dilemma which had weighed upon her for three or four years, she saw the event not so much as a release from emotional upheaval, intellectual frustration, or a misspent youth, as did Augustine, but rather as an initiation into mystical life. She refers to her spiritual conversion as the *"coup de grâce"* granted by God, as she puts it, to set "me on the way He willed that I should travel," namely, the way of mystical ascent. Thus, although her conversion also gave her insight into the idea of liberation from sin due to Christ's redemptive act, she understood the conversion not so much as a sudden and complete turning from a life of sin to a state of grace — a common enough pattern of conversion — but more as the start of a mystical journey, throughout which she was favoured with mystical "graces," as she calls them.

Writing to her son in 1656 in response to questions which he had asked about the vision of 1620 Marie explains:

> I have indicated to you what this impression brought about and its effectiveness, which is always new for me in remembering the great grace which I received at that time: which has always made me call that day the day of my conversion, and like a large door which has given me entry into the mercy of my divine Liberator, who penetrated the depth of my soul and spirit to change me into a new creature. (E II 374)

Marie saw her conversion not only as the event which gave her access to the mercy of Christ, but also as an ongoing spiritual turning which was renewed and nourished by the constant memory of that "great grace." Many years later she judged that this grace kept transforming her long after the day of her conversion; indeed she stresses that it was because of

---

[26] Joseph De Guibert, *The Jesuits. Their Spiritual Doctrine and Practice*, trans. W. Young, ed. G. Ganss, 3rd print., St. Louis 1986, p. 355.

the long-term spiritual impact or "effectiveness" of this experience in later years that she called it her conversion.

The theological understanding, powerful imagery and personal nature of this experience were carried through in her subsequent mystical experiences. Not just the fact that she felt herself changed on a given day, but also the very contents of that experience accompanied her on her spiritual journey. Thus Marie's conversion can be termed ongoing not just in the sense that she was constantly conscious of this turning-point in later years, but also because it continued to affect her unconsciously; for the image of Christ's blood and the message of his redemptive sacrifice were to resurface in her mystical, and later in her missionary, experience. One of the major consequences of her conversion was her renewed desire for religious life. But many years passed between the day of her conversion and the day on which she professed her vows.

During this time, which Dom Oury points to as the most delicate period of Marie's spiritual evolution, her conversion took the form of a rich mystical life which unfolded in a series of visions and illuminations, leading her, in spiritual and psychological terms, beyond the normative framework of ordinary religious practice and teaching, to an extraordinary and direct personal experience of God; the term "mystical," then, is used in this sense of a transforming *cognitio Dei experimentalis*.[27] In much of the literature on Marie's spirituality the conversion of 1620 is referred to as her first mystical favour, or the "extraordinary grace" which marks her entry into mystical life proper.[28] But whereas some scholars tend to see the conversion simply as a first step in her mystical life which was followed by other, more significant mystical moments, for Marie it was much more than this.[29] It marked a new spiritual mode of being and acting. The mystic herself declares that she was changed into a "new creature" as a result of

---

[27] G. Oury, *Ce que croyait*, p. 22. Alois Haas also sees this "experiential perception of God" as a basic working definition. See *Sermo mysticus. Studien zu Theologie und Sprache der deutschen Mystik*, Freiburg 1979, p. 12.

[28] See Jamet, *Écrits*, vol. II, p. 193, n. 1. R. Michel sees Marie's conversion as the point at which she entered "the way of the spirit "and began her "mystical ascent". See *Vivre dans l'Esprit: Marie de l'Incarnation*, Montréal 1975, p. 18, and p. 19, n. 17.

[29] A. Thiry remarks that traces of the memory of the conversion experience were perceptible later in Marie's life, but considers her 1622 vision of God as a sea of purity to be more significant. See *Marie de l'Incarnation. Itinéraire spirituel*, Paris 1973, p. 43. Dom Oury, on the other hand, does stress the importance of the conversion and its attendant vision of Christ's blood, and notes that this image recurs even at a much later stage in her spiritual journey, when, for example, regarding the salvation of pagan souls she mentions her happiness at seeing them bathed in the blood of Christ. See *Ce que croyait*, pp. 111–113.

Christ entering the "depths of her soul and spirit" and, as we shall see, this process of Christ penetrating and taking possession of her soul was a gradual one.

At this early stage in her mystical life, with the vision of Christ's sacrifice still fresh in her mind, Marie was absorbed in the thought of her essentially sinful nature and preoccupied by the concern for her salvation.[30] She writes "for more than a year after this divine operation in my soul the impression of (being immersed in) our Lord's blood remained with me, along with a new impression of His sufferings." (A 15) She explains "I beheld in the shedding of the blood of the Son of God the remedy enabling me to attain happily to my last end." (A 17) In order to make herself worthy of that remedy, she devoted herself "to acts of thanksgiving, to blessing God, to detesting what was not God, to acts of loving compunction," and began to do penances, frequent the sacraments, attend sermons and cultivate solitude. (A 17)

Marie's conversion to a more spiritual life, however, was not only motivated by her gratitude for Christ's redemptive act and sorrow for her sins. A central element of her conversion experience was the sensation that her heart was snatched up and lovingly "transformed" by God. She was moved then, not just by worry over her personal salvation but also by the desire for spiritual perfection and union with God, who was beginning "to communicate Himself" to her in an immediate and extraordinary manner. (A 16) She notes "that my heart should speak so intimately and so eloquently to Him was for me quite incomprehensible." (A 16) The image of Christ's blood which stood at the centre of her conversion experience was perceived not only as the key to salvation which inspired her with remorse for her moral imperfection, but also as the key to sanctification, since it was for Marie the "life and nourishment" of her soul in its "continual colloquy" with God. (A 17, 24) Spurred on by several "new lights," or illuminations, regarding the purity of soul required for attaining proximity to God, she embarked on a path of purification, virtue and prayer and felt even more drawn to contemplative life.

After dealing with all the matters involved in liquidating her husband's defunct business Marie went to live in her father's house where she spent a year sewing, reading, and praying. At the end of this year of quiet reflection — a kind of *christianae vitae otium* — she was asked to help in the employ

---

[30] Marie reflects the increasingly "individualized" anxiety regarding personal salvation which led in post-Tridentine society to a heavier emphasis on moral discipline and good works as aids to salvation. See Briggs, *Communities of Belief*, pp. 201, 282–283, 254.

of her sister and her husband, which she agreed to do on condition that she be allowed to continue her devotional practices.[31] At this stage, however, she was still seeking her way in spiritual life, using different methods such as mental prayer, devotional reading, and ascetic exercises. While finding herself caught up in the thick of business matters and the worldly demands of her new role in daily life, Marie felt a profound "aversion for the world and its manner of life" and wished to talk "only about God and about virtue" and "to run in his service." (A 16–17) After reading François de Sales' *Introduction to the Devout Life*, which advocates spiritual perfection as a goal for the ordinary believer, and consulting with her confessor, she also took the vow of chastity, thereby sealing her decision not to remarry.

Marie's most painful dilemma during this period was the inevitable separation from her son Claude, which she realised would be necessary to achieve her religious goals. Abandoning her son was a prospect which she considered unavoidable, but it weighed heavily on her conscience even though it was not unheard of in her day to leave behind one's family or children in order to fulfil a perceived call from God to religious life.[32] For example, Angélique Arnauld, the abbess of Port-Royal, felt that the matter of family ties was a question of an inner struggle between nature and grace and subsequent to her entry into Port-Royal, she consented to face family members only through the screen in the parlour. Jeanne de Chantal, who entered the convent of the Visitation in 1610, was like Marie in that she abandoned her son, Celse-Bénigne, at a sensitive age. He was fourteen at the time, but unlike Marie's son Claude, he was much better off in terms of his financial and family situation. Claude himself made the point that while "many fathers and mothers leave their children to enter religious life," in so doing, they at least leave them their worldly goods. (E I 275) Marie herself was troubled on this point despite her sister's assurance that she would look after Claude, and despite the promise of the Jesuit Jacques Dinet that a place would be found for Claude at the Jesuit school in Rennes. Her sorrow and guilt feelings were doubtless amplified by those who criticized her for shirking her maternal duty.

---

[31] Peter Brown uses this phrase in reference to Augustine's retreat to Cassiciacum following his conversion in 386. Marie, like Augustine, saw this period of withdrawal as a time of quiet reflection in which the implications of her new religious identity took root. See Brown, *Augustine of Hippo*, p. 115.

[32] On similar cases of "abandonment" see Jamet, *Écrits*, vol. 1, pp. 274–275, n. *c*, p. 275, n. *a*; pp. 288–289, n. 5; and Bremond's chapter "Mother and Son," in *Histoire littéraire du sentiment religieux*, vol. 6, pp. 49–71.

THE DYNAMICS OF CONVERSION

Like others before and after her, though, Marie managed to allay her fears and justify her decision in spiritual terms. What sets her case apart from similar instances such as those mentioned above is that we possess a detailed written account of both her and Claude's views on the matter. One would need a great deal of spiritual empathy, or at least some insight into the mindset of the devout souls of the Catholic Reformation, to read Marie's account of the separation with any sympathy. Its ethereal tone, for all the sorrow expressed therein, comes across as cool, calm, at times even callous. In her *Relation de 1633*, written two years after entering religious life, she refers to Claude as "totally resigned" and admits:

> He aroused such compassion in me that it seemed my soul was being torn out of my very being, but God was dearer to me than all this; leaving him therefore in his hands I laughingly bade him farewell, then upon receiving the blessing of my confessor, I threw myself at the feet of the Reverend Mother, who received me with great love and affection. (E I 284–5)

Her farewell speech, in which she tries to reassure Claude while explaining the necessity of her departure, illustrates her concern, but not the degree of sensitivity one would expect:

> Today when I am about to part from you, I didn't want to do it without telling you and asking you to accept it. I could have left you without making any noise and without talking to you about it, for it is a question of my salvation, and when it is a question of saving oneself, one need not ask permission of anyone. But because I didn't want to sadden you and didn't want you to be too stunned to see yourself, all of a sudden, without father and mother, I have asked you here in particular to ask your consent. God wants this my son, and if we love him we must want this as well. It is for him to command and for us to obey. If this separation afflicts you, you must think that it is a great honour which God grants me to have chosen me to serve him, and that it should be a great source of satisfaction to you that I will pray for you day and night. This being the case, do you not then want me to obey God, who orders me to part from you? (E I 281–2)

Writing in retrospect, Claude could rationalize his mother's abandonment of her young son, but he does not disguise the bewilderment and sorrow that he felt at the time in coming to terms with her decision and the manner in which she executed her designs. The young Claude was obviously far from sanguine about the imminent separation, and fifteen days before her entry into the convent he ran away, and was found three days later at the port of Blois. In reference to Marie's farewell speech Claude notes:

> This was the time and the place to give her son a kiss, as a last sign of her

affection, but she did not, just as she had never done in the past, which
seems to me to be rare in a mother, and which always caused me great
amazement until I learned the reason, [one] which shows a quite extraordinary wisdom ... (E I 283)

Marie had explained to her son that since the time of her husband's death,
her inner conviction that she would one day enter religious life and have to
leave Claude, made her avoid overt displays of affection. She had not
allowed him to embrace her either, feeling that this would lessen the blow
of the future separation. Claude claimed that this plan backfired since in
this way there was an even stronger and more deeply-rooted bond between
them which made the moment of separation more difficult for both. There
is no way of knowing to what extent he was soothed by Marie's counsel,
but he gave the consent which she requested, thereby enabling her to enter
the convent with a lightened mind, albeit still very mixed emotions. It is
small wonder, then, that Marie acceded to her son's persistent request
several years later, that she share with him the secrets of her spiritual life.
The resulting account, *La Relation de 1654*, remains one of the classics of
seventeenth-century spiritual writing.

The vision of 1620 is not the most extraordinary of those described by
Marie de l'Incarnation in her *Relation de 1654*, but it is the most important
inasmuch as it precipitated the event which, in retrospect, she singled out
as the turning-point in her life. Marie's spiritual conversion was a pivotal
experience and its fruits were twofold: it set her personal mystical transformation in motion and it also carried with it the seeds of her missionary
vocation. The best source for studying her conversion as an ongoing
process of transformation is her *Relation de 1654*. It is the only full-length
work of Marie's which has survived in its entirety and in the original
version in which it was written.[33] This spiritual autobiography, written
some thirty-three years after the vision of 1620 and incorporating her
subsequent religious experience both as a mystic and missionary, reflects
her mature and calculated assessment of her conversion and its significance
for her spiritual development.

The conversion experience of 1620, which afforded Marie at once a
clearer religious self-image and a stronger conviction of her unique relationship with God, enabled her — insofar as this was possible — to take
the reins of her spiritual life in hand. This is not to say that at this stage in

---

[33] See Oury, *Marie Guyart*, pp. ii–iii; and J. Lonsagne, "Les Écrits spirituels de Marie de
l'Incarnation. Le problème des textes," *Revue d'Ascétique et de Mystique* 44 (1968), pp.
161–182.

her religious development she rejected or relativized her role within the traditional context of Church life and practice. She never saw her extraordinary experiences as grounds for bypassing the formal structure, and even when she came to see herself as the bride of Christ she still considered herself a faithful daughter of the Church. This orthodox element is a constant feature of Christian mystical experience, for however extraordinary or novel such an experience may be, "the 'novelty' is legitimized, as well as domesticated, by the fact of its transmission through the ultimate authority of the Church."[34]

The mystic's religious tradition, i.e., surroundings, upbringing, specific models of behaviour and general formative impulses etc., certainly affects his or her religious development and prepares the ground for a conversion experience. But regardless of how embedded in this tradition and indebted to ideal models the convert may be, he or she also has a distinct sense of the personal nature of the illumination. If, as I have suggested, the *formative* stage of Marie's conversion, i.e., the period leading up to 1620, was characterized by a rather passive reception of theological, sacramental and devotional elements of her faith within the institutional framework of seventeenth-century Catholicism, the *transformative* stage of her experience was much more personal and active, and brought her own experience of religion to the fore. In Marie's case, as in the case of Teresa of Avila, the spiritual conversion signalled a move to a more mature level of religious life, where the desire for salvation was overshadowed by the desire for sanctification, and guided more by love of, than fear of God.[35]

Marie's conversion had to be worked out after the fact, and the composition of her *Relation de 1654* was part of the process. By sifting through, choosing and ordering the meaningful events in her religious development, she came to terms with her mystical experiences and their implications for her active spiritual identity. In his biography of St. Augustine, Peter Brown offers an apt metaphor to illustrate the situation of the new convert who, firm in the conviction that his life has changed course, finds himself for a time in a spiritual harbour but still has many storms to face before his

---

[34] Katz, "The 'Conservative' Character of Mysticism," p. 23. He adds that however radical or extraordinary the mystics' experiences may seem, their lives are models of "traditional piety." See p. 35.

[35] Teresa of Avila's decision to enter the convent was prompted primarily by concern for her salvation, since she felt "that the trials and hardships of the religious life could not be greater than those of purgatory." It was only after her conversion, some twenty years after becoming a nun, that her prayer life became motivated not so much by fear as by "love of God His Majesty" and by the "desire to spend more time with Him." See *The Life*, pp. 32, 69.

new identity becomes firmly rooted.[36] This was the case with Marie, whose new identity was of a mystical nature; she passed through several "states" in her spiritual life, encountering both ecstasies and dark periods or spiritual trials, and ultimately her quest for closer proximity to God culminated in the union of her soul with the divine will and participation in the divine operations.

Marie's subsequent experience as a mystic, missionary and writer testifies to the profound impact of the conversion of 1620 on her religious life. This spiritual transformation was an event which was captured in her writing; it was the first step in a new stage of spiritual growth and mystical experience; and it was lived out in "conversion activity" as she set out to inspire Ursuline novices to a more spiritual faith and attempted to win over Indians to the Catholic faith. Her "formation" did not end in 1620; indeed the period from 1620–1631 is considered by most of her commentators to be the crucial period in her spiritual formation.[37] The fact that she had to grow into her new identity perhaps attests to the impact of her religious formation on her personality; while those early formative influences certainly helped to plant the seed of conversion, they also presented ample obstacles to its actual ripening at a later stage. Thus, though in 1620 there is no immediate total change, the conversion did mark a watershed in Marie's religious life, because it turned her consciously towards an active realization of her religious self in a new spiritual life. Her *formation* continued, but her spiritual, intellectual and psychological development now occurred in the context of the transformation sparked by this event. She now saw herself as being shaped in a personal and direct fashion by God, who she felt had chosen her for a special relationship with him.

In the Catholic tradition in particular, the Church is both the starting point for conversion experience and the destination in which the experience finds its communal expression. Both in its traditional sense and in its manifestation in seventeenth-century religious life, the Catholic idea of conversion manifests certain consistent features which we can designate as its transformative, formative and performative aspects. The transformation is a private and individual affair, both in the sense that the way in which it occurs and is perceived is dependent on the particular personality and circumstances of the person involved, and in the sense that it is only by

---

[36] Brown, *Augustine of Hippo*, p. 177.

[37] Dom Oury refers to Marie's third and final trinitarian vision in 1631 as the summit and definitive seal of her spiritual experience. See *Ce que croyait*, p. 152. Dom Huijben suggests that as of 1633, the date of Marie's profession of vows, "her formation [had] been fully achieved." See "La Thérèse de la Nouvelle-France," p. 117.

virtue of the individual's consciousness of the event happening that the conversion is made known to the outsider. Nonetheless this conversion is always prepared to a certain degree by the cultural context in which the individual thinks and acts. In the case of Marie de l'Incarnation, the tradition and social reality of Catholic life must be taken into consideration as the formative if not directly causal background to the conversion experience.

The religious transformation of the individual — both theologically seen and in historical examples from St. Paul to St. Ignatius — invariably issues in charitable works. Indeed, as the lives of the two saints mentioned illustrate, the service of God and of others often takes the specific form of conversion activity. For this reason it is appropriate to talk of the performative stage of conversion. In fact the stories of such converts have often served as catalysts in the lives of others and it is because of their implicitly practical nature that they have become part of the formative material of tradition. This three-fold pattern should not be seen as a definitive model *per se* for Christian conversion, but rather as a useful way of understanding Marie de l'Incarnation's experience of conversion.[38] Her religious life illustrates that all three aspects of the traditional idea of conversion — the theoretical practical and experiential — are interdependent; and that the three stages of conversion — the formative, transformative and performative — form a circle that perpetuates this tradition.

One of the tasks of the following chapter, which traces this itinerary, is to show how her mystical experience not only accommodated, but in fact necessitated, her mission to convert others, and to examine in greater detail the effects of this ongoing mystical transformation on her self-image and spiritual writing.

[38] See my "Patterns of Conversion in Christianity," *Studies in Spirituality* 2 (1992), pp. 209–222.

CHAPTER THREE

SUBLIME STATES AND DIVINE DUTIES:
MARIE'S SPIRITUAL AUTOBIOGRAPHY

Putting the final touches on her autobiography in 1654, Marie justified its composition in a short preface:

> I have been ordered by him who holds the place of God in the direction of my soul to put down in writing, insofar as I can, the graces and favours which the Divine Majesty has given me by means of the gift of prayer He has been pleased to grant me. I will, then, undertake this task for God's honour and greater glory, in the name of the most adorable Word Incarnate, my heavenly and divine Spouse. (A 1)

Her *Relation de 1654* was not meant as an exercise in self-expression, but rather as a chore undertaken to satisfy her spiritual director and to glorify God's wondrous workings in her soul. By telling the story of how God called her to contemplative life and missionary activity, chose her as his spiritual bride, and indirectly requested her to commit these details to writing, Marie depicts her whole life in terms of chosenness. But despite her emphasis on religious tasks and divine callings, which would lead one to believe that she had no real choice with regard to her spiritual life, missionary calling or even the composition of her autobiography, it is clear that she did make definitive and painful choices in the course of her life. In offering her autobiography as a work "for the greater glory of God" — a phrase which hinges on the comparative "greater" and implies that there are different ways of serving God — she indicates her awareness of the scope and need for individual decision-making in spiritual life.[1] Though distancing herself from the "task" of writing down her mystical graces, by announcing that she had "been ordered" to do so "by him who holds the place of God" with regard to spiritual direction, *La Relation de 1654* is her

---

[1] The direction of one's prayers and actions to "the greater glory of God" or "*ad majorem dei gloriam*" was the Jesuit motto. See De Guibert, *The Jesuits*, p. 84. It has also been interpreted as a call to choose between alternatives for action which best serves God. See W. Ong, "'A.M.D.G.': Dedication or Directive?," *Review for Religious* 11 (1952), pp. 257–264.

undertaking. Though she dilutes the immediacy and extraordinary nature of her mystical experiences by referring to them in a round-about fashion, and although she stresses her passive and humble state, the one immutable fact that comes to the fore in this brief statement is that she saw herself as no less than the mystical bride of God, her "heavenly and divine Spouse." Both the humility and the exaltation which she expresses are very real, and in this sense the preface provides an apt preview of both the traditional Christian self and the very personal mystical self described in the book as a whole. The work highlights her unwavering deference to her spiritual director, her reverence for God, and her wish to serve others, but although ostensibly writing at the behest of and for the benefit of others, she was also giving formal expression to the realization of her own spiritual goals.

In her *Relation de 1654* Marie presents her mystical journey as a series of spiritual states or *"états d'oraison"* as she calls them. Accordingly she divides her life-story into thirteen chapters corresponding to these successive states of interior prayer.[2] While external events and details of day-to-day life are mentioned, it is clear that she is mainly concerned to narrate the story of her interior life. Because she is trying to assess and describe in a single work the religious feelings, emotional states, spiritual insights and external events which were experienced on different planes, both her style and discourse lack uniformity.[3] She is telling her personal story, but at the same time trying to elucidate in theological terms, the significance of her religious experiences. The result is a mixture of psychological insight, theological analysis, and emotional outpourings. The language she uses to

[2] In his translation of Marie's *Relation de 1654*, John Sullivan renders "état d'oraison" as "state of prayer," but following the English translator of Poulain's classic study of spirituality, who refers to "oraison" as "interior prayer," I have used the term "state of interior prayer," which reflects the distinction between verbal, ordinary forms of prayer, and mental prayer or extraordinary contemplation. See *The Graces of Interior Prayer. A Mystical Treatise*, trans. L. Smith, 6th ed., London 1928. Evelyn Underhill's use of "orison" and "infused orison" suggests that she found no adequate English equivalent for "oraison". See *Mysticism*, pp. 243, 254, 306.

[3] Elmer O'Brien makes a useful distinction between different kinds of mystical writing, and rightly notes that any assessment and classification of different works must take into account the intent behind, as well as the content of these texts. In commenting on the literary form of "spiritual accounts," which he differentiates from other types of mystical texts such as confessions, theological treatises, or personal advice, he suggests that they are "child's play. They are direct and to the point. Their purpose is single: to tell what happened." In listing Marie's autobiography under this category, he not only overlooks the pedagogical and confessional character of her narrative but also fails to consider the stylistic and theological complexity of its content. See *Varieties of Mystic Experience. An Anthology and Interpretation*, Toronto 1965, pp. 18–20.

describe her progressive spiritual ascent and its attendant moods conveys her intuitive observations of an initial religious awakening, her heightened awareness of God's presence, the restless anticipation of further illumination, and finally the sovereign conviction of total interior union with God; it not only conveys her spiritual progress at different stages in her life, but also reflects her emotional or intellectual development from a state of insecurity and confusion to one of confidence and understanding.

It is difficult to unravel this web of experiences, for objective statements regarding religious practices and subjective accounts of supernatural occurrences are intermingled throughout the narrative. Apart from having to juggle the thirteen different spiritual stages — which is a difficult task since Marie neither labels each one distinctly nor isolates the precise point at which one state cedes to the next — one is faced with a scheme of ascent which does not seem to slot smoothly into the traditional Christian pattern of the mystical life as a progression through the ways of purgation, illumination and union. Although both the mystics and the spiritual theologians who are their commentators assure us that this threefold scheme is by no means rigid and binding, since God works in an infinity of ways, there is nonetheless a tendency to see such a pattern as the norm. Where allowance is made for variation, the variations are usually seen as minor differences within the traditional model.[4] However, though each of these steps, the purgative, illuminative and unitive, has an important place in Marie's mystical thought, she points to a dimension beyond the ultimate experience of spiritual marriage — usually held to be the highest stage of the way of mystical union.[5] The position and significance of mystical

[4] Dom Jamet notes: "L'histoire de chaque âme ne se déroule pas selon un plan uniforme, déterminé d'avance pour toutes." He hastens to add that while Marie's mystical pattern is not the most frequent it is by no means unique. See *Écrits*, I, p. 258. F. C. Happold refers to the three stages as the usual division of the mystic way, but adds that they should not be seen as a set pattern universally followed by all mystics. See *Mysticism. A Study and Anthology*, Harmondsworth repr. 1971, p. 56. Evelyn Underhill also follows this pattern, see introduction, n. 7. A critical note on Underhill's classic study of mysticism as a way of life is necessary here. For although "many contemporary commentators unhesitatingly endorse [it] as the best one-volume study of mysticism," as one Jesuit puts it, her treatment of the mystical experiences of individual spiritual figures tends to slight the specific Catholic context in which much of this literature was written. To the extent that her personal religiosity must be taken into account, it should be noted that though Anglican, she was particularly influenced by specific modes of Catholic devotion. See H. Egan, *What are They Saying About Mysticism?*, New York 1982, p. 40; E. Cousins, "Francis of Assisi: Christian Mysticism at the Crossroads," in Katz, *Mysticism and Religious Traditions*, p. 169; and C. J. R. Armstrong, *Evelyn Underhill (1875–1941)*, London 1975, p. 395.

[5] Poulain sees it as "the supreme goal." See *The Graces of Interior Prayer*, p. 283.

union in the overall picture of her spiritual life holds the key to her mysticism.

It goes without saying that Marie's *Relation* was influenced by a long tradition of narrative models and themes, but our concern here is not to disentangle factual events and fictitious imaginings which may be inter-twined in the narrative, nor to try to distinguish what really happened from what the mystic claims in retrospect. For the purposes of this study, which highlights the mystic's religious sentiment and self-understanding, such distinctions need not be our guidelines. She was writing from within a perspective which regarded all these experiences — ordinary and extraor-dinary, natural and supernatural — as objective and real. As the historian Judith Brown noted in her study of a lesser-known seventeenth-century mystic, "whether the events did or did not take place, the undeniable fact is that contemporaries thought they did."[6]

Autobiographical writing is useful for the study of phenomena such as conversion and mystical experience. And this is so not just for the obvious reason that we only know about such experiences because the individual convert or mystic believes them to have happened and informs us of them, but also because the genre in itself caters to self-awareness and self-expression.[7] Writing about her spiritual experiences after the fact, Marie was likely to weave into her description and analysis, thoughts and insights gleaned in the years following the events. It has been argued that because a convert not only sees the subsequent events of his life in light of his conversion, but also sees his conversion through the prism of these subse-quent events, the account is in fact a "disguised description of the convert's *present*, which he legitimates through his retrospective creation of a past and a self."[8] But this retrospective moment is important, for increasingly in literary criticism and modern historiography, such narratives are consi-dered valuable not as a "true" and objective description of past events, but rather as a genuine selection and interpretation of happenings by individ-uals whose viewpoints are, to a greater or lesser degree, culture-bound and embedded in a certain tradition. The subjective input into the interpreta-tion and reinterpretation of the past is a key rather than a pitfall to understanding the mentality of individuals and the collective culture of a

---

[6] J. Brown, *Immodest Acts. The Life of a Lesbian Nun in Renaissance Italy*, Oxford 1986, p. 140.

[7] Weintraub, *The Value of the Individual*, p. xviii.

[8] See Paula Fredriksen, "Paul and Augustine: Conversion narratives, orthodox traditions and the retrospective self," *Journal of Theological Studies* New series, 37 pt. 1 (1986), pp. 3–34.

given time and setting. The hallmark of autobiography is that "it is written from a specific retrospective point of view, the place at which the author stands in relation to his cumulative experience when he puts interpretative meaning on his past."[9] Marie's *Relation de 1654*, then, effectively serves as her interpretation of her mystical experience.

In this spiritual autobiography, she not only presents the dichotomies and tensions of her spiritual life but also resolves them. Like Augustine's *Confessions*, the composition of which was "an act of therapy" that forced Augustine "to come to terms with himself," the importance of Marie's *Relation* lay as much in the act of writing as it did in the finished product.[10] In requesting this account of her religious memories and extraordinary experiences, her spiritual director — a trained Jesuit — was not unaware of its therapeutic value. In its formal definition, the word *relation* means not only a finished product but also the process of recounting. Marie's *Relation* was more than a spiritual outpouring, it was a calculated and reflective selection, ordering and assessment of the highlights and discrepancies of her religious life. It was the very act of writing down, or relating to others what she had discovered about herself, that makes her account the very stuff that autobiography is made of.

Since there are literary critics who see autobiography as "a distinct and deliberate undertaking," one which implicitly follows, or is at least accessible to, accepted theories of form, intention and structure, it might be useful to anticipate the question: can we really read Marie's spiritual autobiography as "autobiography" in the sense of an individual's independent and willed assessment and expression of her life and pronounced sense of self?[11] One could argue that the extent to which her account was "willed" is questionable, given that *La Relation* was a commissioned work, one which, at least on the face of it, was written due to external pressure (i.e., her director's request and her son's emotional blackmail). Another objection that could be raised by literary critics specializing in the genre is that Marie's autobiography, like that of Teresa of Avila, has questionable or limited autobiographical value, since Christian autobiography is by definition more an expression of a typical Christian self, than an example of independent self-expression, the implication being that those who define themselves *a priori* as Christian, are governed by the

---

[9] Weintraub, *The Value of the Individual*, p. xviii.

[10] Brown, Augustine of Hippo, p. 165.

[11] E. W. Bruss, *Autobiographical Acts: The Changing Situation of a Literary Genre*, Baltimore 1976, p. 6.

model-life tradition and therefore have limited scope for independent thought and self-reflection.[12] (Some would even suggest that where a moral system or principle is revered *a priori*, i.e., as having more importance than the individual, the life story of such a person is, by definition, of less interest for the student of autobiography.)

The autobiographical value of Marie's *Relation*, then, would depend on the extent to which the individual is exalted in her own right, as distinct from a pre-ordained social, moral, and in this case specifically traditional Catholic framework. This is a topic unto itself and one which can best be addressed in reference to the rich literature which exists on the contribution of the Christian concept of self to the modern idea of the individual. For our purposes, what is important to remember is that she herself saw her life as an essentially interior, spiritual process which unfolded in an unusual fashion particular to her. She was commissioned to write this account for her spiritual director and also felt conscience-bound to share the secrets of her mystical life with her son, but although she was ostensibly writing at the behest of and for the benefit of others, she was also giving formal expression to the fulfilment of her own spiritual self-image. Her original images of both herself as a devout Catholic, and of the "other" encountered in religious life — and this includes God and the Amerindians of New France — were inherited, traditional, preconceived images, but her personal experience as a mystic, missionary, and spiritual author changed her image of others and of herself.

Though Marie defined herself in relation to others, it is clear that she had a pronounced sense of self and conviction of how to realize her own spiritual needs over/against the demands of tradition or those with traditional expectations of her.[13] It is this idea of the self, and more particularly the view that autobiography is not only dependent on, but also constitutive of self-reflection, which long ago made "autobiography" a much-lauded tool for the interpretation of history and culture. Indeed, in the pioneering work on autobiography undertaken by German philosophers before the word came into common usage, before the modern writing of autobiographies became common practice, and long before the subject infiltrated academic disciplines and underwent literary, historical, and philosophical deep analysis, autobiography was heralded as no less than "the highest

[12] See Weintraub, *The Value of the Individual.*

[13] The idea of "self-identification through relation to another" is examined in Mary G. Mason, "The Other Voice: Autobiographies of Women Writers" in *Autobiography: Essays Theoretical and Critical*, ed. J. Olney, Princeton 1980, pp. 207–235.

and most instructive form in which the understanding of life confronts us."[14] Above and beyond how Marie perceived others or portrayed herself, the main point is that the composition of her spiritual autobiography, like so many other decisions she made in her life, marked a necessary step on her path to self-realization, and the resolution of tensions that had marked her spiritual life from her youth.

After summarizing the different stages enumerated by Marie in describing her spiritual itinerary, I shall bring them together in a thematic discussion of her mystical life as a combination of *imitation of Christ* and *union with Christ*, and then demonstrate how her spiritual identity was rooted in the mingling of a mysticism of union and a mysticism of service. I shall be concerned to present her spirituality as she herself saw it and, by elucidating its key features, to show that while compatible with traditional patterns of Christian spirituality, her description of her transformation introduces a personal and innovative dimension to the classic model of mystical ascent.

Marie begins her autobiography by describing a dream she had at the age of seven in which Christ appeared to her and singled her out for a special relationship with him, the secret nature of which she had but an inkling of at this early stage. In this first state, which could be labelled one of *"spiritual disposition,"* she felt that God "willed gently to dispose" her soul for greater favours, for she received not just the rudiments of Christian devotion, but the initial intimations of a mystical calling as well. (A 6) Although this "first grace" or "signal favour" brought with it a strong desire for interior "converse with God," her religious life in the nineteen years covered by this first chapter — which I have referred to as her formative stage — was still very much rooted in traditional modes of belief and practice and was characterized not so much by visions and ecstasies, as by the love of Scripture, prayer, sacraments, ceremonies and sermons.[15] It was only in the second state, with the "more abundant communication of God's gifts" in the wake of her conversion, that her mystical life proper began. (A 5)[16]

---

[14] W. Dilthey, *Gesammelte Schriften*, vol. 7, "Der Aufbau der geistlichen Welt in den Geisteswissenschaften," Göttingen, 1979, p. 199.

[15] This is similar to Underhill's stage of the "awakening of the self to consciousness of Divine Reality." See *Mysticism*, p. 169.

[16] On Marie's "entrance" into mystical life, see F. Jetté, "L'Itinéraire spirituel de Marie de l'Incarnation. Vocation apostolique et mariage mystique," *La Vie Spirituelle*, 92 (1955), pp. 625–626; H. Cuzin, *Du Christ à la Trinité d'après l'expérience mystique de Marie de l'Incarnation, Ursuline de Tours*, Lyon 1936, p. 9; Bremond, *Histoire littéraire du sentiment*

The second chapter of *La Relation*, then, describes the conversion experience and the consequences of entering this second spiritual state, which Marie explains was designed to draw her to "true interior purity." In the third, fourth, and fifth states of her process of spiritual purification her longing for convent life became more intense. As in all other stages of the journey, spiritual joys and trials were intermingled and it was in these three states that the purgative and illuminative paths merged as her penitential efforts seemed to be rewarded with divine lights or spiritual insights. She was living a life of internal and external penance, while at the same time being drawn into closer intimacy with God.

In the third chapter, for example, she describes her entry into a *"state of profound interior abasement"* and her painful longing to possess the "spirit of Jesus." (A 22) She stresses that "all the powers of the soul desire and long for nothing else but to be in Jesus, through the spirit of Jesus, and to follow Him in His life and in His spirit." (A 22) Though she claims to have "very elevated conceptions" about this spirit of Jesus, she does not yet elaborate on its nature in theological or personal terms. (A 22)[17] This desire to possess Christ's spirit was the essence of her spiritual striving but the accompanying awareness that her lowly and impure soul was unworthy of such a lofty goal caused an inner tension which hampered her spiritual journey from beginning to end.

In the fourth chapter she describes the continuation of her interior and exterior abnegation, as well as her new and powerful anticipation of union with God.[18] Up until this point she had enjoyed "a continual colloquy" with God, but she now felt that he wished to put her soul in a *"state of*

religieux, vol. 6, p. 20; M.T.-L. Pénido, "Marie de l'Incarnation. Aperçus psychologiques sur son mysticisme," *Nova et vetera* 10 (1935) pp. 398, 402.

[17] According to the Jesuit, Jean Baptiste de St. Jure, with whose writings Marie was familiar, "spirit of Jesus" can be understood in a self-contained sense, i.e., in reference to God or the Holy Spirit, or to the operations which link the humanity and divinity of Christ; or in its extrinsic sense, i.e., in reference to the Holy Spirit working within us to adopt Christ's teaching and imitate his life. See Sullivan, *The Autobiography*, p. 190, n. 1. See also Cuzin, *Du Christ à la Trinité*, p. 55, n. 54, for an explanation of this difference between the uncreated reality of the Holy Spirit, and the collection of virtues embodied in Christ and accessible to the ordinary Christian.

[18] The division between states three and four is the only one not clearly indicated by Marie in *La Relation de 1654*. The editor established a dividing line on the basis of the outline of the sixty-three points which Marie had grouped under the thirteen stages prior to writing her account. The finished product comprising sixty-eight points does not correspond exactly to Marie's original plan, and the transition between the third and fourth states is not clear-cut. However, his demarcation is appropriate. See the editor's preface, *Écrits*, vol. II, p. 35.

light" and even greater detachment and purity.(A 24) Marie realized that
the higher goal of this process was no less than union with God, and so this
fourth state was characterized by her "striving for the Beloved." (A 30)
Instead of a general longing for some undefined "spirit of Christ" she now
felt an acute desire for "complete possession of that majesty" whom she
was beginning to experience in a more sublime manner. Entry into the new
state was triggered by an illumination in which "God causes it [the soul] to
see that He, the God of infinite purity, is like a great sea, and that just as a
real sea cannot suffer any impurities, so He will not and cannot tolerate
anything of impurity." (A 25)[19] She suddenly saw "to what a degree
impurities must be purged away before the soul ... can attain to that union
for which it has such an ardent desire and constant yearning." (A 25)

In traditional terms, we can see this as an intensification of the well-
trodden *via purgativa.* The "purging" which Marie envisioned for her soul
was not a matter of eradicating specific faults or moral blemishes, but
rather of expunging anything in the soul that was not purely spiritual.
Purification continued on a more elevated level as she perceived God to be
taking an increasingly active role in this process of mystical growth. She
understood that God, the "inexorable censor," required such purity of
anyone seeking interior converse with him that he withdrew from her the
capacity to enjoy his presence through the senses. The spiritual delights
received earlier had been necessary to buoy up the soul in its weaker phase,
but had to be relinquished as the soul gathered strength. Up until this
point, the soul had "in some measure been supported by the senses, which
have been filled with the splendour radiating from our Lord's sacred
humanity," but the soul now felt "itself called to more sublime things." (A
25) The soul was "passively carried along by a divine touch which begets in
it a deeply rooted peace" and "at the same time divine love keeps the soul
in an agony which is indescribable." (A 31) Being deprived of the "sense
support" which had previously given her a delightful sense of "the presence
and companionship" of the "God-man" was necessary for the spiritual
purification which was leading to divine union. (A 24)

Two points are significant at this stage in Marie's mystical ascent. One is
that her mortifications, practice of virtue and interior prayer now reflect
her desire for union with God, in other words, they are not an end in

---

[19] André Thiry, who sees "purity" as the most characteristic feature of Marie's spiritual
life, places rather too strong an emphasis on the centrality of this illumination regarding God
as a sea of purity. The desire for purity is only one aspect of her dual endeavour to practise
virtue and charity in her attempt to emulate Christ in his abasement and goodness. See Thiry,
Marie de l'Incarnation, pp. 27–29.

themselves, i.e., the emulation of Christ in his lowliness and suffering, but rather they are means to an end, namely, union with Christ. Marie was "amazed" that God gave her "the boldness to aspire to the dignity of being His spouse, to consummate union and most intimate converse with Him" and began urging him, "'Ah, my Love, when will this marriage take place?'" (A 29)

The other point worth noting is that in this fourth state, Marie began to perceive the passive nature of mystical life. Realizing that spiritual experience does not necessarily correspond to one's efforts in pursuing the devout life, but could be received regardless of one's merits, she saw that certain experiences belonged to the supernatural as opposed to natural realm of spiritual life.[20] She mentions that "when God calls the soul to this kind of interior life absolute correspondence is required," but feels a certain ambivalence as to the active role which she must play in responding to this call. (A 26) Marie wishes her soul to advance towards union with God:

> there are no works it would not undertake, whether by day or by night, in order to try to acquire that dignity which it lacks, although it clearly sees that it ought not expect it except as a pure gift from God through an excess of His munificence. (A 27)

In her efforts to gain this "possession so exalted and so sublime," she did everything possible, but realized the inadequacy of these attempts when she was riveted by a verse of psalm: *"Unless the Lord build the house, they labour in vain who build it."* (A 27, 29) With this flash of insight that it is impossible to possess God, "if God Himself does not build the house and furnish it with the adornments befitting so exalted a design," she began to understand that the spiritual transformation which she had been trying to further through her own deeds could be effected ultimately only by God's actions. (A 29–30)

In the fifth chapter she describes God's increased initiative in drawing her soul closer to him, as well as the growing tension between her spiritual inclinations and her position in the world, which she considered "to be

---

[20] Teresa of Avila describes the fourth stage of her seven-stage model of spiritual ascent as one which marks the transition from the way of purgation to illumination, or a move from the natural to the supernatural level of spiritual ascent where the mystic realizes that the soul has gained spiritual favours other than by its own efforts. In contrast to spiritual "consolations" this new "spiritual delight" is not something that can be imagined because "however diligent our efforts we cannot acquire it." *The Interior Castle*, trans., K. Kavanaugh and O. Rodriguez, New York 1979, p. 75.

quite contrary to the spirit of Jesus Christ." (A 40) She enters an "interior" or passive state, which could also be termed one of *spiritual betrothal*, for her soul was both enlightened by and "bound" to Jesus as she received new mystical favours in preparation for the turn to the *via unitiva*. (A 41) After receiving a sublime communication regarding the evangelical counsels, especially poverty of spirit, she took the vows of obedience and poverty which, in addition to the vow of chastity she had made earlier, effectively gave her a monastic pattern of life while circumstance kept her in a secular framework.

Marie's strivings, however, went beyond the desire to follow Christ's teaching by making these virtues her personal guiding rule. She understood that there was a difference between taking these vows and acquiring the spirit that lies beyond them and began to see the "spirit of Jesus Christ" as something more sublime which is imparted to certain souls as they gradually move towards "true poverty of spirit." In this heightened state of illumination her "habitual longing to possess Him forever" plunged her into a period of doubt and suffering. (A 35–6) She suddenly felt abandoned, and underwent temptations regarding her penances, her submission to her spiritual director, and her desire to enter religious life. By the time she wrote her autobiography, she had come to regard this first spiritual night of the soul as an essential part of her purification process; "it was necessary," she writes, "for me to pass through fire before I could be admitted to the honour of receiving His embraces." (A 38)[21]

Marie was released from this spiritual turmoil when she entered a new state as a result of an experience referred to as "the union of hearts," in which her heart was "ravished and ... inserted into another heart, and ... even though they were still two hearts they were so well attuned that they were only one." (A 39) She recounts that this "state of union with our Lord, who had entered into my heart," lasted several days and she needed God's help to support her for "this divine pleasure so transfused my soul that my body could not endure it." (A 40) Prior to this experience she had felt her soul "transported by a power which put it in a passive state" (A 38)

---

[21] See Sullivan, *The Autobiography*, p. 193, n. 4. See also Poulain, *The Graces of Interior Prayer*, pp. 574–577 and E.W. Trueman Dicken, "Teresa of Jesus and John of the Cross," in *The Study of Spirituality*, eds. C. Jones et al., London 1986, p. 374, for a discussion of John of the Cross's distinction between the night of the senses and the night of the spirit as two different stages in the soul's progress towards spiritual union. Whereas St. John sees them as preparations for the spiritual marriage, Marie's trials are an ongoing feature of her spirituality and continue after her experience of union to prepare the way for the ultimate spiritual state of victimhood.

and intensified her longing "to gain Him for whom my soul sighed." (A 39) Thus this experience, in which the illuminative merges with the unitive stage of her ascent, reflects her anticipation of spiritual marriage which would require an even greater passivity on the part of the soul, and bring with it delights of an even more sublime nature.[22]

As already noted, Marie's spiritual perception had shifted from the humanity of Christ to a more abstract intimation of his divine nature, and though she seems to be reverting to the emotive terms and sensual imagery of her earlier stages, she is in fact imbuing this image with a more elevated spiritual significance as she struggles to describe the nature of her experience at this stage in her mystical development. This vision of the "union of hearts" was the first of three interior events which established her devotion to the Sacred Heart as a central element of her mystical life.[23] This vision, then, though indicative of her affective perception of spiritual experience, is not so much a sentimental as an intellectual projection of a divine attribute — God's love — onto an image which in Marie's day had a dual significance: the Sacred Heart of Jesus was a theocentric spiritual concept seen to embody his interior essence or spirit; at the same time, in certain devotional groups, it was also an object of worship directed at the concrete and vivid image of the wound in Christ's side, inflicted during his Passion.[24] In this fifth state, Marie had an additional illumination, experiencing the "sacred mystery of the Incarnation" interiorly "in a manner which I had never conceived of." (A 40) Despite the overwhelming intensity of this "state of union," she was still only on the threshold of mystical marriage.

In chapters six, seven and eight Marie describes three trinitarian visions, each of which initiated her into a "new interior state." As a result of the first vision, which "instructed" her in the mystery of the Trinity, she entered the sixth state, one which could be labelled a *passive state of purity and repose*, as her soul received "delicate but ... crucifying" divine

[22] Although the *via unitiva* is considered by spiritual writers to be the highest stage of the mystical ascent, it knows different, progressive degrees of union, the most exalted of which is usually considered to be the spiritual marriage. See Poulain, *The Graces of Interior Prayer*, p. 283.

[23] Oury, *Ce que croyait*, pp. 129–131. Claude Martin compares Marie's vision of the union of hearts to a similar experience in Catherine of Siena's life. See *La Vie de la Vénérable Mère Marie de l'Incarnation*, p. 753.

[24] For a general discussion of this term see "Sacred Heart," *A Dictionary of Christian Spirituality*, London 1983, pp. 347–348.

"touches" in preparation for spiritual marriage, while already languishing in the passive experience of divine lights and love. (A 51)

The first vision occurred while Marie was attending Mass during Pentecost in 1625. She recounts that while looking at the altar her mind was suddenly elevated "in a view of the most holy and august Trinity." (A 44)[25] The imprint of this mystery on her soul caused her "to see in a flash the inner life which exists between the three Divine Persons," and to know "the unity (of the divine essence), the distinction (of the persons), and the operations (which terminate) in the Persons, and the operations (which terminate) outside Them." (A 44) Marie relates that her soul "was quite lost in these splendours, and it seemed that the Divine Majesty was pleased to illuminate it more and more" (A 45); an additional illumination shed light not only on the inner life of the Trinity, but also on the relationship between the human soul and its divine source: the three powers of the soul (memory, understanding and will), were seen to correspond respectively to the Father, Son and Holy Spirit of the Trinity.

Closely linked with this understanding of the way in which the soul is created in the image of God, was her perception of God as "an abyss of love" in which the soul "yearns to be swallowed up ... and to be so lost in it as to be transformed into the Beloved." (A 47) She realized that this transformation of the soul and its three powers into their original source, or the restoration of the divine image, would be possible only through additional spiritual purification, and that God would now be the main agent in this process. While in this sixth state, Marie also received from God "an impression of His divine perfections" or "divine attributes," which she says nourished her soul for about a year, after which she was ready to enter yet a new state. (A 52, 53)

In chapter seven she describes the second trinitarian vision which ushered her into the seventh state of her spiritual itinerary. This second vision not only deepened her understanding of the Trinity, but also swept up her will in union with God. The spiritual marriage completely changed the state of the soul, which was no longer "in a state of constant tendency

---

[25] According to Poulain, the intellectual vision of the Trinity is one of the common characteristics of the transforming union. See *The Graces of Interior Prayer*, p. 283. Marie's description is strikingly similar to that of Teresa of Avila, who writes that in the seventh dwelling place of the interior castle "the Most Blessed Trinity, all three Persons, through an intellectual vision is revealed to it [the soul] ... and these Persons are distinct, ... the soul understands ... that all three Persons are one substance and one knowledge and one God alone." *The Interior Castle*, p. 175. Regarding Marie's familiarity with the works of Teresa see Jamet, *Écrits* I, pp. 246–247, n. 5.

toward and expectation of this exalted grace" but now entered a state of spiritual possession or *deep permanent union*. (A 58) This was a pivotal point in the mystical ascent because, according to Marie, this state of union remained constant throughout her subsequent states and was not affected by later changes in her spiritual life. The ensuing states, then, can be seen as sub-states within this unitive framework.

Although she encountered in this vision the "Father, Son, and Holy Spirit," the focus is on the second person of the Trinity or "the Word" who is "truly the spouse of the faithful soul." (A 56). "The Word," she writes, "held my soul and all its powers captive in Himself, who was my Spouse and my Love, and who desired my soul entirely for Himself." (A 57) At the moment of her insight into the nature of the Trinity, and into how the Second Person relates to the soul, "this most adorable Person took possession of [her] soul and, embracing it with an inexplicable love, united it to Himself and took it for His bride." (A 56) The mystical transformation which is recounted here has both a noetic as well as an affective quality. The mystical *cognitio Dei experimentalis* entails an elevated apprehension of God or the Trinity, but one which is the result of a direct and personal experience, as opposed to mediated or acquired knowledge:[26]

> The powers of my soul, being engulfed and absorbed and reduced to the unity of the spirit, were all taken up with the Word, who in the role of Spouse, granted to my soul great intimacy with Himself and the power to enjoy the dignity of bride. (A 57)

She writes "no longer being myself, I abided in Him through intimacy of love and of union, so that I was lost to myself and no longer aware of myself, having become Him by participation." (A 57)

Although Marie stresses the ineffability of this mystical union, her account of "the mutual embraces of the soul and this most adorable Word

---

[26] As Henri Bremond notes, Marie's account illustrates two points which lie at the heart of any enquiry into mystical experience, namely the assertion that there is, beyond intellectual knowledge, a kind of direct knowledge which establishes an immediate contact with God, and that this experience has as its object not the idea of God but the divine reality itself. See *Histoire littéraire du sentiment religieux*, vol. 6, pp. 175–176. Recent studies rightly sidestep the opposing claims of theologians and psychologists as to the ontological or subjective nature of the experience and address instead the more tangible issue of the extent to which the mystic's experiential knowledge, or personal perception of a direct and extraordinary encounter is nonetheless shaped *a priori* by the religious tradition or "received knowledge." On the dynamic relationship between mysticism and tradition, experiential knowledge and received faith, see the volume edited by Katz, *Mysticism and Religious Traditions*, especially the articles by S. Katz, pp. 3–60; and R. Gimello, pp. 61–88.

who by the kisses of His divine mouth fills her with His spirit and with His life" echoes the erotic imagery of the *Song of Songs*. (A 58) In her religious lexicon spiritual marriage was not just a general metaphor for the traditional idea of the cloistered nun as the bride of Christ, it was a lived reality.[27] For Marie, as for a long line of mystical writers before her, the *Song of Songs* offered the best literary approximation of the experience of the soul's union with God. This text served the mystics well, not just as an allegory for the close bond between Christ and the Church, or Christ and the individual soul, but as a literal paradigm of the emotional dimension of human love for God.

Especially in the medieval commentaries we see not just the tendency to imbue the sensuous imagery with the pure and elevated idea of a spiritual link to the divine, but also the acknowledgement that in psychological terms, the human experience of love — comprising various elements such as insatiable desire, intimate knowledge, physical closeness, self-giving and loss, as well as the emotional and moral responsibilities implied by the total bond of two human lives — provided an aid to comprehending the powerful affective impact of the spiritual encounter with God.[28] Marie's identification with the spouse of the *Song of Songs* is reflected in her description of her soul which in this state "is entirely penetrated and possessed by Him. It is consumed by caresses and acts of love which cause it to expire in Him by suffering deaths the most sweet; moreover, these very deaths constitute the sweetness." (A 58) She is careful, however, to temper the erotic overtone of her description by stressing that no human words or images and "nothing which falls within the scope of the senses" can adequately convey "what transpired in this ecstasy and rapture of love." (A 57)

As opposed to earlier states in her spiritual life in which she had taken active part in trying to grow in spiritual perfection, the soul is now totally passive for it "no longer lives in itself but in Him who holds it completely absorbed in His love." (A 62) And because God "so restrained [her] faculties that they could attend only to Himself" she had difficulty saying the rosary, or vocal prayers, or even reading devotional books. (A 61) She explains that her soul so enjoyed the "sweet intimacy with this Divine Spouse" that even "short intervals for sleep and for the discharge of one's

---

[27] Underhill, *Mysticism*, p. 138.

[28] For a standard study of the development of ecclesiological and mystical interpretations of the *Song of Songs* see F. Ohly, *Grundzüge einer Geschichte der Hoheliedauslegung des Abendlandes bis um 1200*, Wiesbaden 1958.

duties" constituted a kind of "martyrdom for the soul" which could not bear to be separated from its spouse. (A 66, 60) On the other hand she admits: "without the brief moments of respite from this loving activity which are granted to the soul to enable it to release a bit of the pressure from the plenitude which its Beloved has communicated to it, these excesses would kill the body." (A 64) And so Marie writes that although her soul was passive and her spirit "entirely abstracted from the things of this world and ... caught up in a loving ecstasy," which was both delightful and violent, she was nonetheless drawn to works of charity. (A 60)[29]

As a result of her mystical transformation or divine union Marie became preoccupied with serving her divine spouse. Acts of charity towards and instruction of others were now undertaken "in order to gain them for her Beloved." (A 59) In this chapter, then, there is an ambivalence with regard to the relation between passive contemplation and the whole issue of spiritual action, but there is also a first indication of the performative turn which her spiritual life would take as a direct result of her elevation to and participation in the divine life:

> The soul has no more desires, for she possesses her Beloved ... She performs her duties in order to seek His glory in and through all things according to the lights He has given her, and to promote His reign as absolute Master of all hearts. (A 59)

Her total commitment to make God reign in all hearts, however, came only at a later stage when she was ripe for this special vocation to spiritual service. The soul, she explains, sees that it will have its "opportunity to make a free return of love ...; but when [it] is in this state of suffering it is not the time for that." (A 63) For the time being "there is nothing to do but suffer the divine domination" of her soul and enjoy the "divine excesses" with which it has been favoured. (A 63) Marie's transforming experience eventually lead to active service "in keeping with His loving plan," but at this stage her sole concern seemed to be to escape from "the corruption of the world," and to enter religious life. (A 64, 68) She concludes the chapter, then, with an account of her growing conviction of this contemplative vocation which was sealed by "an interior voice" telling her "'Make haste, for it is time; there is nothing more for you to do in the world.'" (A 71)

Chapter eight describes Marie's first days in the Ursuline monastery and

---

[29] For the theological explanation of how exterior occupations are possible even at the stage of permanent union "in such a manner that the two different operations do not interfere with one another," see Poulain, *The Graces of Interior Prayer*, pp. 189, 283.

then details her final and most sublime trinitarian vision, which lifted her into the eighth spiritual state, one characterized by *the mutual possession of the Trinity and the soul*. At first she received an "impression," or mental imprint, of the words *"If anyone loves Me, My Father will love him, and We will come to him and make Our abode with him."* (A 79)[30] As was the usual pattern with her visions or impressions, she first understood the general meaning of these words and then felt their effect in her soul, which was "penetrated by the reality which they signified." (A 79) As a result of this new "communication of the three Divine Persons," which occurred one evening as Marie knelt at prayer, she experienced that she possessed the Trinity and it possessed her in a new and absolute way. She explains the significance of this vision in relation to the two previous ones:

> In a manner more distinct and intelligible than by means of any words, I was enlightened as follows: "The first time that I manifested Myself to you it was in order to instruct your soul in this great mystery; the second time, it was in order that the Word might take your soul for His spouse; but this time the Father, the Son and the Holy Spirit give and communicate Themselves in order to possess your soul entirely." Then the effect followed, and just as the three Divine Persons possessed me, I also possessed Them in a plenitude of participation of the treasures of the divine magnificence. The eternal Father was my Father; the most adorable Word was my spouse, and the Holy Spirit was the one who by His operation acted in my soul and caused it to receive the divine impressions. (A 79)

In contrast to the first vision which helped her to "understand" how the powers of her soul (memory, understanding and will), correspond to the three persons of the Trinity in derivative, analogous fashion, and the second vision which united her with the second person of the Trinity, this third vision restored Marie's soul finally and fully to its divine source; her soul no longer mirrored the different persons of the Trinity, but was restored to its full image through participation in its inner life. She writes: "Ah! Who could tell the greatness of the honour God does the soul which He has created to His image when it pleases Him to elevate it to His divine embraces?" (A 80) In this eighth state the soul enjoyed a spiritual repose in which it could do nothing but love God "who disposes it for great things

---

[30] Teresa also refers to this scriptural passage (Jn.14:23) in discussing the effects of the spiritual marriage: "Here all three Persons communicate themselves to it, speak to it, and explain those words of the Lord in the Gospel: that He and the Father and the Holy Spirit will come to dwell with the soul that loves Him and keeps his commandments." See *The Interior Castle*, p. 175.

which He keeps secret." (A 77) Soon after donning "the holy habit of religion," and still confused and distressed by the discrepancy between God's sublime nature and her nothingness, she was inundated by temptations and eerie imaginings which she took to be the work of the devil. These spiritual trials, which continued for nearly two years, signified God's purifying action in her soul in preparation for new mystical favours, and they disappeared after she took her final vows.[31]

Marie made her solemn profession in 1633 on January 25, a day of particular spiritual significance for her since, as she notes, it was a special feast day commemorating the conversion of St. Paul. The same day, while in prayer, Marie heard God telling her that from now on she "would fly continually in His presence and in His holy service," and that "in imitation of the Seraphim spoken of by the prophet Isaias," her "love and ... correspondence (with grace) were to know neither interruption nor limits." (A 86) This mystical illumination makes explicit the idea of mystical love or divine union as a kind of springboard for active service. The link between love of God and love of others, or the combination of contemplation and action in spiritual life, was a common enough characteristic of Catholic Reformation spirituality, but in the development of Marie's mystical thought these two aspects became so intertwined that she would eventually come to see the highest reaches of mystical life as the setting for active service, and conversely would experience her actions as an intensification of the mystical reality in which she was permanently ensconced. At this stage, however, she did not yet have that clear and unequivocal understanding of her active vocation and, content for the time being to possess the "happiness of being in the house of God and a portion of His heritage," she revelled in convent life which she saw as "thoroughly filled with the spirit of God." (A 82)

Marie proceeded to the ninth state of her journey — the state of *"apostolic spirit,"* which revealed to her the new direction of her life of mystical union. As the result of a dream of a vast unknown country — later identified as Canada — and a subsequent "rapture" in which God said that he wished her to go there to help establish his Church, she saw her call to holy service in specifically missionary terms. (A 99) The anguished longing which she had once felt for both the religious life and for union with God was now transferred to the mission of saving souls, and her desire for the salvation of souls became focused on the Indians of New

---

[31] For a comparison of Marie's experience of spiritual trials with that of Teresa of Avila and John of the Cross, see Sullivan, *The Autobiography*, pp. 195–196, n. 6.

France. Her desire to give active expression to the message of salvation, which had accompanied her from the time of her conversion in 1620, now made convent life burdensome:

> My spirit was far distant from the place where my body was, and this separation caused my body much suffering because even when taking my meals I was traversing in spirit the country of the savages in order to work for their conversion and help the preachers of the Gospel. (A 100)

Even the other nuns, she tells us, became convinced that "God wanted something of me in particular and that His Divine Majesty would withdraw me from the monastery for something pertaining to His glory." (A 97–8)

In chapter ten Marie recounts how her restlessness concerning the conversion of pagan souls was stilled when she entered the *state of spiritual repose*, the tenth state of her journey, and one in which the ever-present ideal of martyrdom became a vital concern. One day while praying for the salvation of souls she experienced a spiritual ecstasy which gave her a strong desire to become actively involved in the work of winning souls for God, even to the extent of becoming a victim herself in pursuit of this goal. She then had another experience in which she felt her will being captivated by God, and her impatience concerning the salvation of souls was stilled. Marie tells us that God caused her soul to die to its own desires, even those pertaining to the missionary venture, and showed her that he alone would be master in the execution of his designs regarding the mission to Canada. After a year in this state of spiritual repose she felt instructed by God to reveal her special missionary vocation to her superiors, thereby launching the project in concrete fashion.

Chapter eleven gives a detailed account of the arrangements and obstacles involved in making possible the missionary venture to Canada, and of the dangers faced in the voyage itself. Marie tells how contact was established with Madame de la Peltrie, a devout woman who felt called to help finance the Québec project; how companions were chosen for the trip; how she received episcopal approval; and how, after revealing the secret of this undertaking to the Ursuline community, she managed to overcome the opposition of Church officials and family members. In terms of Marie's interior life the eleventh spiritual state was characterized by *"love of the cross,"* that is, by a readiness to suffer whatever she might encounter in serving God.

The twelfth chapter documents the missionaries' arrival in New France, their first impressions of the native Indians and the difficulties involved in settling into a new and harsh environment. In spiritual terms Marie entered a new and "much more crucifying" state of lowliness, which she refers to as the *"revolt of my passions."* (A 140) This twelfth state, which lasted several years, was a final painful night of the soul, or necessary purifying prelude to her ultimate mystical state. She experienced temptations to despair, lost confidence in others, and a conviction that she was "vile and wretched." (A 141) This spiritual trial revealed to Marie more clearly than at any previous stage in her spiritual life the magnitude of the purity which God expected of the "soul which He maintains in an habitual and intimate union with Himself." (A 143) She went to confession to further purge her soul of any "spiritual impurities" and to achieve total self-renunciation, since "a soul which God calls to lead a continual life of the spirit has to pass through many a death before arriving at the goal." She adds that it is:

> difficult to believe the degree to which the soul must abandon itself to be guided by God whithersoever He wills to lead it. It is said, and in a sense it is true, that contemplation is idle; and yet it has great tasks to perform which leave it no repose night or day in these paths along which the spirit of grace leads it... (A 149)

In the thirteenth state, the final one of her mystical journey, Marie was delivered from the "interior crosses and temptations" which had lasted almost eight years. As the "revolt of the passions" subsided, she entered *"a true state of victimhood and continual consummation".* (A 172) This transpired on the Feast of the Assumption of the Virgin Mary in 1647 when, after praying to the Virgin Mary to help free her from her trials, she felt "an influx of peace" in her soul which was thus "freed from its bonds and reestablished in all that it thought it had lost." (A 153, 155) It was at this stage that Marie attained that "true and substantial spiritual poverty" which had been the goal of her spiritual life ever since she received her first illumination concerning this virtue in the third state. (A 172) In this thirteenth state, she tells us:

> the union with my Divine Spouse through His holy impressions effected in me the fundamental virtues of His divine maxims in so spiritual a manner that I could perceive them only through their effects ... [which] consisted in an extraordinary sweetness and a profound sense of destitution so that what I had previously possessed of these virtues now seemed to me to be nothing. (A 160)

This poverty of spirit, which includes all others and is the essence of the spirit of Jesus, meant nothing "other than that pure love which in its simplicity looks only to God." (A 172)[32] This state was unlike all the preceding states in that she now entered this poverty of spirit to such a degree that she felt herself to be helpless:

> I am constantly engaged in this converse with the Divine Persons, in a manner so delicate, simple, and deep that it defies expression. It is not an action; it is an atmosphere in the center of the soul wherein God abides, which is so pleasant that, as I've already said, I can't find words suitable for expressing myself. (A 179)

Her sanguine disposition served her in good stead in the face of the dangers and disasters which she faced in the mission. Referring to the Iroquois massacre of missionaries, and the Iroquois persecution of the Huron Indians, she explains that because she had made the interests of God her own, "the misfortunes of His Church constituted an interior crucifixion" for her. (A 160) When fire destroyed the monastery in 1650 Marie felt her sins were responsible for this calamity, but she was also totally submissive to God's workings: "the depths of my soul were bathed in a love of complacency for God's holy will." (A 165) Explaining that "the interior state into which our Lord has led me" was "one of a continual victim, but in a more perfect and intense degree than has ordinarily been the case with me," she describes the various steps which God took to purify her soul and make it die completely to all its desires — paradoxically even to the desire for loving union with God. (A 171) Having suspended the "will's power of loving" God allowed the soul to enjoy "at its center an actual love through the embrace of its Spouse." (A 177)

Marie sums up:

> This state is like a gentle and loving respiration which continues without interruption. It is a communication of spirit to spirit and of spirit in spirit ... which causes the words of St. Paul to be verified in the soul, *Jesus Christ is my life and my life is Jesus Christ. It is not I who live, but Jesus Christ who lives in me.* (A 177)

But God continued to purify and consume the soul. "Herein," she says, "is the sacrifice of the victim, here finally is true and substantial spiritual poverty of spirit." (A 178) And those "great interior and exterior trials"

---

[32] This experience of pure love is considered to be a mystical act of self-surrender, marking the death of selfhood and entry into a state of intimate repose in the divine life. It should not be confused with the Quietist notion of spiritual indifference which saw passivity as a goal in itself which precluded any activity on the part of the contemplative. See De Guibert, *The Jesuits*, pp. 402–413.

faced by the soul were necessary so that "St. Paul's words may be verified from every aspect, *He has conformed them to the image of His Son.*" (A 178) Ultimately, she explains, "the high point of the spiritual life and the consummation of the perfection of the saints consists in living only through Him." (A 180)

Marie finishes her autobiography on a suitably sublime and typically humble note, expressing both the splendour of her exalted mystical favours, as well as her reservations with regard to her salvation and progress in sanctification. She describes her experience as:

> something so elevated, so ravishing, so divine, so simple, and so far removed from what can be expressed in human language that all I can say is that during it I am in God, possessed by Him, and that He would soon consume me by the intensity and force of His love if I were not sustained by another impression which follows upon the former. This second impression doesn't cause the first to disappear but merely tempers its splendour, which is too great for one to bear in this present life. (A 180)

She then notes "my infidelities give me reason to fear" and so she closes her story with a prayer which recalls the content of her conversion vision some thirty-four years earlier, asking God "to be pleased to drown them all [her infidelities] in His precious blood and to have mercy on" her. (A 182)

At the time of writing her autobiography in the summers of 1653 and 1654 Marie considered this thirteenth state to be the final station on her interior journey. As far as we can tell from letters written between 1654 and 1672, she did not update her spiritual itinerary. This is not to say that in the last twenty years of her life her spiritual life drew to a standstill or that her mystical experiences ceased, but rather that she considered the stage of spiritual victimhood to be the ultimate spiritual state or the framework within which God would "bring to completion His designs in my regard through His Holy Spirit." (A 171) She saw these thirteen states not as a series of disparate, fleeting visions but as a slow and arduous succession of mystical states — each one lasting several months or even several years — and all contributing to God's grand design for her. This design comprised both sublime states and divine duties, and was experienced in mystical union and a missionary vocation.

The period covered from the first chapter of the *Relation*, which opens with Marie's childhood dream in 1607, up to the final account of her initiation into the state of victimhood in 1649, spans roughly forty-two years, and in chronicling her story Marie describes a myriad of interior experiences, visions, ecstasies, trials, and personal events and decisions which gave her spiritual life its stamp. In outlining these thirteen spiritual states, I have characterized each stage in terms of one main feature or key term — even where Marie eschews distinct labels — and have indicated how her itinerary corresponds to the basic pattern of mystical ascent, which is usually divided into the three stages of purgation, illumination and union.[33] While such a sketch is not intended to summarize her mystical life, it may serve as a useful frame of reference for the thematic discussion below, which elucidates the key features of her spiritual identity. Her spiritual ascent conformed to the Christian mystical norm, that is, it was a process of transformation in the divine image, a process which comprised both the imitation of Christ and union with Christ. For Marie, however, being transformed in the divine image or sharing in the inner life of the Trinity found its highest expression in service of others. Her mystical life took on a performative quality and her transformation was continued on another plane as she expressed her spiritual self by serving others.

In living out her conversion, Marie found herself engaged in what Dom Oury refers to as "the quest for Him who alone is perfect and can suffer near Him only those who are transformed in his image."[34] This is an apt formulation given that Marie's mystical experience was a twofold process of spiritual growth, combining both her quest for God and what she saw as God's initiative in transforming her. Her ongoing conversion thus entailed a gradual transformation of her soul into the image of God; it was a process in which she sought to emulate Christ in his goodness and suffering, and perceived God elevating her soul to himself, regardless of her spiritual efforts. Her transformation can thus be characterized as a combination of *imitatio christi* and *unio christo*, or the active process of conforming to Christ through her own ascetic endeavours, and the passive experience of being united with him through extraordinary mystical grace.

In theological terms, the spiritual life is a process of recovering or renewing the image of God, in whose likeness man was originally created (Gen. 1:26), and which became obscured as a result of original sin.[35] This

---

[33] For a comprehensive table summarizing Marie's thirteen stages, which is based both on the points she drew up before writing *La Relation de 1654* as well as on the content of the final text, see Jamet, *Écrits*, II, pp. 391–400. A nutshell summary is found in O'Brien, *Varieties of Mystic Experience*, pp. 227–229.

[34] Oury, *Ce que croyait*, p. 98.

[35] See W. Riehle, *The Middle English Mystics*, London 1981, p. 143; and also Spitz, "Reformation," pp. 60–69, on the idea of personal reformation as the restoration of the original image of God.

idea of the restoration of the divine image is closely linked with an essential point in Christian mysticism, namely that the soul has a *"capacitas Dei."*[36] Accordingly, the way in which the soul conforms to the original divine image can be seen either as a process of reformation, the combined working of divine grace and human effort in becoming more "like" Christ who is the image of God; or an experience of transformation, which results from an infusion of extraordinary grace "in the soul of the contemplative who feels and recognizes God's presence in himself through his love which enables the soul to know and love him in the act of complete surrender."[37] This process, then, knows two modes in the spiritual life. Ascetic efforts to conform to the perfection embodied in Christ are a way of growing in likeness to God by imitating his son; but there is another way of understanding the image of God, one which pertains to the passive or mystical aspect of spiritual life, i.e., not what is attained through one's own efforts, but what is given in extraordinary fashion by God. At the higher stages of spiritual life, then, the restoration of the divine image in the soul does not refer solely to the process of spiritual growth, or the human capacity for perfection, but rather signifies the soul's ultimate attainment of the "divine likeness" through union with God.[38]

If we consider again Marie's thirteen states, states two through five indicate that her transformation initially followed the "imitation of Christ" pattern. These states, which in terms of the three-fold mystical scheme, correspond roughly to the ground covered in the purgative and illuminative ways, illustrate her attempt to purify her soul and attain the spirit of Jesus through her own efforts at virtue and prayer. After her conversion she took the vows of chastity, obedience and poverty, performed penitential acts and looked for opportunities to be of "charitable assistance" to others. She kept her talents hidden and welcomed the "hidden status of a poor ignorant creature fit only to be the servant of the servants of the house." (A 23) Still under the impression of the vision of Christ's blood, and overwhelmed by his self-sacrifice, she undertook "the most lowly and humiliating works" in order to emulate his abasement and goodness. Thus, in keeping with the traditional view, she saw Christ as the model for spiritual life, for as Jaeger has noted, in Christian terms, it is this model "which we must emulate, or rather so dispose ourselves as to let Christ take shape in us."[39]

---

[36] Riehle, *The Middle English Mystics*, p. 144.

[37] Ibid., pp. 147–148.

[38] Ibid. p. 143.

[39] Jaeger, *Early Christianity and Greek Paideia*, p. 93.

Marie's actions and prayer-life, then, were part of a process of purification which grew in intensity as she advanced in spiritual life.[40] Immediately following her conversion she felt remorse for her earlier faults and errors of judgement. Then, upon receiving additional illuminations, she began to confess even "the least atom of imperfection." (A 28) Dom Oury notes that the 1622 revelation regarding God's boundless purity confirmed her conversion experience and "impelled her to enter more deeply into imitation of God's son."[41] As she felt herself being drawn to God interiorly she became intent on purifying her soul of anything which might hinder this divine proximity. As her son explains in his biography of Marie, the intention behind her ascetic acts was "to entirely die to herself and to the most secret inclinations of human nature in order to pass into a state which was entirely God-like [*déiforme*] in its essence and powers."[42]

This path of *imitatio christi* then merged with a new path leading to union with Christ. Sensing that her active efforts at spiritual perfection were gradually diminishing in importance as God infused her with new, extraordinary experiences, Marie began to see her own role in a more passive light. (A 29) The "exercise" of imitation of Christ was yielding, as it were, to an "experience" of the imminence of union. She understood that the spiritual transformation could ultimately be effected only through God's initiative, and so began to acquiesce to the divine favours received rather than trying to achieve the anticipated divine union through her own efforts.

The *leitmotiv* of the "spirit of Jesus" which runs through Marie's account, resounding in a new and higher key at different stages in her mystical ascent, lay at the heart of her desire to be more like Christ, the source and epitome of perfection. Her particular devotion to the spirit of Jesus did not change during the course of her life, but the shifting modalities of her spirituality reflect a gradual development in her understanding of this spirit, and how the soul experienced it. Her pronouncement that her soul longed "for nothing else but to be in Jesus, through the spirit of Jesus and to follow Him in His life and in His spirit" suggests that this "spirit" was both the *object* of her spiritual endeavours, which was to be "followed" or emulated, as well as the *means* by which she could reach her

[40] André Thiry sums up Marie's spiritual development as a double movement of purification and union. See *Marie de l'Incarnation*, p. 27. M.T.-L. Pénido suggests that she experienced this purification process on three levels: the moral, metaphysical and mystical. See "Marie de l'Incarnation...," pp. 418–419.

[41] Oury, *Marie Guyart*, p. 76.

[42] Martin, *La Vie de la Vénérable Mère Marie de l'Incarnation*, p. 586.

ultimate spiritual goal of being "in Jesus." (A 22) The "spirit of Jesus," then, signified both the qualities which she felt drawn to imitate, and the vehicle of ascent and entry into the divine life. The "spirit of Jesus" was the fulcrum of Marie's spiritual life, balancing the imitation of Christ and union with Christ.

In the initial stage, as I have mentioned, this spiritual aspiration fostered Marie's attempt to imitate Christ in his goodness and share in his suffering. She writes "apart from prayer, my heart was in a state of being constantly drawn to His goodness, for I looked on nothing as good or beautiful or desirable except to possess the spirit of Jesus." (A 22) At a more advanced stage in her journey she perceived this spirit not in terms of the virtues represented by Christ, but more in terms of his divine nature in the inner life of the Trinity — a life which she came to share through her experience of union. Ultimately, the spirit of Jesus became identified with the divine plan of salvation, in which she took an active part through her missionary role.

The pivotal stage of Marie's mystical life was her experience of spiritual marriage, or the union of her soul with God's will, which was anticipated in the sixth state, fulfilled in the seventh and sealed in the eighth. At this point, having reached what is usually termed the "unitive path" in mystical life, she was not so much shaping herself on a model, but rather being elevated and transformed in the divine image. She was no longer consciously *imitating* Christ, because she now *participated* in his life, and shared his likeness as a result of her soul's union with God. Marie's progression from *imitatio christi* to *unio christo*, and the very nature of this transformation in the divine image — particularly its active implications — must be seen in their trinitarian context.

In the western mystical tradition, the teaching on the trinitarian nature of the divine image is central to this concept which is considered to be a traditional metaphor for the goal of the mystical quest:[43]

> the capacity for likeness to God is actualized through the Son but refers to the Trinity. If the soul is made in the image of the Son of God, as Paul taught, then in fact it is made in the image of the Trinity, since Christ said: "I and the Father are one." The image can be reformed only by the Trinity.[44]

The idea of the total substantial unity of the Trinity as a force working in

---

[43] Riehle, *The Middle English Mystics*, pp. 142–150.

[44] M.T. Clark, "The Trinity in Latin Christianity," in B. McGinn & J. Meyendorff eds., *Christian Spirituality: Origins to the Twelfth Century*, New York 1985, p. 283.

the human soul is compatible with the doctrine concerning the Trinity's internal dynamics: though the Holy Spirit is considered to proceed from the Father and from the Son, this does not detract from the co-equality of the three Persons.

In the sixth state, the one preceding her entry into spiritual marriage, Marie had an illumination regarding the manner in which the soul is created in God's image, namely that the soul's higher faculties, the memory, the understanding, and the will, correspond in analogous fashion to the three members of the Trinity. She was drawing on a tradition of analogical thinking stemming from Augustine who taught that the image of the Trinity consists in the three powers of the soul, the memory, the intellect, and the will.[45] Marie explains that her soul perceived:

> how it was created to the image of God; that the memory relates it to the eternal Father, the understanding to the Son, and the will to the Holy Spirit, and that, just as the most Holy Trinity is threefold in Person, but one in essence, so also the soul is threefold in Person but one in essence. (A 45)

Closely linked with this understanding of the way in which the soul is created in the image of God, was her recognition of God as "an abyss of love" in which the soul "yearns to be swallowed up ... and to be so lost in it as to be transformed into the Beloved." (A 47) Marie already anticipated, then, the restoration of the divine image, or the transformation of the soul and its three powers into their original source.

Throughout her account there is a growing abstraction in the way she describes her spiritual experiences and goals. For example, the concrete image of the blood shed by Christ dominates the second state in her journey, but in the fourth and fifth states this yields to a more abstract concern with the spiritual qualities which Jesus represents, and culminates here in the speculation on the paradoxical nature of his life in the Trinity. In state seven, her soul was wedded not to Jesus, but rather to the "second person of the Trinity"; and though she refers to her marriage in terms of a particular member of the divine body, it becomes clear in the eighth state that her experience of union encompassed all three persons of the Trinity. When she writes "just as the three Divine Persons possessed me, I also possessed Them in a plenitude of participation of the treasures of the divine magnificence," she is indicating that in the aftermath of this vision, the soul was no longer just similar to the Trinity, but in fact participated in it. (A 79)

---

[45] Louth, *The Origins of the Christian Mystical Tradition*, p. 152.

The difference between Marie's illumination in the sixth state regarding how the soul is by analogy "related" to the Trinity, and her soul's immersion in the inner life of the Trinity in the eighth state, reflects a traditional distinction made in the teaching on the divine image, which maintains that there is "not only derivation from the trinitarian God but also an implied likeness and a dynamic note of tendency toward the Exemplar-Principal."[46] In the initial states, her spirituality was characterized by just such a spiritual inclination, or "tendency" as she terms it, towards God, which ceased when she entered the state of permanent union. Thus, for her, the soul's higher powers were no longer tools for perceiving or desiring likeness with the Trinity, but were rather transformed into the image itself.

In spiritual theology, the state of union is described as one in which the soul is habitually conscious of the divine cooperation in all its higher operations and in the depths of its being. No union of a more intimate kind can be imagined. This grace can be considered under another, more sublime aspect:

> in concurring in our supernatural acts God makes them His own; He renders them divine and shows that He does so. There is therefore a transformation of the higher faculties with regard to their manner of operation.[47]

As a result of this intimate union with God and the transformation of the soul's powers or "higher faculties," then, the soul is seen to operate within the context of the divine life; the soul's activities are governed by God who "makes them His own." It is this notion of "divine cooperation" that provides the key to the apparent paradox in Marie's mystical account, which includes both her claim that spiritual union renders the soul totally docile and able only to "passively receive" God's favours, and her assertion of a burning ambition to actively seek the conversion of others. For this mystic, then, transformation in the divine image was not an end in itself, because sharing in the inner life of the Trinity meant participating in the execution of its will in external actions. Theologically speaking, "it was more than the 'signified will' of God (what He wanted her to do); it was the

---

[46] Clark, "The Trinity...," p. 277. See also Louth, *The Origins of the Christian Mystical Tradition*, p. 152: "the soul must learn what it means to be the image of God in its memory, understanding, and will and learning that learn how to pass beyond the image to God Himself in contemplation of Him."

[47] Poulain, *The Graces of Interior Prayer*, p. 287.

'essential will' of God (which is identical with His essence)."[48] As one commentator notes, Marie's "awakened desire for a life of missionary activity was submerged in the will of God, and consciousness of her own will, as distinct, was lost."[49]

Marie's christological thought reflects the increasingly sublime nature of her progression from the imitation of Christ to union with Him in the life of the Trinity. Her preoccupation with the passion of Christ who "had so lovingly shed His precious blood," was followed, as her spiritual life deepened, by a sense of distraction from Christ's humanity. (A 16) Christ's divinity or the mystery of the Incarnation began to loom large in her spiritual perception. To compensate for her inability to concentrate on Christ's passion when praying, God gave her insight into the unity of the humanity of Christ with the Sacred Word Incarnate. Finally, she advanced from the consideration of the God-man, or Incarnate Word, to an appreciation of the more sublime aspects of the Trinity.

Henri Cuzin has suggested that it was this increased centring on the ineffable nature of the Trinity which gave Marie's mysticism its final imprint.[50] Her spiritual journey led her from a desire to share in the virtuous life and suffering of the human Christ to her enjoyment of the secret life of the Trinity. However, if we peruse the five states which followed her trinitarian visions and mystical marriage, it seems that Marie's christology had come full circle and reverted to its initial model: that of the suffering Christ. Given that she designates the state of victimhood and the aim of total self-sacrifice as the apex of mystical life, her mystical scheme seems regressive rather than progressive insofar as it suggests a return to an exercise in imitation.

The explanation for this apparent incongruity in Marie's mystical development lies in the nature of the trinitarian union, which she perceived in terms of an identification of wills. (From the point of view of doctrinal orthodoxy this is important, for the assertion of an identification of essence would make the mystic's claim heretical.) As a result of her transformation in the divine image she shared the concerns of the Trinity and was penetrated by Christ's redemptive spirit to such an extent that she was willing to become a living sacrifice to further the goal of saving souls.[51]

---

[48] Ibid., p. 228.

[49] O'Brien, *Varieties of Mystic Experience*, p. 228.

[50] See Cuzin, *Du Christ à la Trinité*.

[51] In this respect her spiritual self-image is similar to that of the recently canonized Québec missionary and mystic, Catherine de Saint-Augustin. See G.-M. Oury, *L'itinéraire mystique de Catherine de Saint-Augustin*, Chambray 1985, pp. 161–162.

Marie's perception of the degree to which her spiritual acts and desires reflected the divine will reached its peak in her thirteenth and final spiritual state where she notes, "my soul was possessed by the spirit of the Son of God and ... I acted in keeping with that spirit," and claims "I have made the interests of the divine spouse my own." (A 157, 160)

In a letter written to her son three years before she began composing her spiritual autobiography, she explains that within the experience of mystical union — even in its most sublime form — there is a gradation in the soul's state of spiritual poverty, and a difference between the works and suffering which are embraced in "imitation" of Christ, and the total self-sacrifice through which one's service of others betokens a "resemblance" to Christ:

> Our union is never more eminent than in the works suffered in imitation and for the love of Jesus Christ who, at the time of his suffering and most of all at the time of his death, was in the highest degree of union and love for man with God his Father. The gentle and loving union is already the beatitude begun in mortal flesh and its merit is in acts of charity towards God and others ... But with regard to the union of which I am speaking, which is nevertheless a continuation of that one, it is a question of giving one's life in a consummation of works which carry the resemblance to Jesus Christ. (C 397)

After progressing to this intense state of union, she was thus no longer imitating a model of the suffering Christ, but suffering together with Christ, to whom she was united and whose desire for redemption of souls she bore as if it were her own. Marie was not reverting to the exercise of her own will in pursuit of spiritual goals. Rather, she experienced her participation in the life and interests of the Trinity in such an absolute fashion that she felt her will was, as it were, totally subsumed in the divine will and that her actions were an expression of this divine will. This view of spiritual service is akin to the Augustinian idea of transformation in the Trinity leading to action, and the attainment of the divine image, not as an end in itself but rather as a "dynamic process of involvement in God, society, and the world through love."[52] Her understanding of mystical service through participation in the Trinity recalls this Augustinian view which is summed up by one commentator as follows: "in intimacy with the divine persons the soul attains likeness to wisdom and shares in divine creative and providential action, illuminating and loving action."[53]

However, though theologically sound and well-rooted in patristic thought, this pattern of active service in and through union with the

[52] Clark, "The Trinity...", p. 283.
[53] Ibid., p. 283.

Trinity is not commonly considered to be either the norm or even a representative form of Christian mysticism. This is not to say that in the Christian spiritual tradition mystical contemplation and active service are considered to be mutually exclusive or incompatible. Indeed, in the Quietist controversy of the seventeenth century, the Church attacked the extreme Quietist stress on contemplative passivity as a goal in itself to the exclusion of all action; in countering the Quietist position the spiritual theologians emphasised that the experience of mystical contemplation by no means precludes charitable actions, and the latter should in fact be seen as the fruits of extraordinary spiritual states. However, there has long been a tendency in the history of Christian spirituality to view "the contemplative mystical life" and the "active life of works" as "two distinct ways of perfection" and to present the contemplative life — especially in its pristine monastic form — as the superior of the two.[54] Even in cases where groups or individuals — perhaps most notably in the Catholic Reformation — felt that true Christian spirituality, or living in the spirit, must be expressed through active service to others, the traditional tension between action and contemplation still existed.[55]

There has been a tendency in studies on Christian spirituality to classify and contrast spiritual patterns and types and to assess mystical writing according to existing models. Passive spirituality is generally set over/ against different forms of active spirituality; or the bridal mysticism which centers on "the image of Christ as the Beloved ... after the imagery of the Song of Songs" is usually sharply distinguished from the ascetical "suffering Christ" pattern.[56] There is also an implicit dependence on the traditional purgation-illumination-union model of mystical ascent which, though useful in itself, tends to arrest our thoughts at the experience of union as the summit of mystical life instead of prompting further reflection on the different forms of mystical experience which can develop within this unitive framework.[57] Poulain's remark that "since St. Teresa's time,

[54] D. Knowles, *What is Mystisicm?* London 1967, p. 37.

[55] Knowles suggests that by the time of the Catholic Reformation, changes in doctrine and religious sentiment had loosened the rigid dichotomy between actives and contemplatives and challenged the presumed superiority of the latter. Ibid., p. 40. However, while new groups were formed to balance these two modes of religious life, the respective value of each was still an object of debate.

[56] Katz, "The 'Conservative' Character of Mysticism," p. 46.

[57] E. Trueman Dicken offers a defense of the systematic presentation of these stages of spiritual life, noting that "the outlines of this 'normal' pattern of Christian spiritual growth ... had already been established well over a thousand years." See "Teresa of Jesus and John of the Cross," pp. 375–376. Poulain is critical of what he sees as elaborate, multi-stage schemes

descriptive mysticism seems to have made but little progress" attests to the existence of an unofficial literary canon of spirituality, which serves as a frame of reference in which certain spiritual writers are seen as standard-bearers and against whose schemes other mystics are evaluated.[58] As a result, the unique features of individual spiritual writers are often overlooked.

Unlike other mystical writers, Marie does not present the experience of mystical union or spiritual marriage as the ultimate stage of the spiritual journey. In Teresa of Avila's *Interior Castle*, which renders the soul's progress in mystical life as an ascent through seven levels, from the outer courtyard to the innermost chamber, the crowning experience of spiritual marriage occurs in the final stage.[59] In Marie's *Relation de 1654*, however, the spiritual marriage occurs not in the final state, but rather at the mid-point of her spiritual journey, in the seventh of thirteen stages. Like Teresa of Avila she describes, or rather tries to describe, the ineffable ecstasy of the spiritual marriage with Christ:

> This most adorable person took possession of my soul, and embracing it with an inexplicable love, united it to Himself and took it for His bride. When I say that He embraced it, this of course was not after the manner of human embraces. Nothing which falls within the scope of the senses is like this divine operation, but it is necessary for me to express myself in terms of our earthly life, since we are composed of matter. (A 56–7)

Here she uses the bridal imagery common to Christian mystical literature since the Middle Ages when the *Song of Songs* was drawn upon by monastic writers to express the inexpressible. Marie cautions the reader not to think of these embraces in human terms but only as a metaphor for a divine operation whose force is, nonetheless, best captured through the use of erotic imagery. She continues her account in the same vein:

> The spiritual marriage completely changes the state of the soul. It is entirely penetrated and possessed by Him whom she loves. It is consumed by caresses and acts of love which cause it to expire in Him by suffering deaths the most sweet; moreover these very deaths constitute the sweetness. (A 58)

The erotic imagery, insistence on the ineffability of the experience, and the use of paradoxical language to express that which is beyond words and

of the spiritual life: "Let us not multiply divisions without necessity." See *The Graces of Interior Prayer*, p. 549.

[58] Poulain, *The Graces of Interior Prayer*, pp. 540–541.

[59] Teresa of Avila, *The Interior Castle*.

conceptions, as for example in oxymora such as sweet suffering or the
sweetness of death, is typical in this regard — none of this is new in
spiritual writing. What is rather new or unexpected is the fact that this
sublime experience is not the be all and end all of Marie's spiritual journey.
As already noted, the spiritual marriage she describes occurs in the middle
of her ascent, in the seventh of the thirteen states presented in the *Relation*.
Marie is aware of the need to explain:

> It might seem that there is nothing more to say about such communication
> of spirit with spirit. But no: divine love is an inexorable censor; its lamps are
> fire and flames. It wishes to purify the soul yet further ... and herein is the
> sacrifice of the victim, here finally is true and substantial poverty of spirit.
> (A 177, 180)

And indeed, Marie traversed many more stages of purification and illumination on a mystical journey which led her from the cloister in Tours to the
colony of Québec, and required additional material and mental sacrifices
before she finally reached the thirteenth and final state of her spiritual
itinerary, the state of victimhood. The general idea of spiritual sacrifice
and the desire to achieve total identification with Christ by becoming a
"victim" are thematic concerns which surface in other seventeenth-century
spiritual writing, and they are by no means peculiar to New France.
However, it is important to note that Marie herself saw the sum total of
her mystical experiences and their culmination in a state of victimhood, in
definitive terms of her missionary vocation in New France. In sifting
through all the events, images and set notions that characterized her
spiritual life from early childhood to her adult years, Marie saw her
specific mystical experience as inextricably linked to the New World, both
as a preconceived idea and as a lived reality. Indeed, it was in New France
that she came to see the meaning of her spiritual roles and to balance them
through her choice of words and images while composing her account of
the central events of her life.

At the end of her *Relation de 1654*, Marie analyzes her sublime experiences and brings them sensibly down to earth by offering some sage
comments on the effects of her ultimate mystical state, which was characterized by:

> an annihilation, along with a deep-seated knowledge that one is nothingness
> and weakness itself, a low estimate of oneself and of one's own activity,
> which is seen as always mixed with imperfection ... which serves to keep it
> profoundly humble, no matter how elevated it might be[;] ... a certain fear
> ... lest one be deceived in the ways of the spirit and mistake therein the false
> for the truth[;] a great patience with one's crosses and a whole-souled

inclination towards peace and benignity with everyone ... [;] ... this state also causes one to accept sufferings in a spirit of love[;] it begets a great love of the vocation and state to which God calls the soul ... [and] an ever greater love for everything done and practised in the Church of God, in which one sees only purity and holiness[;] ... and an all-embracing urge to permit oneself to be guided by those who hold the place of God and to submit one's own judgment to them. (A 181–2)

Deferring to tradition, the Church, and her spiritual directors in this manner is not a denial of self, for lurking behind her humble portrayal of the faithful and unworthy daughter of the church, we can discern a very healthy appreciation of self and the conviction that she had forged a spiritual path that was hers alone. Regardless of how many times she resorts to the humility topos, she still reveals in self-conscious fashion a very pronounced, albeit uneasy awareness of her own worth as a mystic chosen by God for a unique spiritual task.

Marie's *Relation* can be seen on the one hand as a solid portrait of a mystic, missionary and humble servant of God, but on the other hand as a somewhat shaky sketch of a bemused woman engaged in self-reflection and self-expression. Her narrative bridges the gap between her active and contemplative convictions; between her sense of chosenness and the necessity to be humble; between her love of family members and her willingness to disappoint them for the sake of her role in the grand divine scheme of things; between her conviction that she was "in God, possessed by Him" and her feeling that she was "the lowest, most debased, and most contemptible person in the whole world"; and between the ineffability of her experience and her literary attempt to express it. (A 180, 131)

It reveals its author not as a passive representative of a religious trend or period, but as a highly motivated individual, who, in reflecting on her life and relating it to others, left behind an intriguing spiritual autobiography — one that is nonetheless autobiographical for being spiritual. When read as autobiography Marie's account allows us to see things from her point of view. Ultimately, she defined her life in spiritual terms and the axes of her self-definition were her mystical encounter with God and her missionary encounter with the Amerindians with whom she spent more than thirty years of her life. It is by trying to gain access to her point of view, and the underlying process of self-reflection, that we not only gain a more accurate picture of her life (to complement what we know from biographical sources), but also learn much about the workings of religious experience and self-expression in Early Modern times, and in the significant New World context.

CHAPTER FOUR

NEW FRANCE: FROZEN EARTH, HEAVENLY SPLENDOUR

Marie's first encounter with the New World was in a dream she had after becoming a full-fledged contemplative. No sooner had she fulfilled her wish to become a cloistered nun than the outside world beckoned, in the form of a call to New France. After professing her solemn vows in 1634, she had a vivid dream about a snow-covered land in which the Virgin Mary was seen whispering a secret to the infant Jesus:

> Finally we came to a beautiful place at the entrance to which was a man dressed in a white garb like that in which the apostles are commonly pictured. ... He admitted us and gave us to understand that this was the way we had to pass, since there was none other except the one he pointed out. ... Silence reigned here, and this constituted part of the beauty of the place. Advancing within, I saw at some distance to my left a little church of wrought white marble, on top of which was the Blessed Virgin, seated on the pinnacle. She was holding the Child Jesus on her lap. This place was very elevated, and below it lay a majestic and vast country, full of mountains, of valleys, and of thick mists which permeated everything except the little building which was the church of this country. (A 90–1)

Marie relates that the Virgin Mary seemed to whisper to Jesus something "about this country and about myself and ... had in mind some plan which involved me," and although the meaning of this dream "remained a complete secret" she felt an extraordinary inner peace when she awoke. (A 91, 92) She recounts how she was ushered into a new spiritual state:

> Then at the age of thirty-four or thirty-five, I entered upon the state which had been intimated to me and which I was awaiting. This was a communication of the apostolic spirit, which was none other than the Spirit of Jesus Christ, which took possession of my spirit in order that I might no longer live except in and through Him and be wholly devoted to the interests of this divine and most adorable Master through zeal for His glory, so that He might be known, loved, and adored by all the nations which He had redeemed by His precious blood. (A 95)

This "Spirit of Jesus Christ," which in earlier stages had been identified with the virtues of chastity, poverty, and obedience, and later with the sublime divine spirit embodied by Christ, is now an active principle of the divine mission for the redemption of souls. Marie became obsessed with the idea:

> 'O Father, why dost Thou delay? ... I plead with Thee for the interests of my Spouse. Thou wilt keep Thy word, O Father, for Thou hast promised Him all the nations.'... I didn't at all cease to petition the eternal Father on our Lord's behalf, as though I had been His advocate. (A 96, 97)

Intent on totally annihilating her spirit so that God would hear her prayers, she soon received another illumination, "a divine infusion and ray of light" in which God told her to pray "'through the heart of Jesus, my most beloved Son; it is through it that I shall hear you and grant your requests.'" (A 98) In the fifth state of her journey, the image of the heart of Jesus represented his suffering and death as a human, as well as his embodiment of divine love and justice. In this state, she sees it as an instrument for effecting, or a vehicle for carrying, the grace of redemption.

A subsequent illumination revealed the specific meaning of her earlier dream of the snowy wilderness:

> One day, ... I was praying before the Blessed Sacrament when my spirit was of a sudden ravished in God. ... Then this adorable Majesty said to me, 'It is Canada that I have shown you; there you must go to make a home for Jesus and Mary.'... Then I experienced a loving ecstasy during which this infinite Goodness bestowed on my soul such caresses as human tongue could never describe. (A 99)

This mystical ecstasy serves to underline the fact that the divine call to missionary service was not just an addendum or supplement to Marie's contemplative life of prayer, but rather the crux of her spiritual identity, in which interior stillness and active service were fully intertwined. In addition to having been chosen by God to become a contemplative, as well as his spouse, she now felt chosen as his emissary, or co-worker in the divine plan for the salvation of souls. The longing which she had once felt for both the religious life and for union with God was now transferred to the mission of saving souls. The idea of salvation of souls was not just a valid abstract principle, it became a pressing concern which she felt personally compelled to bring about, and so her participation in the mission was essential to her spiritual fulfilment.

In her *Relation*, in an unusually detailed and extensive account of the subsequent intrigues occasioned by her attempts to bring about the

planned departure for the New World, Marie reveals herself in a refresh-
ingly human light, embroiled in a test of wills rather than pursuing a
course of pure spiritual detachment. Having learned that her former
spiritual director, Dom Raymond of St. Bernard, was also seeking permission to join the Canadian mission, she wrote to him, and he in turn
wrote to a friend explaining his plan in the hope of diffusing any opposition
it might engender. But his friend was vehemently opposed to the idea
which would mean a great loss for their order, and came immediately to
accost Marie for encouraging the plan. She was astonished that this
brother would oppose "a project so noble as that of the conversion of the
savages," and reiterated her firm commitment to the plan, much to the
irritation of her opponent (A 107):

> When he had finished listening to me he was as nettled as a person in his
> state of life could be, and he began to tell me point-blank that I had surely
> known of the plan of [Dom Raymond] that he had caused me to lose my
> head, that I was supporting his cause, that he had written to me and had led
> me astray with his fantasies. On my part, instead of being agitated by his
> talk I smiled to see him attack me on this subject. He left me in his
> resentment, and I told [Dom Raymond] that he would have done well not
> to have informed his friend of his project, for he was going to make it known
> and oppose it. And that's just what he did. He also came each day to
> torment me, insisting that I tell him whether I desired to go to Canada.
> When I saw the extent of his anxiety I told him plainly that I did, but that I
> was not worthy to go there, being a poor creature of no account and also
> that my state as a religious was an obstacle to the actual execution of such a
> plan in my case. ... He was so indignant that quite often he made use of
> abusive language and invectives and even sent me sheets of paper filled with
> them. What mortified him the most was the fact that I remained calm
> amidst all of his contradictions. (A 107–8)

This brother enlisted the help of a friend to try and thwart Marie's plans. "I
told both of them," she writes, "that they would change their ideas, that
they themselves would want to go to Canada, but that neither of them
would ever actually go. At this they both laughed at me." (A 108) Having
prayed that the two would have a change of heart, she was delighted when
she received soon after a letter from one of them, who wrote "to apologize
for all that he had said to me and to tell me that he felt strongly attracted to
the mission of Canada." (A 108) In describing how his companion was
also subsequently moved to regret his actions and support her plan,
Marie's triumphant tone reveals her personal satisfaction that by "invoking
the Holy Spirit" she had not only overcome a major obstacle to her own

vocation but had also helped win others to the cause:

> This father was so powerfully touched by grace that he passed the whole
> night without sleeping, filled with remorse of conscience for the way he'd
> conducted himself; and he was so fired with zeal for the salvation of these
> poor savages and with the desire to go labour among them, ... that he
> couldn't have done more in the matter. He came to see me but was now
> thoroughly humbled and did not dare to raise his eyes. He began by asking
> me: 'What have you done for me? I can't go on living. Pray God to be
> merciful to me. On my life, I won't oppose any vocation to the mission of
> Canada.' (A 108–9)

Marie's drawn-out description of the nasty confrontation with religious
figures who used their authority and influence to try to foil her plan, only
to be themselves converted to a missionary mentality, indicates that she
saw divine providence at work behind the scenes every step of the way,
orchestrating events and moving about the players in the drama which was
unfolding. Her account also indicates her conviction that her spiritual life
was destined to find its expression in New France, regardless of any
obstacles encountered. It was in New France that she undertook — at the
behest of her spiritual director — the task of outlining the course of her
spiritual life, and fashioning her self-image as mystic and missionary.

The idea of the New World mission occasioned an identity crisis for
Marie as a cloistered nun, but it was in fact in the stark reality of colonial
life that she came to terms with, and made her written assessment of, the
tension which can arise between action and contemplation — especially in
the advanced stages of spiritual life — and the resolution of this tension.
Marie grew up at a time when the blending of quiet devotion and active
service, or contemplation of God and charitable works, was being increasingly recommended as a goal for the ordinary Catholic. In fact, given that
she is renowned both as a mystic and as one of the founders of the colonial
Church in Canada, it would seem that she represents a perfect blend of
contemplation and action. However, she trod a long and difficult path
before achieving a synthesis of the two in the New World, and the special
link which she perceived between them in her new spiritual setting is the
key to her mystical thought. In the Christian tradition action and contemplation are seen as two modes of the spiritual life, or two kinds of religious
calling, the adjectives "active" or "contemplative" referring to the relative
emphasis placed on active ministry or prayer as the central expression of
one's spiritual life.

It might be useful at this point to say a few words about the term
"contemplation." The word "contemplative" generally brings to mind the

idea of a way of life, one devoted to prayer, be it in the structured framework of a religious order, or in the looser context of life in the world, where ordinary men and women, married or single, opt for a more devout form of life. Apart from this basic notion of a life devoted to prayer, "contemplation" in Catholic spirituality is also seen as a specific kind or rather state of prayer associated with an advanced stage in spiritual life.[1] Like other forms of prayer, this state of contemplation consists in conversation with God but it is conversation of a different order — one in which God is seen to be taking the initiative and leading the conversation. At this stage the mystics talk of passive as opposed to active prayer, extraordinary as opposed to ordinary contemplation. Since in this spiritual state the senses are stilled, the reasoning faculties incapacitated and the soul rendered passive, the mystic's role is limited to acquiescence to the grace infused in the soul. This infused as opposed to acquired contemplation is usually reached at an advanced stage of the spiritual journey and is often associated with the mystical experience of union with God.[2] In theological terms, the discussion of the relative merit of contemplation and action does not revolve solely around the question of the intrinsic value of these two sides of the spiritual life, but must also take into consideration God's prerogative in establishing different vocations for different souls. In the Christian tradition the active life, insofar as it may be seen as a particular vocation aimed at furthering God's will for the world, can in some instances be deemed superior to contemplation.[3]

The relation of contemplation to action poses two particular problems depending on whether one sees contemplation as a life devoted to prayer or as an extraordinary mystical state: first, what should be the role and nature of action in the contemplative life, that is, in a life devoted to prayer — be it inside or outside the monastery walls? And second, what is the role and nature of action when one reaches the passive mystical state of spiritual life known as extraordinary or infused contemplation? Marie faced both these problems before eventually finding harmony between action and contemplation. In the course of her spiritual life she had to deal with her strong desire to become a contemplative — in the strict sense of entering religious life — while at the same time fulfilling family, marital

---

[1] On the distinction between acquired and infused contemplation see Poulain, *The Graces of Interior Prayer*, pp. 59–63. See also J. De Guibert, "Goûter Dieu, servir Dieu", *Revue d'Ascétique et de Mystique* 7 (1926), pp. 337–353.

[2] "Contemplation" refers here to "the wholly supernatural and infused knowledge of God and of divine things." See Knowles, *What is Mysticism*, p. 27.

[3] De Guibert, "Goûter Dieu, servir Dieu", p. 349.

and work obligations in the outside world; later on, she had to deal with her desire to go out and serve others in the world once she had reached her contemplative goal — that is, after experiencing the grace of mystical contemplation and after becoming a nun. In other words, she had to find a way to reconcile her life as a contemplative nun and mystic with the desire for active service. In both its senses, then, contemplation was a problematic proposition for Marie.

From the time of her spiritual conversion in 1620 when she had begun to "taste the goods of the spirit and to know the vanity of earthly things," Marie saw herself as a contemplative "called to the religious life." (A 32) But as long as the care of her son kept her tied to the world she had to reconcile herself with the activities and distractions involved in working for her brother-in-law. And "so," Marie tells us, "I bore this necessary obstacle in a spirit of acquiescence to the divine will, which nevertheless enclosed my heart in a cloister even though my body was in the world." (A 32) In the early stages of her spiritual life she tried to approximate the contemplative ideal as best she could while enmeshed in her temporal duties, but despite her ability to simulate to a certain degree the religious state, through intense prayer and by taking vows, she still "suffered greatly in the world." (A 40) As her mystical experiences increased, eventually leading to her spiritual marriage at the age of twenty-seven, she felt even more strongly "that life in the world was unbearable." (A 67) The extraordinary graces which she received in this permanent state of contemplative union made her longing for the cloister more acute: "this vocation followed me everywhere and I spoke to my Divine Spouse about it in my most intimate converse with Him." (A 67)

Marie had become accustomed to combining her interior prayer life with service to others. It is interesting to note that when considering which religious order to enter, she had been drawn initially to the more austere Feuillant and Carmelite orders, but ultimately opted for the Ursulines, a newly-founded teaching order of women, because she had heard that they were devoted to helping souls, "a thing to which I was powerfully attracted." (A 69)[4] But this inclination to serve was clearly seen within the context of cloistered life where action must be subordinated to contemplation. When she finally entered the Ursuline convent four years after her spiritual marriage and embraced the contemplative life proper, that is, one which is by definition and rule devoted to prayer, Marie's problems regarding

---

[4] See M. de Chantal Gueudré, *Histoire de l'Ordre des Ursulines en France*, 2 vols., Paris 1957–60; and P.-G. Roy, *À travers l'histoire des Ursulines de Québec*, Lévis, 1939.

action and distraction seemed to be over. Indeed, she writes

> It is impossible for me to tell how delightful I found the religious life after
> such confusion at that which I left behind, how delightful to see myself as a
> novice, who has only to devote herself to the observance of the rule. The
> total exclusion of distracting affairs was quite in keeping with my nature
> which, of itself, did not care for entangling activity. (A 74)

By entering the convent she escaped from a way of life which had been at
odds with her religious identity. Indeed, cloistered life seemed to provide
the best framework for living out the dual contemplative ideal — a life
centred on prayer, and an extraordinary state of mystical contemplation.

The importance of spiritual direction in Marie's mystical life, especially
with regard to her understanding of the role of action in contemplation,
cannot be overemphasised. In 1631, after Dom Raymond, her spiritual
director of twelve years' standing, left Tours to become the prior of the
Feuillants, she was left without special guidance and "couldn't find help
from anybody" in her difficulties. (A 86) She "felt drawn to have recourse
to the fathers of the Society of Jesus" who had begun to visit the Ursuline
convent, but "for fear of being guilty of fickleness" she decided to consult
only the Feuillant fathers whom she knew, still hoping that her old
director might return. A couple of months after taking her solemn vows,
she "felt a strong impulse to speak" with Père George de la Haye, a Jesuit
who had preached at the monastery several times and with whom she had
become acquainted. (A 87) At her superior's suggestion Marie met with
Père de la Haye, who subsequently became her spiritual director. As was
usual for spiritual directors of mystics he had her write an account of her
spiritual experiences from childhood to her present state, on the basis of
which he concluded that she had truly "been guided by the Holy Spirit."
(A 87) Marie reports that after pouring out her soul to her director, "all my
sufferings disappeared, as though he had delivered me from a captivity"
and "from that time on the direction of my interior life has always been in
the hands of the Jesuit fathers." (A 87, 88)[5] It is significant that her
exposure to the Jesuits and the avowed therapeutic effect of de la Haye's
guidance occurred at this juncture in her spiritual life, when she was about
to turn to the way of action as the continuation of her mystical union and
life in the Trinity.

No sooner did Marie fulfil her calling to leave the world and take

---

[5] On spiritual direction in mystical life see Poulain, *The Graces of Interior Prayer*,
477–486.

contemplative vows than she experienced a call to leave the cloister and take on active service. The dream which she had of wandering in a vast, unknown country, and the subsequent illumination regarding her call to join the Canadian mission, triggered a spiritual dilemma of sorts and shifted the focus of her prayer life to the goal of saving souls.[6] She writes:

> Although bodily I was actually living the life of the rule (in the monastery), neither my spirit nor my heart abandoned these journeys, which consisted in a loving activity, more swift than any speech, whereby I entreated [God] for the salvation of the many millions of souls which I presented to Him. (A 95–6)

A few years earlier she had complained that God enclosed her heart in a cloister even though her body was in the world. Now she tells us:

> My body remained within the confines of our monastery, but my spirit could not be confined for it was bound to the Spirit of Jesus. This Spirit transported me in spirit to the Indies, to Japan, to America, to the East, to the West, to parts of Canada among the Hurons, and to all the habitable parts of the earth where there were souls, all of whom I saw as belonging to Jesus Christ. (A 95)

Marie's new-found apostolic zeal, however, seemed to her to be "opposed to common sense," especially given her "condition as a religious who ought to live and die within a cloister." (A 104) It aroused misgivings with regard to both her contemplative position and her interior state of contemplative union. First of all it would mean leaving the Ursuline convent

---

[6] Paul Renaudin suggests, wrongly in my view, that already after her conversion Marie was oriented more to an apostolic than to a contemplative vocation. See *Une grande mystique française au XVIIe siècle, Marie de l'Incarnation, Ursuline de Tours et de Québec. Essai de psychologie religieuse*, Paris 1935, p. 105. Jetté notes that the "the precocity of mystical marriage" in the case of Marie de l'Incarnation makes her an exception to the rule, but adds: "Her itinerary does not break the classic framework of spiritual life, it simply expands it a little by adapting it to the world of action." The special grace of spiritual marriage, in Jetté's view, can be explained in part by the requirements of Marie's particular vocation: "usually such favours are reserved for souls who reach the end of their career, but God wished to grant them to Marie very early, both for the good of the young Church in which she had come to work, and also to teach those who would follow her ... the ideal of holiness to which they should aspire." But he also stresses that "the spirit of the Incarnate Word," which is the moving force of Marie's mystical experience, is perceived by her both as a gift received early on in her spiritual itinerary, as well as an ongoing grace which finds new expression in her subsequent experiences, especially in her spiritual marriage and missionary calling. See Jetté, "L'Itinéraire spirituel de Marie de l'Incarnation", pp. 642–643.

in Tours, which had previously represented for her the ideal place for leading the contemplative life. She writes, "I could not imagine that our Lord intended that I should be bodily present in a strange country and actually serving Him in it, seeing that I was a religious leading a life of seclusion in a monastery." (A 97) Marie ultimately kept her monastic framework in the new colony, where she founded an Ursuline convent governed by the same conditions and rules as in France; however, at the time of her apostolic vocation she felt confusion in this regard. Moreover, her desire for missionary action seemed totally at odds with the state of infused contemplation, which she tells us was characterized by a permanent inner conversation with God, in which "the powers of the soul ... are bound and silenced; all is in a passive state." (A 52) If as a result of the spiritual marriage "the soul has no more desires, for she possesses her Beloved," how could the soul so ardently desire the salvation of souls? (A 59) How could she entertain the notion of going out into the world as a missionary?

Marie was able to resolve the apparent discrepancy between her contemplative state and her active calling and the seeming paradox of being in a passive state of mystical repose while yet desiring to take an active part in the business of saving souls, because she saw the missionary call as an integral part of her mystical life. She notes that at the very moment she accepted God's interior command to go to Canada her will was "united to that of God" and she "experienced a loving ecstasy during which this infinite goodness bestowed on my soul such caresses as human tongue could never describe." (A 99) What is particularly significant about this passage is the recurrence of the mystical language which she had used earlier to describe her experience of union. Marie came to the conclusion that, since in mystical union her will was united to God, any activity which she undertook or desired was an expression of the divine will and not of her own.

In her *Supplément à la Relation de 1654*, Marie elaborates on the active aspect of this divine indwelling which instilled in her the conviction "not just that God is present to it [the soul], but also that he dwells in it and acts there through his divine Spirit." (E II 384) The difference between acquired and infused contemplation, or between "the soul acting by itself or being activated by the Holy Spirit which governs it," is that in the latter instance, the soul "loses itself in this source, having no other operation than by the [Spirit's] movement." (E II 384) The reality of this divine indwelling and activity became clear to her one day as she was urging God to save more souls:

All of a sudden He removed from me all power and capacity for such commerce and ravished my soul in an ecstasy which ... caused it to enjoy His divine caresses and embraces in an unspeakable love and familiarity. (A 102–3)

She suddenly realizes that she had been trying to influence God's will:

"O my great God! I wish for nothing, I am unable to wish for anything because Thou hast captivated my will! How could I will anything, since Thou hast captivated it and rendered it incapable of willing. Do Thou, then, O my Love, will for me whatever pleases Thy just and divine will." (A 103)

She elaborates on the implications of this captivity of her will:

By means of certain special graces given to me, the divine will guided me in the ways of peace in a manner which until then had been unknown to me, so that I no longer suffered any agony of spirit for the salvation of souls ... although I still had the same views regarding the missions ... all the while experiencing that this divine will did everything for me. (A 104)

Because her will in mystical union was caught up by God and transformed into his will, and because his will was the salvation of the Indian souls in Canada, this goal became the focus of her contemplative life. Her desire for missionary activity, then, was no longer seen as conflicting with mystical union or mystical contemplation of God, but as issuing from the union of wills.[7] In effect she came to see missionary activity as the crowning of her contemplative life.

In writing her autobiography, Marie portrayed the contemplative ideal — both her stint in the convent and her mystical experience of contemplative repose — as having prepared the ground for this active calling. As far as she was concerned, the reason for her early experience of mystical union, or spiritual precocity as one scholar puts it, was that union was a necessary preparation for the special mission which God had chosen for her.[8] In reference to the state of infused contemplation she claims that "in this repose the soul cleaves to the sweet impressions of the sacred Word Incarnate, who disposes it for great things which He keeps secret." (A 77)

---

[7] In her autobiography, Marie indicates that her rich interior life was the necessary foundation for her apostolic activity, but she does not present her life of union with Christ solely as the means to an end, or as a preparation for her mission — as some of her commentators suggest. She sees it rather as an ongoing experience of participation in the divine life. See Huijben, "La Thérèse de la Nouvelle-France", p. 99; and A. Rétif, *Marie de l'Incarnation et la mission*, Paris 1963.

[8] Jetté, "L'Itinéraire spirituel de Marie de l'Incarnation", p. 642.

Marie writes:

> I also knew that God's purpose in bringing me into the religious life was that
> I might be prepared by means of it to spend myself and be spent in that place
> to which [He] was calling me. (A 118)

But her active role did not replace her contemplative experience. Her
mystical life was still unfolding, for as she says "whatever be the degree of
union with God which the soul experiences in this life, there always
remains a higher degree of union, God being infinite in His gifts." (A 158)
And it was precisely in this context of mystical progress in union that
Marie understood her missionary calling: it was an extension of the life of
union, or an expression of the mystical state of contemplation. On the one
hand she saw contemplation as the highest form of spiritual life, but on the
other hand she felt that contemplation, even in its most sublime form,
must be lived out in service to others. And action was not just one of many
aspects of her spiritual life, a complementary addition to balance prayer
life or a means of expressing her love of God, but rather, as far as she was
concerned, it was the continuation of her mystical experience in another
form.

Perhaps the best illustration of Marie's view of apostolic action as
contemplative prayer is found in a letter to her son in which she states:

> I never find myself better in God than when I leave my repose for his love in
> order to speak to some good Indian and to teach him to perform some
> Christian act ... I tell you this to make you see that the mixed life of this
> quality gives me greater vigour than I can tell. (C 187)

She is referring not to a voluntary "mixture" of contemplative union and
apostolic activity, but to a "mixed life of this quality," namely, one in
which there is no perceptible difference in mystical terms between resting
in God and exercising his will in the work of converting the Indians. She
sees herself as a divine agent of sorts, helping God not so much of her own
volition, but rather as a consequence of having attained the divine likeness
through a shared life in the Trinity.[9] Both interior prayer and external

---

[9] In Thomistic theology this idea of being a divine agent or "cause" of other things is seen
as the height of spiritual perfection, but Aquinas is referring to the human initiative in
seeking perfection or approximating the divine image and not to the mystical experience of
participation in the divine life and action once one has attained this likeness: "While then a
creature tends by many ways to the likeness of God, the last way left open to it is to seek the
divine likeness by being the cause of other things, according to what the Apostle says, Dei
enim sumus adjutores." Quoted in Underhill, *Mysticism*, p. 428.

service were considered equal ways of being fully "in God." Action was not an addition to contemplation, it was contemplation. For her the *vita contemplativa* — both as a chosen way of life and as a received mystical state — found its meaning in the *vita activa*.

Almost all of what we know about missionary activity in New France is to be found in the *Jesuit Relations*, annual reports on life in the colony and the progress of the mission, which were published in Paris from 1632–1672.[10] Marie had probably heard about the mission to Canada in sermons and intercessions during Mass, though she claims to have read a Jesuit report, or *Relation*, concerning Canada only after receiving her secret vocation. (A 100) Based on the Ignatian principle of epistolary thrift, or the idea that letters were meant to inform others of the fruits of missionary labour and were therefore to contain only edifying material, these reports were carefully edited so as to remove inessential or possibly damaging descriptions. They were, as one Canadian historian notes, "works of propaganda first and works of history only second".[11] These accounts, however, not only informed the faithful in France of the progress of the mission in order to elicit donations and prayers, but also had an important impact on the spiritual lives of French Catholics in the Old World. They highlighted the spiritual journey or path of sanctification of certain devout souls involved in the endeavour, appealed to the sense of piety and heroism in their readers by telling tales of the unwavering faith of martyrs who met their death at the hands of the natives, and imparted a sense of the aura of the *mirabilia dei* — instances of daily divine intervention in their lives — which fuelled the spiritual and missionary zeal of these latter-day apostles. The reports were instrumental both in drumming up funds and winning new recruits for the mission. Marie tells us not only that her own missionary vocation was spurred by one of the accounts "of what was going on in Canada," but that Madame de la Peltrie, who donated all her wealth to support the mission, "had been powerfully affected" and "won over by the appeal God directed to her through the Relation of Father Le Jeune." (A 101)

In the early years especially, before they became an institution, the *Relations* were novel, exotic and expressed the awe of those confronting

[10] The standard English edition is that of R. G. Thwaites, ed., *The Jesuit Relations and Allied Documents*, 73 vols., Cleveland 1876–1901. A new critical French edition containing previously unedited material is being prepared by Lucien Campeau: *Monumenta Novae Franciae*, 5 vols. Rome 1967–   .

[11] B.G. Trigger, *The Children of Aataentsic: A History of the Huron People to 1660*, 2 vols., Montreal 1976, vol. 1, p. 5.

this new reality.[12] As Stephen Greenblatt has recently noted, "the expression of wonder stands for all that can scarcely be believed"; this could apply equally to an experience of culture shock or mystical illumination, for in the New World context, wonder meant both the "shock of the unfamiliar" or — as Descartes phrased it — "'a sudden surprise of the soul.'"[13] Marie's image of the New World was also suffused with wonder and couched in terms of religious challenge and supernatural expectation. In fact, from the outset she depicted the missionary venture in terms similar to those used in describing the splendour afforded by her mystical experiences. The departure for what was to be a harrowing journey across the ocean is remembered and depicted in sublime terms:

> When I set foot on the ship's boat, which was to take us to the place where our ship rode at anchor, it seemed to me that I was entering paradise, for I was taking the first step towards the state in which I would risk my life for love of Him who had given it to me. (A 122)

Before her departure Marie had two interior visions in which she anticipated the "terrible solitude of spirit" which she was to suffer as part of God's plan. (A 118) The first was a terrifying image of a huge building "entirely made up of crucified persons instead of stones," each of which bore a cross. This vision was followed by a second unnerving experience which gave her a preview of all the trials and "crosses" which awaited her in Canada, as well as a foretaste of the total alienation of spirit, or abandonment which she was to undergo. Prompted by a desire for total self-sacrifice, she immediately abandoned herself "to His will in this enterprise" and "to suffer whatever was the good pleasure of His Divine Majesty." (A 118) She began to understand her contemplative vocation and mystical life as having been ordained from the outset to this missionary end and now aimed for total self-renunciation. Despite the mishaps, and the lack of food, fresh water, and sleep which made the voyage so hazardous, she assures us "my spirit and my heart enjoyed a very great peace through union with my sovereign and unique Good." (A 124)

For Marie, as for others who went to New France, the missionary call was a special form of service since, by bringing the Gospel message to distant lands, they were actively furthering the course of salvation history. But in her case, this vocation was also the result of an interior illumination

---

[12] L. Pouliot, *Le Père Paul Le Jeune S.J. (1591–1664). Textes choisis et presentés par Léon Pouliot*, Paris 1957, p. 11.

[13] S. Greenblatt, *Marvellous Possessions. The Wonder of the New World*, Oxford 1992, pp. 2, 20.

which meant release from spiritual turmoil. It is perhaps not surprising that in describing the farewell blessing offered by the archbishop of Tours, prior to the nuns' departure for New France, Marie mentions both his "fine exhortation on those words which our Lord spoke to His apostles when He sent them out on mission," and also his request that they "recite the psalm *When Israel went of Egypt.*" (A 119) In a way the departure for the overseas mission signified nothing less than a personal exodus to a promised land where her spiritual drama was to be resolved.

Arriving in New France in 1639, Marie embarked on her new religious path and despite the hardship of a "manner of life so entirely different from that of our monasteries in France," soon made it her new spiritual home. (A 128) In her *Relation* she writes:

> Now that I have seen this country I recognize it as the one which our Lord showed me in a dream six years ago. These great mountains, the vast areas, the site and the configuration, which were still engraved on my mind as at the time of the dream — all this was exactly as I had seen it, except that I don't see as much fog as I did then. (A 128)

As long as she was in France her missionary effort was limited to the level of praying for the salvation of "pagan" souls. As far as she was concerned the conversion of the Indians was essential in order that justice be done to Christ, and she was determined to make sure that his suffering and death had not been in vain. In praying for these souls which had "cost Him so much," she saw their conversion as a fairly straightforward matter: if God so willed, the pagans would convert and could thus be saved. (A 159) The reality of mission life and the interaction with the natives, however, soon led her to a deeper understanding of conversion and of her role in it.

Once Marie encountered the natives, she came to "nourish in [her] heart a tender affection for them all" and devoted herself to the work of conversion out of personal concern for their welfare. (A 129) She was no longer just interceding to God in abstract fashion for their salvation on behalf of her mystical spouse. Her first impressions of the Indians in New France, as recorded in her autobiography, suggest that the momentous and rather unsavoury task of teaching them not only the truths of the Gospel, but also French norms of civility and basic hygiene, was a welcome challenge for the missionaries:

> The filthiness of the savage girls who were not yet used to the cleanliness of the French, sometimes caused us to find a shoe in our soup pot, while daily we would find hair and charcoal in it; but this didn't cause us any disgust. The persons who visited us, and to whom by way of recreation we would

recount this, couldn't understand how we could get used to that sort of thing, nor how we could caress and take on our knees the little savage orphans who were given to us, for they were greasy from a little grease-stiffened rag which covered a small part of their bodies and gave off a very bad odour. And yet all of this was actually a source of delight for us much greater than one would even begin to suspect. (A 128–9)

For those determined to build a new life and meet new religious goals in the New World, "tradition, experience and expectation were the determinants of vision" and each of these components had an impact which varied depending on the individual in question.[14] Like others who were guided by a naive image of the noble native and by wishful thinking with regard to the chances for civilizing and evangelizing the indigenous peoples of America, the missionaries in New France had "to accept from an early stage that the inhabitants of this idyllic world could also be vicious and bellicose, and sometimes ate each other."[15] But unlike many utopians and others who sought a new and pristine life in the wilderness, the missionaries — even when confronted with obstacles to their missionary goals — could see the silver lining in any cloud: paradoxically, any danger, threat, hardship etc. was a considered a welcome ingredient of their spiritual self-fashioning in the New World.

On a personal level, the spiritual growth of the missionaries was nurtured by the harsh conditions and by the constant danger of death in which they lived. Missionary life facilitated the spiritual goal of total identification with Christ through suffering, and also seemed an apt preparation for the specific mystical goal of sharing in the divine life through union with Christ. The mystical experience of *mors mystica*, or dying to oneself as a pre-condition for union with God, was much more tangible in a situation where martyrdom was an immediate threat. Calling to mind scenes or moments of suffering from Christ's life was not so much a meditational exercise, such as those taught in the spiritual manuals circulating in France; it was more of an identification process experienced in realistic terms. Referring to the terrifying sea voyage the missionaries had endured, Paul Le Jeune stressed "it is one thing to reflect upon death in one's cell, before the image on the Crucifix; but quite another to think of it in the midst of a tempest and in the presence of death itself."[16] The ascetic

---

[14] J.H. Elliott, *The Old World and the New 1492–1650*, (1970), new edition, Cambridge 1992, p. 20.

[15] Ibid., p. 27.

[16] Thwaites, *Jesuit Relations*, vol. 5, p. 13.

exercises of self-denial, fasting and bodily mortifications, ordinarily taught as the basis for spiritual progress through the numbing of the senses, was not an artificial practice, but a lived reality. To illustrate that "the life which one conducts in the company of the barbarians is a continual martyrdom," the Jesuit Jacques Bruyas described the daily martyrdom of the senses by enumerating how one's sight was affected by the smoke in the cabins; one's hearing by the natives' "importuning cries"; one's sense of smell by the stench of the natives' oiled hair and bodies; one's sense of touch by the cruel cold of Québec; and one's sense of taste by the "insipid food which is fit for dogs."[17]

Although there is no marked homogeneity of spiritual thought in the writings of the missionaries, it is clear that they saw themselves collectively as a nascent Church; living under primitive conditions in a hostile environment, they identified closely with the apostles and martyrs of the early Church. They were both an ecclesiastical elite, chosen for the difficult mission of converting souls in a far-flung land, and a spiritual elite, singled out by God for spiritual favours. Taking special measures to ensure that "only men of the elite" would be sent to the missions, the superiors of the Society of Jesus measured the stature of prospective candidates in spiritual terms and closely queried them to establish whether their calling was based on "supernatural motives," i.e., divine inspiration, or passing enthusiasm.[18] Those chosen to be sent overseas felt fortunate to be taking part in the work of salvation. Those who, in addition, felt themselves graced to be making progress in their ascent to mystical heights, also nurtured the physical and spiritual state of lowliness in which they found themselves. In their view, Canada was both a country of sin and a heavenly paradise.

In revising their initial conception of and workplan for their mission in New France, missionaries such as Marie de l'Incarnation discovered that preconceived or inherited notions (*imitatio christi*, sacrifice, redemptive blood, communion of saints, pagan customs, struggles with the devil) had become experiential and personal aspects of their spiritual life in New France. The missionaries certainly did not abandon tradition, but apprehended it differently in light of their concrete and acute experiences. Echoing Le Jeune's sentiments, Père Bruyas aptly pointed out that "there is some difference between meditating on the Canadian mission in one's

[17] Thwaites, *Jesuit Relations*, vol. 51, pp. 134–136.

[18] L. Pouliot, *Étude sur les "Relations" des Jésuites de la Nouvelle-France (1632–1672)*, Paris 1940, pp. 207–208.

oratory [in France] and in finding oneself in the exercise of the Canadian mission."[19] Because of the objective circumstances of missionary life, the subjective spiritual experience took on a pronounced biblical-apostolic quality and imparted a sense of spiritual immediacy similar to that enjoyed by the early Christians. With regard to this new religious context the missionaries firmly believed that "if the consolations of the earth are lacking there, those of Paradise may already be enjoyed."[20]

In a letter written to her son after nearly two decades in the New France mission, Marie de l'Incarnation says that her apostolic life, "emanating from sources which I have just discussed, is a kind of 'interior prayer' since it comes from God and ends in God." (C 597) She indicates not only that her state of permanent union with God gave her strength for her missionary tasks, but that these tasks themselves were of a mystical nature. At first, she had found the Indian dialects impossible to learn, suffering many headaches in the process until she "spoke lovingly to our Lord about it," after which she soon "had a very great facility in the language." (A 127) But she explains that not only was her "interior life ... neither hindered nor interrupted," by the linguistic challenge, but that such "study was a prayer, which made this language delightful." (A 127)

The New World was the final destination on Marie's spiritual journey. This *locus amoenus*, which she saw in her dream as a beautiful place, "a majestic and vast country, full of mountains, of valleys, and of thick mists," became her existential niche and lost none of its splendour even in reality, for in coping with the hardships and hostilities in their new-found frozen land, the missionaries were advancing on their respective spiritual paths. (A 91) The gatekeeper, who in the dream points out to Marie and her companion that "this was the way we had to pass," that "this was our destination," represents Marie's own view that her path in spiritual life was specific, undeniable, and preordained. In recounting the story of her life then, she indicates that her dream of 1634 had contained not only a foretaste of the place and task which awaited her, but also the first hazy hints of the full-fledged interpretation of religious life which she was eventually to set forth in her spiritual account. It was after having been in Canada some six years that Marie made a special vow to do everything possible to seek her "greater perfection" or "greater sanctification," and "the greater glory of God." (A 148) She viewed her own ongoing conversion

---

[19] Thwaites, *Jesuit Relations*, vol. 51, pp. 134–136.
[20] Thwaites, *Jesuit Relations*, vol. 5, p. 33.

or pursuit of sanctity as inextricably bound up with promoting the salvation and sanctification of others for the glory of God.

Marie's *Relation de 1654*, which was written some thirty-three years after her conversion experience, and twelve years after her arrival in New France, incorporates and assesses both her mystical and missionary experiences. Her retrospective interpretation of her life — a life which she defined in spiritual terms — not only points to a new summit of spiritual experience, but also and more importantly gives primacy of place to her experience in the New World. Indeed, life in New France was in effect the context and culmination of her spiritual self-definition.

As we shall see, Marie's missionary activity deepened her understanding of conversion, a term which still denoted for her the concrete, sacramental event of baptism as a condition for salvation, but now had added connotations as a complex process influenced by a variety of socio-economic and psychological factors. Her description of both negative and positive factors in this process reveals her growing recognition of conversion not just as a theological fact or divinely orchestrated gift of grace, but also as an emotionally loaded and culturally shaped experience in which religious role models could play a key role.

CHAPTER FIVE

THE HARVEST OF SOULS: MARIE'S MISSIONARY ACTIVITY

Heightened missionary activity in the sixteenth and seventeenth centuries was an inevitable result of European exploration in the new age, which led to the discovery of new lands and peoples who knew nothing of the Christian faith. The evangelization process went hand in hand with the colonial enterprise and trade policies pursued by major European countries, whose political leaders — especially those in staunchly Catholic countries such as Spain, Portugal and France — saw the missionary cause as both a worthy and advantageous endeavour.[1] The Church's missionary work in this period was carried out by a variety of religious orders who were spurred by the common conviction that each individual soul won over to the faith was an important component of the ultimate divine plan of universal salvation. Missionary goals and methods varied from country to country and depended to a large degree on the attitude of the missionaries to the indigenous peoples. Indeed, members of different religious orders were sometimes at odds with one another over the question of effective and permissible means of converting pagan souls.

In the early sixteenth century, the bulk of the missionary initiative was taken by Franciscan and Dominican priests and friars; the Society of Jesus, a new order which came into existence in 1540, played a key role in the Catholic Reformation movement as a whole, and in particular produced some of the most famous figures in the annals of the Christian missions. By the middle of the seventeenth century, the Jesuits had "laid their bones in almost every country of the known world and on the shores of almost every sea" and had been both praised and censured for the methods they developed in their conversion activity.[2] Convinced of the need for careful discernment and decision-making to achieve their mis-

---

[1] See K. Scott Latourette, *A History of the Expansion of Christianity*, vol. 3, Three Centuries of Advance A.D. 1500–A.D. 1800, London 1940; and S. Neill, *A History of the Christian Missions*, London (1964) 2nd ed., 1986.

[2] Neill, *A History of the Christian Missions*, p. 127.

sionary goals and thereby promote the greater glory of God, the Jesuits kept the *"ad majorem dei gloriam"* motto uppermost in their minds and used their special training, linguistic skills and flexibility as means to this end.

Jesuit activity in the Far East and the Americas reflected, albeit to varying degrees, the spirit and practice of cultural flexibility or "accommodation" which governed the Jesuits' encounter with foreign cultures. Like other missionaries the Jesuits were guided both by their preconceived notions regarding "pagans", as well as by the specific social or political circumstances which confronted them in each instance. Their tolerance of and adaptation to local custom were determined by a sliding scale — the long-established civilizations of the East were recognized as such by the Jesuits and treated with more respect and tolerance than were the customs and myths of native American peoples. It was in Japan that the first fledgling experiments of cultural flexibility were made. In China and South India the call for accommodation likewise carried the day. By the beginning of the eighteenth century the policy of accommodation pursued by the Jesuits in the Far East and elsewhere met its demise when Rome issued a series of bulls requiring all Christian missions to follow traditional Roman Catholic practice down to the last detail. In the preceding two centuries, however, the Jesuits had adhered to the simple notion that "in dealing with a great and ancient civilization, it is necessary to proceed with great circumspection and respect" and in so doing, had reaped considerable fruits.[3]

Missionary activity in the Americas was governed — at least at the outset — by quite a different set of assumptions than those underlying the missions in the Far East. The missionaries seemed to concur with the prevailing European opinion that the Indians of the Americas had "no rellish nor resemblance at all, of the Arts or learning, or civility of Europe," nor indeed "of the arts or industry of China or India or Cataia or any other civill region along that border of Asia," as one seventeenth-century geographer phrased it.[4] In South America, missionary spheres of influence were divided between Spain and Portugal, each of which received a grant of patronage from the Pope, that ensured direct control over missionary activity in their designated areas.[5] As a result, the Spanish and

---

[3] Ibid., p. 140.

[4] Quoted in M. Hodgen, *Early Anthropology in the Sixteenth and Seventeenth Centuries,* Philadelphia 1975, p. 315.

[5] Neill, *A History of the Christian Missions,* pp. 121–122.

Portuguese missionaries were as much agents of colonial expansion as they were emissaries of God. In most areas, apart from Mexico and Peru, where the missionaries had to contend with ancient indigenous civilizations, conquest rather than accommodation was the operative word — at least at the outset. In their relatively "easy and rapid conquest of this new world" the missionaries encouraged the natives to lead a settled and Christian life in return for religious instruction and protection from their enemies.[6] Mass conversions were common in these early missions, estimates of baptized natives running into the hundreds of thousands.

The French missionary venture in the New World was conducted in the context of colonial expansion and indeed, royal and ecclesiastical interests in New France were mutually supportive. In fact, the establishment of the colony was from the outset furthered as much by the Christian ideal of salvation of souls as by the commercial and political aims of the French. The colony as a whole benefited from the presence of the missionaries and from the new local Church, which had an important stabilizing influence on settlers, traders and Indians alike. The missionary project in turn benefited from the support of the French authorities — especially the trading companies who effectively ran the colony in its first decades.[7] New France did not in fact come under direct French rule until 1663 when the Crown took over political and economic control of the colony. The famous trading company, the Company of the One Hundred Associates, also known as the Company of New France, arranged for the Jesuits to have exclusive control over the New France mission. Paul Le Jeune, the first Jesuit superior of the mission, acknowledged the support of the Company of New France, noting that "since they interest themselves in the glory of God, in the spread of the Gospel, in the conversion of souls, we feel an inexplicable and affectionate interest in their affairs."[8]

Individual traders were also instrumental in establishing good trade relations and friendly contacts with different Amerindian tribes, thereby preparing the ground for the missionaries, who first needed to make a positive impression on the natives before beginning the more delicate and complex process of converting them. Though zealously devoted to different causes, the local French traders and missionaries cooperated with one another in pursuit of their final goals. Not infrequently however, the

---

[6] Ibid., p. 144.

[7] L. Campeau, *Les Cent-Associés et le peuplement de la Nouvelle-France (1633–1663)*, Montréal 1974.

[8] Thwaites, *The Jesuit Relations*, vol. 5, p. 85.

traders and missionaries found themselves at cross purposes, for as Marie de l'Incarnation wryly notes in one of her letters, "each aims for what he likes, the merchants to earn money, the reverend Fathers to win souls." (C 678) The "reverend Fathers" were the Jesuits, who had been active in Acadia on Canada's east coast as early as 1611 and who were granted a monopoly over the New France mission when England returned the captured territory to the French in 1632.[9] The Jesuits continued and upgraded the missionary endeavour of the Recollets, who had made little progress in advancing the cause of the faith. Compared with their Recollet predecessors, who had advocated a policy of settling and civilizing the Indians as a strategic prerequisite for their conversion, the Jesuits proved more flexible in their approach to winning the confidence and religious allegiance of the natives.[10]

Although the first cross was erected in New France in 1534 when Jacques Cartier claimed the new-found land for the Crown, serious settlement did not begin until Samuel de Champlain founded the French colony at Québec in 1608. The missionary campaign began in earnest in 1632 when the colony once again came under French control. The New France mission shared some common features with those of Latin America, most notably with regard to the learning of local dialects, the founding of schools and the attempt to settle native Indians into Christian villages — *réductions* or reserves — in order to facilitate Christian instruction and the exercise of discipline. However, there were some important differences, many stemming from the Jesuits' initial assumption that contrary to other missionary endeavours, the New France project was directed at a people who had no culture of their own. In one of his first reports on the New France mission, Le Jeune assessed the situation as follows:

> Great fruits have been obtained in the East Indies and in South America, although there have been found in those countries not only vices to combat, but also strange superstitions, to which the people are more attached than to their lives. In New France, there are only sins to destroy, and those in a

---

[9] Several vintage studies offer a useful, if uncritical, overview of the Jesuits' early years among the Amerindians: J. Wynne, *The Jesuit Martyrs of North America*, New York 1925; T.G. Marquis, *The Jesuit Missions. A Chronicle of the Cross in the Wilderness*, Toronto repr., 1964. Critical new perspectives on various aspects of Jesuit missionaries' interaction with the Amerindians are found in James Axtell, *After Columbus: Essays in the Ethnohistory of Colonial North America*, Oxford 1988 and *Beyond 1492: Encounters in Colonial North America*, Oxford 1992; Cornelius Jaenen, *The Role of the Church in New France*, Ottawa 1985; and Bruce Trigger, *Natives and Newcomers*, Montréal 1986.

[10] Trigger, *Natives and Newcomers*, pp. 202, 294.

small number; for these poor people, so far removed from all luxury, are not given to many offenses. If there are any superstitions or false religions in some places, they are few. The Canadians think only of how to live and to revenge themselves upon their enemies. They are not attached to the worship of any particular Divinity. ... In truth, anyone who knew their language could manage them as he pleased.[11]

Like most Europeans, the Jesuits had made their initial acquaintance with the natives of America in the Old World where, after reading travelogues and other accounts of explorers and early missionaries, they formed their first impressions of the natives of the wilderness of New France.[12] Like others who had read this travel literature, the Jesuits were intrigued by the noble and exotic qualities of the "wild men" but also appalled by their "barbaric" habits; while horrified by their cruelty on the one hand, the Jesuits marvelled at certain virtues such as the natives' patience and generosity which far surpassed those of the average Frenchman.[13] Notwithstanding this basic ambivalence with regard to specific character traits of the Indians, the Jesuits seemed to have no doubts as to the task at hand: the natives would have to be tamed, then evangelized.

The Jesuits brought to the New World their European, pre-conceived image of the Amerindians as primitives — devoid of reason, religion and culture, who would first have to be civilized before they could be christianized. After their initial satisfaction at the apparent success of their missionary efforts — a satisfaction which found expression in the reports of numbers of Indians baptized, which were sent back to France — the Jesuits began to realize that the supposed conversions were not always deep or lasting; quite often in fact, the Indians "went out from amongst us, but were not of us" (I Jn 2:19). This led them not only to identify and remove obstacles to their goals, but also to amend their approach to native culture and, by trial and error, to refine their practice of conversion accordingly. Thus, the missionaries' experience in the New World — and particularly their discovery of Amerindian culture — forced them to abandon their Old World perspective, and to reassess their view of the planned harvest of souls.

Though the Jesuits had exclusive control over the running of the mission, they were helped by members of other religious orders, most notably by the Augustinian or Hospital nuns and the Ursulines who

[11] Thwaites, *The Jesuit Relations*, vol. 5, pp. 33–35.
[12] Dickason, *The Myth of the Savage*, p. 205.
[13] Thwaites, *The Jesuit Relations*, vol. 5, pp. 29, 133.

arrived in the colony in 1639 as the first female missionaries in North America. This large-scale involvement of women in missionary campaigns was quite an innovation in the history of Christian missions; the Ursulines and Augustinians set up a school and a hospital respectively, and the educational, medical and social services which they provided for both the colonists and the natives formed the indispensable infrastructure for the expansion of the colony and mission.[14] The Jesuits were instrumental in helping Marie realize her missionary goal, by helping to win official Church approval for the plan to establish both a seminary for the education of French and native girls in the colony, and a hospital to serve the colonists and their new-found Indian allies.

Both Marie de l'Incarnation and Madame de la Peltrie, the woman who provided financial backing for the project, were part of this contingent of religious and laywomen who arrived in New France in 1639 to serve the fledgling community. Their work was considered an invaluable contribution to the modest expansion of the missionary and colonial enterprise. Marie's views on conversion activities were coloured by those of the Jesuits who orchestrated the whole missionary operation, and her descriptions of missionary attitudes and strategies were naturally indebted to their oral or written reports of encounters with the Indians. Marie, however, also drew on first-hand experience of this interaction, and the letters which she wrote from New France, though in many instances based on Jesuit reports, differed from the latter in tone and intent. Her writings are considered an important supplement to the Jesuit *Relations* since they were written without the constraints governing the composition of the Jesuit reports, and thus contain valuable insights concerning the shifting aims and approaches of the missionaries.[15] Because they were written informally and were not subject to official scrutiny, they present a more candid, personal view of the Indians, as well as of the nature, mechanics and consequences of conversion.

In general terms, Marie saw the conversion of the Indians as a "great harvest" of souls, with each additional soul reaped compensating, as it were, for the loss of the apostate angels who had caused man's initial fall and still sought his eternal damnation. (C 810, 193) Her image of a door opening to the nations, and her allusion to the conversion of all, promised

---

[14] Latourette, *A History of the Expansion of Christianity*, vol. 3, p. 100.

[15] Her letters are particularly important in this regard. Of the several thousand letters which she is believed to have written, only two-hundred and seventy-eight remain. These have been edited by Dom Oury. (see Introduction, n. 10)

by the Gospel, reflect the theological view of universal conversion underlying the missionary aim to convert each and every newly-discovered tribe. (C 501, 181) Elsewhere, she reveals the pronounced eschatological underpinning of this "quantitative" approach to the conversion project, in her comment, "I don't know if the end of the world is near but the faith is spreading greatly." (C 278) The Indians' presumed transformation from "demi-beasts" into "children of God" was a clear sign that the devil's machinations were being thwarted. (C 902) For to the missionary mind, the wild terrain of New France was the devil's turf, and the devil jealously guarded his domain, intent on preventing the missionaries from winning Indian souls. (C 149, 169, 591) Hence the enthusiasm with which Marie marvels at how God caused the natives' "frozen souls" to melt, "took possession" of their hearts, and inscribed on their souls "the law of simplicity and love." (181, 160, 154)

Underlying the many metaphors Marie uses to describe the Indians' adoption of the Christian faith is her fundamental belief in the necessity of baptism as a precondition for salvation. The idea of conversion conjured up for her the cause-effect image of souls being "freshly washed in the blood of the lamb" and thereby purified of original sin. (C 91) Indeed, the above images suggest a simple equation of conversion, baptism and redemption, and evoke the notion that in baptism, "the 'name of Christ' was applied to the Christian like a vaccination," to use Peter Brown's phrase.[16] In fact, in cases of imminent death it was usual to baptize quickly — often large numbers at one time. It was felt that since death removed the danger of further occasions of sin, these newly "purified" souls would rise straight to heaven. Paul Le Jeune wrote of "the joy that one feels when he has baptized an Indian who dies soon afterwards and flies directly to Heaven to become an Angel."[17]

It is estimated that members of the different tribes — the Algonkin, Huron, and Iroquois being the predominant ones — numbered between 125,000 and 150,000 when the French arrived in the New World; in forty years of missionary work, approximately 16,000 converts were baptized, of whom roughly a third were infants, children and adults baptized before death.[18] As far as the Jesuits were concerned, such death-bed conversions certainly counted in the grand scheme of things, i.e., God's redemptive plan, but were not of much practical use to the missionaries in their

---

[16] Brown, *Augustine of Hippo*, p. 41.
[17] Thwaites, *The Jesuit Relations*, vol. 8, p. 169.
[18] Pouliot, *Étude sur les "Relations" des Jésuites*, pp. 223–224.

immediate task. Citing the numbers of baptized in 1640, Père Lalemant noted the high number of those who had died shortly after baptism and lamented the fact that so few "active" converts had been gained: "We have busied ourselves this year with augmenting the Church triumphant rather than the Church militant."[19] The missionaries knew that new converts were an invaluable resource for the progress of the mission. "They do more than we for instructing the other Indians," notes one Jesuit, the explanation for the natives' success in propagating the faith being that the "Indians aren't so surprised to see the French behaving well and believing strongly in God; they think this is required from birth," but when they see their own kinsmen "who are, like them, accustomed to superstition and immersed in vice, come out of baptism pure and clean they are greatly impressed."[20]

Baptism had its drawbacks, however. Because of the close correlation in the native's mind between baptism and subsequent death, some natives began to view the religious rite as the cause of death and the Jesuits were at pains to convince them that baptism does not kill, and that disease, once it afflicts the body, takes its natural course and often leads to death regardless of whether one has been baptized. The Jesuits did not deny that although its primary function was spiritual, baptism sometimes led to recovery. Père Brébeuf explained this to a woman seeking baptism for her sick granddaughter and hoping that it would save her life: "'You care only for the body," said he, "we care for the soul, which is purified by this Sacrament, ... baptism always cures the soul, and does no harm to the body, but on the contrary often restores it to health.'"[21] So convinced were they of the importance of the sacrament that the Jesuit fathers sometimes resorted to devious means when a dying child's parents refused to let him or her be baptized. One account tells of a priest who, under the guise of offering the ailing child a drink of sugar water, used some drops of unsweetened water to brush the child's forehead and secretly administer the sacrament.[22]

Below the surface of the symbols which Marie used in reference to conversion, a more sophisticated view of conversion was developing, which on the one hand took for granted its theological implications and technical aspects, i.e., the required baptismal act, but which on the other hand became self-adjusting insofar as it incorporated her growing recog-

[19] Thwaites, *The Jesuit Relations*, vol. 19, p. 122.
[20] Ibid., vols. 23, pp. 102–4; and 20, p. 230.
[21] Ibid., vol. 5, p. 232.
[22] Ibid., vol. 14, pp. 40–42.

nition of conversion's cultural and psychological dimensions. When used in a collective sense in reference to all those who had joined the Church, "conversion" signified a technical and tangible religious change: it meant that the Indians had undergone the rite of baptism. However, throughout her correspondence Marie repeatedly emhasises that before baptism was possible, the Indians had to "convert" to the faith, i.e., show interest, respect and docility with regard to Christian teaching and practice. In recounting for example, how new Indian converts spread the word to other members of their tribe, she implies that conversion was a matter of the personal conviction which precedes baptism: "They explained to them points of faith as they had learned them, so that they converted a great number of them, whom they brought to Trois Rivières to be baptized there." (C 279)

The anthropologist Bruce Trigger argues that for the missionaries it was imperative to instill in the Indians the desire for baptism, even if it became evident that the prospective converts had ulterior motives.[23] Marie, how-ever, suggests that sincerity was required of those turning to the faith, and cites an instance in which baptism was refused on the grounds that it was motivated by temporal desires. (C 286) In her view, conversion — or "submission to the faith" as she refers to it — and baptism were essentially two distinct steps. (C 802) In another letter she refers to Indians interested in baptism as Christians in their hearts, but catechumens in actual fact. (C 399) The term "conversion" then, could refer either specifically to the initial display of interest in the Christian message, or more generally to the end result of the process as a whole, once submission to the faith, instruc-tion and baptism had taken place.

It soon became clear that if getting the natives to accept the faith in the first place was difficult, keeping them Christian was an even more compli-cated task. While conversion and baptism were essential for the salvation of souls, the missionaries required not only that a convert submit to the faith and be baptized, but also persevere in the faith and battle all subse-quent temptations. It mattered little, from the missionary's point of view, that certain Indians were nominally Catholic if they remained lax with regard to behaviour and beliefs. Marie worried that one could as easily lose one's soul within the faith as without, and refers to "weak souls" who began stumbling after their conversion. (C 299) Baptism was seen as a necessary but not sufficient condition for the ultimate goal of salvation; the sacraments of communion, confession and confirmation were seen as

---

[23] Trigger, *Natives and Newcomers*, p. 20.

safeguards, which helped make the conversion a lasting one. Marie mentions confirmation as a means by which converts could be strengthened in their struggle against the temptations of the devil. (C 731)

Marie indicates that the chances for perseverance were better if a native submitted to the faith of his or her own volition, rather than as a result of coercion, explaining "the human heart is a strong thing, God takes it when it is offered to him willingly, but he forces no one." (C 293) This was the reason that the Indian girls were not kept in the convent against their will and received instruction only if their parents requested it. (C 802) The only exception with regard to "forced" baptism was in cases where the soul was deemed to be in imminent danger, in which case the question of prior preparation and subsequent perseverance was of little consequence; in such cases the imperative was to transmit the sacramental grace of baptism without which salvation was impossible. On these grounds Marie justified the policy of mass conversion, i.e., the large-scale and sometimes hasty baptism of the sick and elderly, with little regard for the personal significance of the religious change thus wrought.[24] Referring to new converts who died shortly after their baptism, she states that God had called them perhaps "out of fear that malice might change their hearts." (C 735)

A most gruesome illustration of the principle that in cases of imminent death a technical conversion was better than none at all, is Marie's account of how captured Iroquois warriors were brought for baptism by the French's Indian allies after having been tortured, and, in Marie's words, thus "died as Christians" and "in hope of their salvation." (C 621) She also mentions a captive who underwent a "sudden conversion" before being taken to his death, and was said to have uttered the words "'you say that those who believe go to heaven.'" (C 338) In such cases where "conversion" was synonymous with baptism there was little or no possibility of either preparing the individual for conversion or of verifying the ongoing effect of the religious act in the individual's life; but though one could hardly contend that a genuine inner change had taken place, such an assumption is implicit in Marie's claim that these victims did in fact believe in the possibility of their salvation.

When conversion entails joining a group, that group has its own criteria for what constitutes a real conversion, but religious authorities can only judge an individual's conversion on the basis of its subsequent external

---

[24] On the rationale behind the new policy of mass conversion see Trigger, *Natives and Newcomers*, pp. 265–267. The policy was eventually reassessed due to the alleged insincerity of those Indians who abandoned Christian practice upon recovering from their illness.

manifestations. In describing the apparent consequences of "conversion" in her letters, Marie indicates what proofs were sought by the missionaries as a guarantee that the conversion was genuine. Apart from her frequent observation that the Indians became docile as a result of the encounter with the Christian faith, she also claims that conversion caused the savages to "lose their natural traits" and become sedentary, or willing to be restricted in movement and lifestyle. (C 119) Beyond this, the missionaries sought indications of the personal significance of the convert's new religious identity, and in so doing sometimes projected onto the convert their own spiritual sentiments, as they looked for familiar signs — such as effusive prayer, zeal for confession, acts of piety, tears of joy or remorse, and even spiritual visions. (C 260, 261, 285) In describing her own pupils, Marie praises their "innocence and interior grace," "angelic modesty," "purity," "ardour and desire to be united to our Lord." (C 95, 97) From the missionaries' point of view, the most gratifying consequence of a "successful" conversion was its translation into zealous preaching activity on the part of the new convert, who set out to persuade friends and relatives to accept Christian "truths." (C 119, 544)

However else they may have viewed the nature of conversion — whether as a native's initial display of interest in adopting the faith, or as the moment of baptism, or as an ongoing display of fidelity over time — missionaries such as Marie saw conversion as no less than a miracle; she felt that God was the prime mover in winning the Indian converts and that he alone knew the "moments of their conversion." (C 672) Yet even though she saw God both as the main agent behind conversion and the ultimate judge of its validity, she acknowledged the role of others in realizing this divine plan. She considered the missionaries, for example, to be indispensable in preparing the actual conditions for conversion. It was "through the ministry of [God's] servants," she claims, that the "barbarians" were able to receive "the light which alone can illuminate them on the way to heaven." (C 902) By way of rationalizing the French settlers' plan to destroy the warring Iroquois nation, whose attacks on both the French and the Indian allies of the French were endangering both colonial and missionary interests, Marie asks: "when there is no more Christianity, nor missionaries, what hope will there be for their salvation?" (C 649) She insists that if there were no missionaries left, the conversion of the natives would require "a quite extraordinary miracle," the implication being that while nothing is impossible for God, he prefers to accomplish his will with human aid. (C 649) Hence her reference to priests as both God's representatives and instruments on earth. (C 139, 124)

If Marie viewed the missionaries as instrumental to the work of conversion, she regarded the martyrs amongst them — those killed during and because of their attempt to spread the faith — as even more important. Their contribution was twofold: through their suffering and sacrifice they atoned for sins of those on earth, and as companions of God in heaven they could make a direct appeal to Him to prevent danger and advance the conversion of the souls in New France. (C 356, 338, 349) She saw the lot of the martyrs as the most desirable way of serving God and would gladly have followed them "in their crosses" and risked martyrdom. (C 860) The missionaries' self-image as a "new Church" was modelled on and infused with the spirit of the apostles and the martyrs of the Early Church. (C 139)[25] Indeed, Marie remarks that the new Indian converts also reflected "the fervour of the Church's first Christians" in their purity and eagerness to observe the law of God. (C 119)

Because she saw prayer as the most essential, albeit intangible instrument of conversion, Marie often concluded letters to friends with a request to pray for the salvation of souls. She believed that by virtue of their intercessions, the recipients of these letters were also influential agents of conversion and active participants in the "amplification of God's kingdom." (C 154, 157, 232, 294) She was applying the lesson of her own experience, for as mentioned earlier, after receiving her missionary vocation while in the convent in Tours, she was able to "help the preachers of the Gospel" only by praying and inveighing upon each of the nuns "to do what she could for the conversion of the savages in Canada." (A 100, 105)

Although Marie envied the Jesuits their more active role and considered herself but a "poor instrument" of God's mission, her writing suggests that once she reached New France, her own efforts were by no means negligible. She laments the fact that her work was limited to the confines of the Ursuline convent, but at least felt able to contribute to the conversion of the Indians in a more direct and tangible fashion:

> It's true that our enclosure doesn't permit us to follow the workers of the Gospel to the nations being discovered every day; being nonetheless incorporated, as I am, in this new Church, our Lord, having done me the honour of calling me here, ties me so strongly to them in spirit, that it seems I follow them everywhere and that I work with them in these so very rich and noble conquests. (C 734)

---

[25] This theme is central to Ghislaine Boucher's study of the nascent Church in New France. See *Le premier visage de l'Église du Canada. Profil d'une Église naissante. La Nouvelle-France 1608–1688*, Montréal 1986.

She also emphasises that efforts to educate the colonists' daughters and keep them from "becoming wild," was as important as the indoctrination of the Indian girls entrusted to the nuns. Keeping the colony not only Catholic but also pious was essential to the missionary project. (C 734) With regard to the Indians themselves, Marie informs us that at first the nuns were kept busy nursing the many who had fallen ill during an outbreak of smallpox. (A 126) Soon thereafter, they began to learn "the language of the savages," in order to instruct them "in everything that was necessary for their salvation." (A 127) There were "a large number of savages of both sexes" and from different nations who came to the convent for instruction and conversations with the nuns. The latter, Marie notes, "exercised continual charity on behalf of these poor savages ... from the different nations," but she does not describe their activity in any detail, mentioning only that they received the Indian "students" in order "to prepare them for baptism and other sacraments." (A 127)

The Indians themselves were agents of conversion. Although the official view was that the new converts, even the holiest among them, did not have a "nature suited to the ecclesiastical functions" and should therefore not be encouraged to proselytize, Marie praised the informal efforts of these "dear neophytes" in glowing terms. (C 396, 150, 161, 181, A 126) She felt that their enthusiasm made some converts effective preachers, quite capable of "winning hearts," and tells of an Algonquin widow whom the nuns accepted for instruction despite her age because of her zeal for the Christian faith. (C 566, 333, 730) This woman began preaching only after receiving the sacrament of confirmation which was considered "something great and holy" and required considerable preparation on the part of the recipients. (C 730) Another Christian convert, an Iroquois woman who also spread the Gospel message enthusiastically, was described as having a perfect grasp of "the holy mysteries." (C 860) Preachers cut from local cloth, these newly converted zealots had to display a certain knowledge of Christian teaching, as well as intense devotion, before they were encouraged to evangelize among their brethren.

Children were also seen as excellent channels for conveying the Christian message, and because of the Indians' extreme respect and affection for their offspring, the latter were often successful in persuading others to come to the seminary for instruction. (C 565) And yet, despite the prolonged and often sympathetic encounter between the Ursuline nuns and native girls placed in their charge, the work of instilling in them the Christian faith was an arduous task, and whatever interim success was reported by Marie and others, the fact remains that by the end of the seventeenth century, there were no longer any Indians receiving instruction in the Ursuline convent.

On the whole, the mechanics of conversion proved to be quite complex — affected by a myriad of obstacles and ultimately by the new and often ingenuous approaches developed by the missionaries. Addressing those back in France who were "astonished that they hear nothing about the conversion of Savages during the many years that we have been in New France," Paul Le Jeune explained "it is necessary to clear, till, and sow before harvesting."[26] From the outset the missionaries had faced concrete, practical obstacles to the conversion of the Indians. Sometimes the problems were of an obvious, practical nature, such as the nomadic lifestyle of certain tribes which effectively removed them from the Christian sphere of influence for several months of the year; the intimidation of the "traditionalists," natives who bribed, threatened or killed kinsmen who converted to Christianity; the fierce attacks of enemy tribes on French settlers and on the latter's Indian allies; and the circulation of alcohol among the Indians.[27] The French offer of the "king's protection" in return for the Indians' becoming "faithful subjects," and the exclusive supply of guns to converts, presented the latter with serious incentives for a change of allegiance. (C 940) If the attacks of the Iroquois threatened to obliterate the mission altogether, the sale of alcohol was seen to be slowly eroding its existing base. In face of these threats to the success of the mission, the Jesuits sanctioned drastic measures such as military action against warring enemy tribes, and the excommunication of French traders who sold alcohol to the natives.[28] In justifying the plan to destroy the Iroquois, lest "all the Christians and Christianity perish," Marie indicates that the end justified the means — means which she herself admits seemed contrary to the spirit of the Gospel. (C 649) Elsewhere, noting that French force made the Iroquois "as mild as lambs" and willing to be instructed like children, she concludes that "God makes use of everything for the salvation of souls." (C 939) Even nature — in the form of the earthquake which shook the colony in 1663 — was seen as an awe-inspiring instrument of salvation which could effect conversions. (C 711)

To a large degree the difficulties faced by the missionaries were of a less tangible nature and rooted in the Indian way of life and of seeing the world. To begin with, the temperament or "nature of the Indians" who

---

[26] Thwaites, *The Jesuit Relations*, vol. 5, p. 113.

[27] Trigger, *Natives and Newcomers*, pp. 258–278.

[28] Ibid., pp. 258–278.

were considered proud, melancholy and untamed was seen as an impedi-
ment to conversion. (C 553, 718, 809) Marie also observed that if they were
not well-versed in Christian morality they tended to follow the habits and
customs of other members of their tribe. Writing to the Mother Superior
of the convent at Mons, that "it is hard work converting the savages," she
suggests that, given their superstitions and belief in sorcery, it is no less
than a miracle if they do indeed convert. (C 855) On the other hand, Marie
was very sceptical about the French policy of *francisation* — or the
attempt to make Frenchmen of the natives as a method for converting
them — admitting "frankly I don't know where it will end, it seems
difficult." She felt that "civilizing" the Indians and making them adopt
French manners and customs was not only a nigh impossible proposition,
but was also unnecessary for their conversion. (C 828)[29] In this she echoes
the sentiments of Paul Le Jeune, who felt that it was more important to
bring the natives to Christ's universal kingdom than to turn them into
loyal subjects of the French king.[30]

At first the Jesuits had been concerned to inculcate Christian values and
customs, almost as if they believed that "people who could be made to act
like Christians would also come to think like them"; they gradually came
to the conclusion, however, that the missionaries would have to act like
Indians in order to make the latter think like Christians.[31] As Père Vimont
admitted, a missionary could hope to make progress among the Indians
only if he "has penetrated their thoughts; has adapted himself to their
language, their customs and their manner of living; and when necessary,
has been a Barbarian with them in order to win them over to Jesus
Christ."[32] Thus, the missionaries diligently learned the different Indian
dialects in order to make their message more accessible. "Before knowing
a language," wrote Paul Le Jeune, "it was necessary for me to make books
from which to learn it."[33] And instead of trying to pin down the natives to
one location, they set up roving missions to service those whose hunting

[29] Dominique Deslandres suggests that Marie de l'Incarnation, as well as the Jesuits,
advocated *francisation* as part of the missionaries' socio-religious acculturation process, but
as Trigger has noted, this policy was not of Jesuit origin, nor did they implement it
enthusiastically in all cases. See Deslandres, "L'éducation des Amérindiennes d'après la
corréspondance de Marie Guyart de l'Incarnation," *Sciences Religieuses* 16/1 (1987), pp.
91–94; and Trigger, *Natives and Newcomers*, pp. 293–294.
[30] Boucher, *Le premier visage de l'Église du Canada*, p. 24.
[31] Trigger, *Natives and Newcomers*, p. 295.
[32] Thwaites, *The Jesuit Relations*, vol. 23, pp. 207–209.
[33] Ibid., vol. 5, p. 113.

patterns removed them from the Christian sphere of influence for several months of the year. Unlike their Recollet predecessors, then, who had advocated a policy of settling the Indians to keep them under French supervision, as well as teaching them French language and customs, the Jesuits proved in the long run to be more flexible and practical. And once it became evident that the natives' apparent acceptance of Christianity often meant no more than a superficial appropriation of Gospel stories and a syncretistic adoption of Catholic rites to supplement their own myths and rites, the missionaries began to relate to native myths and customs more seriously, and to adapt their approach to conversion accordingly.

In order to achieve a "genuine" conversion, then, they sought not only to convey a surface knowledge of the teachings and rules of the new religion but also make it a living personal faith. Instilling this component of religious experience was a much more difficult proposition than teaching the prospective converts what beliefs to profess and what actions to adopt, but this is precisely what the Jesuits set out to do. And the key to their strategy was a close consideration of the compatibility of aspects of native and Christian culture. Their acquaintance with native culture enabled them to manipulate those aspects of Christian life which might make a fair impression on the prospective convert, and to accommodate certain native customs and beliefs, especially those which could serve as a useful bridge to the Christian outlook. They came to the conclusion that in principle at least, the natives' preservation of their culture did not by definition prevent them from being excellent Christians — on the contrary, a certain syncretism could in fact make a "genuine" conversion possible.[34] In fostering this emphasis on the moods and motivations which underly religious life, the Jesuits were in effect treating both Amerindian cosmology and Christianity as "cultural systems" in Clifford Geertz's sense of the term.[35]

A distinction was made, however, between those aspects of their tradition which were unacceptable and those which seemed compatible with Christian teaching. One of the most interesting and insightful expositions on native culture found in Marie's correspondence is a letter which she wrote to her son in 1670, in response to his queries regarding the beliefs and practices of the natives. Marie claims that before the arrival of the

---

[34] Axtell, *After Columbus*, p. 117; on shifting missionary strategies see J. Axtell, "Harvest of Souls", chapter six of *The Invasion Within: The Contest of Cultures in Colonial North America*, Oxford 1985.

[35] Geertz, "Religion as a Cultural System", pp. 94–98.

Europeans, the Indians had no knowledge of the true God, even though

> some of them, reflecting on the movements of the sky, the disposition of the
> stars, and the constant order of the seasons, knew by natural reasoning that
> there was some powerful genius, who having created all these things, ruled
> them with such wisdom. (C 915)

The Indians' notion of "an Author of all the things we see in the world"
was for Marie not just a valid way of looking at the world, it was a useful
bridge to the Christian outlook. She happily notes how "they were praying
to the one who made everything, and those who became Christians kept
this way of praying so that when they went to pray to God they say: 'You
who made everything ... '." (C 915) If certain small details of native
cosmology and worship were permissible, there were many which were
considered errant if not abhorrent:

> Some were worshipping the Sun and offering it sacrifices, throwing bear
> fat, or moose fat, or fat of other animals in the fire, or burning tobacco or
> corn flour. Some believed in a certain Messou, who redeemed the world.
> This belief is beautiful, and is well in agreement with the coming of the
> Messiah, who was the Redeemer of the world. However, the blindness of
> infidelity stained this beautiful light by the most ridiculous story: the
> Hurons who had this belief pretended that this Messou redeemed the world
> with the help of some muskrats. Some others believed in a certain genius
> whom they said ruled over the waters, the woods, mountains, valleys and in
> other places. But all of them were obeying their dreams like a divinity, doing
> exactly what they saw in their sleep. If a man had dreamt that he was killing
> another man, as soon as he woke up he went to look for him, surprised him,
> and killed him. Those who did not receive the Faith are still doing that,
> because they felt obliged to obey their dreams; and this evil is one of the
> obstacles to the Faith. (C 916)

Obviously, those native practices which were clearly incompatible with
Christian life were not tolerated. The traditions of offering sacrifices to the
sun or blindly obeying commands perceived to have been conveyed in
dreams were condemned outright. New converts were required to renounce
their attachment to dreams as a prerequisite for baptism.[36] Taking issue
with the centrality of dreams in the life of the natives, Paul Le Jeune
recounts how he was approached by an Indian who had dreamed that Le
Jeune would give him a piece of tobacco:

> I refused him, saying that I did not give anything on account of dreams, that

---

[36] Pouliot, *Étude sur les "Relations" des Jésuites*, p. 225.

they were only folly, and that, when I knew his language, I would explain to him how they originated. He replied to me that all nations had something especially their own; that if our dreams were not true, theirs were; and that they would die if they did not execute them. According to this idea, our lives depend upon the dreams of a Savage; because, if they dream that they have to kill us, they will surely do it if they can.[37]

On another occasion, fighting fire with fire, Paul Le Jeune brushed off native threats with the light-hearted retort, "If you dream that no one will be converted, we will dream that you all will be converted."[38] In one of her letters Marie also derides the Indians' obedience to the supernatural commands which they claimed to receive in dreams, saying, "Look at the blindness of these pagan people, walking more than a hundred leagues to obey a dream." (C 916) On the one hand, this dismissive stance is a good illustration of Montaigne's oft-quoted adage "each man calls barbarism whatever is not his own practice"; on the other hand, Marie is condemning a practice which should not, strictly speaking, seem so alien to her.[39] She seems to have forgotten that her own presence in New France was the result of her obduracy in obeying a divine call, received in a dream — one which entailed travelling a much greater distance.

When Marie de l'Incarnation first arrived in New France she saw conversion as a fairly simple matter of teaching the natives the good news that they could be saved, and of softening their hearts and winning their souls through a display of temporal and spiritual charity. Her autobiographical *Relation de 1654* describes her first encounter with the natives:

> We met many savages when we went ashore, and this was a great joy to us. These poor people had never seen anyone dressed up as we were, so that they were filled with wonder; and when they were told that we had left our country, our relatives, and all comforts out of love for them, they were utterly amazed. And they were even more amazed when told that we had come to teach their children so that they would not have to burn in the fires of hell and would learn what they must do to be eternally happy. (A 124)

On the surface this quotation simply reflects one missionary's rather naive assumptions concerning her task, but at the same time it also indicates those aspects of the missionary approach which were deemed effective means of making an emotional, aesthetic impact on the natives. For the

---

[37] Thwaites, *The Jesuit Relations*, vol. 5, pp. 159–160.

[38] Ibid., vol. 11, p. 203.

[39] Quoted in Axtell, *After Columbus*, pp. 37–38.

missionaries came to recognize and use to their own advantage the natives'
attachment to their children, their understanding of kinship ties, their
attraction for European apparel, gadgets and trinkets, as well as their
belief in an after-life, and their fear of the hell-fire described by the
Christians. The missionaries sought ways of making the conversion meaningful on the cultural and emotional level and not just on the level of
behaviour. Apart from the removal of obstacles, then, the conversion
process required the careful manipulation of those aspects of Christian life
which might make a favourable impression on the prospective convert. It
also involved a positive look at those elements of Indian life and lore
which might be compatible with the Christian faith. Marie points out, for
example, that

> their fables have something in common with what Scripture says about the
> flood. The Abnakiouois (Abenaki's) who are a people from the south talk
> about a Virgin who gave birth to a big Nan. These people had less contact
> with the Europeans than with the other Nations of America, so this know-
> ledge of the Virgin Mother is extraordinary and amazing. The same goes for
> this big Nan whose Mother she is, because it is this Messou I spoke about
> whom the Hurons pretend redeemed the world with muskrats. (C 917)

In the Jesuit *Relations* we also read that some tribes believed "that there is
one named Messou, who restored the world when it was lost in the
waters," a belief which was not irreconcilable with the Christian idea of the
redemptive coming of the Messiah.[40] From the missionary stand-point
this was also a promising indication that "they have some traditions of the
deluge, although mingled with fables."[41] Already in 1632, Paul Le Jeune
cautioned that "it is a great mistake to think they have no knowledge of
any divinity." He continues:

> I confess that the Savages have no public or common prayer, nor any form
> of worship usually rendered to one whom they hold as God, and their
> knowledge is only as darkness. But it cannot be denied that they recognize
> some nature superior to the nature of man. As they have neither laws nor
> government, therefore there is no ordinance which concerns the service of
> this superior nature; each one acts according to his own understanding.[42]

The order of the stars, the movements of the sky and the cycle of seasons
were attributed to "a certain one whom they call Atahocan, who made all

---

[40] Thwaites, *The Jesuit Relations*, vol. 5, p. 155.

[41] Ibid., p. 155.

[42] Ibid., p. 153.

things."[43] This being could easily be linked with the divine creator of monotheistic religions. The Jesuits found it encouraging to see that the natives had not only "some idea of God," but also "some form of sacrifice," and found further scope for cultural bridge-building in the fact that "there are some men among them who make a profession of consulting their Manitou. It seems ... that by this word 'Manitou' they understand as among us, an Angel or some powerful being."[44]

The "Manitou" concept in native tradition proved even more useful to the missionary cause when the Indians began to use the term in reference to the Jesuits who seemed to display supernatural powers. On the subject of "traditions of their past" and how they were transmitted from generation to generation, Marie informs her son that although the natives themselves did not have an alphabet and depended on oral tradition to preserve their stories and customs, they were intrigued by the seeming magical power of the writing used by the Christians, and were consequently more amenable to missionary overtures:

> They can not understand how, by letters, we are able to know what is happening in France and other places. Their faith becomes stronger when we tell them that writing teaches us our Mysteries. If they are three or four hundred leagues away, and when their people who come here for the fur trade, go back carrying letters to the Fathers who look after them, they are amazed that these Fathers tell them all they did and said in Quebec. They can not understand how this letter they carried could tell such amazing truths without ever making an error. That is why they think of the Fathers as "Manitous," from whom nothing can be hidden and for whom nothing is impossible, and this helps a lot in their faith. (C 918)

Because the natives themselves did not have an alphabet and depended on oral tradition to preserve their stories and customs, they were intrigued by the seeming magical power of the writing used by the Christians, and this made them more open to missionary overtures. It was the Jesuits' awareness of the power of print which was in part responsible for their relative success in the New France mission as compared to their Protestant counterparts in New England.[45]

Because of their belief in reunion with the deceased, the Indians could be made to see the desirability of baptism, for the missionaries assured them that baptism would enable them to be joined with family members in

[43] Ibid., p. 153.
[44] Ibid., p. 157.
[45] Axtell, "The Power of Print in the Eastern Woodlands," in *After Columbus*, pp. 86–99.

heaven, or to use the natives' phrase, the "land of the setting sun."[46] Marie
mentions an interesting variation on this theme in her account of a tearful
Indian mother, distressed by the fact that her children had died unbaptized,
who was consoled by the assurance that at least the children were in limbo
and would not burn in the fires of hell. (C 730) Conducting the baptismal
ceremony within the framework of a communal feast, which was a popular
Indian custom, heightened the appeal of the Christian initiation rite. In a
similar way, the signing of peace treaties was also accompanied by the
distribution of gifts and Indian gestures in order to establish a congenial
rapport between the Indians and the French. (C 333, 563, 258) Marie
stressed the importance of "regaling them splendidly in their fashion, for it
is thus that one must attract them." (C 565)

Along with teaching Christian moral values, the Jesuits introduced the
catechism as a means of indoctrinating the Indians and rooting religion in
their minds by activating their reasoning faculties. Noting the natives'
progress in learning, Marie notes with delight "the great care they take
that God be served as he should ..., that the laws of the Church be rigidly
adhered to, and faults be punished to appease God." (C 278) The Jesuits
observed that "the Savages listen to reason readily, — not that they always
follow it, but generally they urge nothing against a reason which carries
conviction to their minds."[47] The Christian truths were taught in a
straightforward manner because the missionaries felt that the simplicity of
the natives, "who act fairly with God," was an advantage in getting them to
grasp and keep the faith:

> These good folk do not philosophise as much as our Europeans; once they
> have received the faith and believe that he who obeys the will of God will be
> saved, and that if he commits an offense it will be forgiven if he is duly
> contrite and confesses, they expect that God for his part will keep his
> promise.[48]

But the missionaries were concerned to speak not only to the minds but
also to the hearts of the natives. And so the rational explanation of moral
rules, the basic tenets of faith, and the Gospel stories were commonly
supplemented by pictorial representations in order to make the Indians
visualize what was being preached, and to fill them with lively religious
sentiments, of both a positive and negative kind.[49] These pictures included

[46] Thwaites, *The Jesuit Relations*, vol. 15, p. 109.
[47] Ibid., p. 195.
[48] Ibid., vols. 21, p. 148; and 32, pp. 206–208.
[49] See F.-M Gagnon, *La Conversion par l'image. Un aspect de la mission des Jésuites*

magnificent illustrations of the glories of paradise and of heavenly angels who gracefully elevated to God the souls of deceased Indian converts. Paul Le Jeune noted the importance of having "all the mysteries of our faith well illustrated [since] these images help greatly and already speak for themselves."[50] The Jesuits paid close attention to native sensibilities and aesthetic preferences and if they noticed that a specific picture "greatly pleases our savages" they would order extra copies to be sent from France. One such request referred to pictures depicting "some handsome Jesus who has no beard ... or not much of one, for example at the age of eighteen or thereabouts."[51]

Marie discusses at some length the paintings of the Jesuit Jean Pierron, who used "painted figures to make them [the Indians] see with their eyes what he preaches to them in words," and whom the Iroquois considered "one of the world's greatest geniuses" — presumably because of this "admirable invention." (C 839) Père Pierron's pictures, with which, Marie says, he was "working miracles," included a representation of hell replete with fire, serpents and demons who tormented the damned Indians with torture instruments and far surpassed the bounds of cruelty familiar to them. In stark contrast was the portrayal of paradise and the celestial angels who carried off the souls of deceased Indian converts. (C 857) Marie suggests that these aesthetically pleasing pictures were as effective as their fear-inspiring counterparts, for "these poor people were so delighted to see these figures that ... they followed the Father [Pierron] everywhere." (C 857) She was particularly impressed by this mode of conversion and suggests its effectiveness in getting new converts to adhere to Christian practice. Pierron not only painted appropriate pictures, but also devised a picture game which engaged the imagination of the natives in various details of Christian doctrine and tradition.[52]

Describing the devotion of one of the Indian girls who had not yet been baptized, Marie indicates the emotional appeal of such images, as well as the importance of trying to instill in potential converts a filial attachment to traditional Christian figures and make them feel — at least in psychological if not in cultural terms — part of the family:

The greatest pleasure one can give her is to explain these truths to her by

auprès des Indiens du Canada au XVIIe siècle, Montréal 1975; and F.-M. Gagnon and N. Cloutier, Premiers Peintres de la Nouvelle-France, vol. 1, Québec 1982, pp. 9–43.
   [50] Thwaites, The Jesuit Relations, vol. 5, p. 259.
   [51] C. Garnier, Lettres de Charles Garnier, Québec 1931, p. 37.
   [52] Thwaites, The Jesuit Relations, vol. 52, p. 118.

> means of images; she has such devotion towards the Holy Virgin that she
> trembled for joy at the sight of her portrait; she calls her mother, kisses her
> and cherishes her alone. (C 91)

Elsewhere, recounting how she had one of the "neophytes" make an
examination of conscience out loud each evening, she adds:

> To encourage him more I said to him: I want to give you a candle and some
> pictures so that you can pray in the morning and at night, when you're
> hunting. ... that is fine, he said to me; I'm going to show you how I put up my
> altar and how I pray to God. He set up his pictures; then he got down on his
> knees and having made the sign of the cross, he prayed for some time with
> such ardour, and entered into such profound contemplation that it seemed
> he was enchanted. (C 123)

The emotions or little speeches attributed to the native converts in missionary reports are excellent illustrations of the didactic, aesthetic or
emotional approaches which the missionaries employed in teaching the
Indians, and of the kind of behaviour and discourse which they looked for
as proof of a convert's sincere turning to the Christian faith. Marie
describes an Indian captain addressing his companions at a Christian feast
in honour of the Virgin Mary. She reports that, pointing to the candles
which had been distributed by the priest, he said:

> 'Ah! my brothers, what an obligation we have to this Father for having
> taught us such beautiful truths. Do you understand what this fire, which
> you are carrying in your hands means? It teaches us that Jesus Christ is our
> day and our light; that it is he who gives us the spirit by giving us the faith
> and the knowledge of the truths of Heaven: That it is he who reveals to us by
> his light the way of happiness; that these flames teach us that Jesus Christ
> was consumed on earth for our salvation; that these same flames are being
> consumed in our hands to teach us that we must also be on fire for his love
> and be consumed in his service.' (C 333)

Marie indicates that for the natives, communication was possible on many
levels, and that the language of gestures was as important as the spoken
word. On one occasion when the French and the Indians met to conclude a
peace treaty the latter "erected two poles and stretched a cord from one to
the other to hang and attach there, so they said, the words they were to
bring, that is to say, the presents they were to give us; because everything
speaks among them, and their actions are significative, as well as their
words." (C 254) Images and painted statues, rosary beads and candles,
which were often carried by hunters on their trips, were an important
means of cultivating religious habits, and instilling in the converts a filial

attachment to traditional figures (the infant Jesus, the Virgin Mary, and the saints) to help them feel part of the Christian family and rooted in its ancient tradition. Referring to painted statues of St. Ignatius and St. Xavier, Paul Le Jeune noted, for example, that the natives "looked upon them with awe, believing them to be living persons; [and asking] if they were Ondaqui." "The word Oqui and its plural Ondaqui," he explained, "signifies among them some divinity; in a word, what they recognize as above human nature."[53]

In effect, the Jesuits pursued a policy of adapting "new Christian forms to old functions" which, as James Axtell has noted, involved encouraging the natives to substitute "sacramentals for traditional stone amulets," and "to seek their fortune from God alone by supplicating him with the aid of Christian amulets — crucifixes, medals, rings, rosaries, and relics."[54] Archaeological evidence from Indian villages in these areas supplements information we find in the Jesuit *Relations* regarding the importance of inscribed medals, rings and crosses in missionary activity.[55] Apart from visual images and devotional instruments there were other aspects of Christian practice, and even mundane objects and simple utensils which attracted the Indians. Bruce Trigger notes that even before they became interested in the functional tools which the traders possessed, the Indians were most impressed by the trinkets, beads, bells and tin ornaments proferred by the French.[56]

Among other items which, in Marie's account, held an emotional as well as an aesthetic appeal were the clothing of the missionaries — who were referred to by the Indians as the "black robes," their processions, singing and sacramental rites. The nuns in their "choir ceremonies" captured the imagination of the Algonquin widow mentioned earlier, because she saw the nuns as imitating the angels and saints in heaven. This same convert was so moved by the Good Friday liturgy and story of Christ's Passion that she "melted in tears." (C 730) Marie notes that the Iroquois were very taken by the singing of the Indian children and expresses her own joy at hearing them "tamed and singing praises" in their own language. (C 531) Singing, then, which for the natives was considered a traditional form of recreation and devotion, proved to be a particularly fruitful bridge to

[53] Ibid., vol. 5, p. 257.

[54] Axtell, *The Invasion Within*, p. 112.

[55] See G. Irving Quimby, *Indian Culture and European Trade Goods: The Archaeology of the Historic Period in the Western Great Lakes Region*, Madison 1966.

[56] Trigger, *Natives and Newcomers*, pp. 126, 129.

Christian worship. Thus, while on the one hand working on the assumption that "fear is the fore-runner of faith in these barbarous souls," the missionaries also applied the pleasure principle and used games, singing and a crude form of theatre to root the Christian message in the natives' hearts and minds.[57]

We cannot judge whether the reported conversions were genuine, any more than the attendant priests could — indeed the debate about the quality and sincerity of such conversions is still being waged among ethnohistorians to this day.[58] What is clear, however, is that the missionaries themselves were aware of the problems involved in trying to effect, assess and sustain a *bona fide* conversion. Their experience led them to adjust their view of conversion, to see it as an ongoing process rather than a single event, and to develop new approaches to the task at hand. The accounts we have illustrate the missionaries' attempt to create a congenial religious atmosphere, elicit a positive emotional response, and engage the memory, even as a short-term measure — all to the end of trying to instill in the natives a "genuine," i.e., deeply-rooted commitment to the Christian faith.

Perhaps unwittingly, the missionaries channelled their own attachment to tradition into their conversion effort. Of course they could not replace native tradition, but they tried to make Christian tradition — both its concrete forms and its supernatural elements — more appealing. On the basis of Marie's missionary correspondence, it is not possible, nor is it our aim, to prove that the missionaries were successful in effecting a genuine religious change in those they counted as Christian converts. She came to recognize the function of language, imagery, mentality, ritual and tradition in mediating faith; she saw the need to accommodate aspects of Indian custom where possible, to instill in them a sense of belonging to Christian tradition; and to look for effective methods and avoid those that were counter-productive for the purposes of conversion. Her testimony — in particular her emphasis on the aesthetically and emotionally appealing facets of Catholic tradition — suggests that the practice of conversion drew on the principle of formation, or inculcation of tradition, which is often a necessary ingredient or starting-point for personal conversion. In

[57] Thwaites, *The Jesuit Relations*, vol. 11, p. 88.

[58] Bruce Trigger challenges the notion of "sincere" Indian conversions, claiming that baptism was sought primarily for economic, political or military reasons. See *Natives and Newcomers*, pp. 254–256. James Axtell challenges the sceptical position in his essay "Were Indian Conversions Bona Fide?" in *After Columbus*, pp. 100–121. See also *Beyond 1492: Encounters in Colonial North America*.

the case of the Indians who, as the missionaries grudgingly came to concede, had a religious culture of their own, this formative ground had to be prepared somewhat artificially; before the new seed could be planted the old cultural ground had to be uprooted, or at least carefully weeded. Even if we do not take at face value the emotions and behaviour Marie ascribes to the Indian converts, her comments on the approaches and methods of the missionaries, as well as the obstacles encountered, give us considerable insight into how she herself came to view conversion — both as an individual religious experience and as a collective missionary enterprise.

CHAPTER SIX

THE ASCENT OF SOULS: MARIE'S SPIRITUAL TEACHING

Marie's activity in the Canadian mission was in effect the ultimate manifestation of her mystical repose in the Trinity. She herself perceived her
mystical experience not as union for its own sake, but rather as union for
the sake of others. She had chosen the Ursuline order as the framework for
her religious life specifically because the Ursulines combined contemplative
austerity with a vocation for "helping souls." And her missionary effort
was certainly the most readily identifiable example of such religious
service. Indeed, it was shortly after making her solemn profession that she
had the dream which presaged her missionary calling, and gave her
contemplative life its indelible apostolic stamp. From that time on she
turned her inward gaze on the pagan souls in distant lands and prayed for
their salvation.

Marie's emphasis on the "apostolic" nature of her spiritual experience
and her self-professed preoccupation with the problem of the salvation of
souls, have led many commentators to view her missionary work among
the Indians as the utmost, almost exclusive expression of her active
spirituality.[1] This focus, however valid in itself, has overshadowed the
other form of conversion activity that was an integral part of her apostolic
identity, namely, her promotion of a spiritual turning in religious life. It
was shortly after entering the convent and before receiving her missionary
vocation that she felt "strong impulses ... to leap and clap [her] hands and
urge the whole world to sing the praises of this great God." (A 80) Her
eagerness to engage others in the pursuit of spiritual elevation reflects her
sense of a divine call:

> the goodness of this Divine Spouse had led me to a rich and fertile pasture

---

[1] See Rétif, *Marie de l'Incarnation et la mission*; and S. Labelle, *L'Esprit apostolique
d'après Marie-de-l'Incarnation*, Ottawa 1968. Labelle sees Marie's "apostolic spirit" as
comprised of several "fundamental intuitions" which were received prior to her apostolic
call. These key formulas include "the service and the glory of God, the Church and the
Kingdom of Christ, the salvation of souls and the blood of Jesus Christ." See p. 67.

where my soul was well nourished and supplied with good things to pass on to others, about which I could not keep silent. (A 81)

The scope of her conversion activity was thus more far-reaching than her missionary work, and the term "apostolic" should be extended to include her efforts to effect in others an inner turning to a purer form of religious devotion.[2]

In considering Marie's active promotion of spiritual change a further distinction must be made, for her insights and instructions on the spiritual life reveal a dual approach to spiritual conversion. Depending on whom she is writing for, she in fact seems to be promoting two distinct, though linked, kinds of conversion, one of which could be termed "spiritual" in a general sense and is characterized by human initiative in turning to the path of holiness; and the second of which could be termed "mystical" since it is perceived as a divine initiative which transforms and unites the individual's soul with God.[3] In some instances she not only suggests how one should turn wholly to God and pursue perfection, but also hints at the mystical favours which are sometimes received when God turns to the believer in extraordinary fashion and effects, as it were, a mystical conversion. In view of these two levels of her spiritual discourse, Marie can be seen as both teacher and guide — for her approach to spiritual conversion was both pedagogical and mystagogical.[4]

Interspersed among the numerous letters in which she describes the details of missionary life are several letters devoted to the subject of the spiritual life. Inasmuch as this correspondence exhorts to and explains the intricacies of the pursuit of perfection, it exemplifies her promotion of

---

[2] F. Jetté uses the term "apostolic life" in the limited sense of missionary work, although he does assert that Marie's mystical union with God early on in her spiritual life was meant both for "the good of the young Church" and to teach holiness to those who followed her in the apostolic life. See "L'Itinéraire spirituel de Marie de l'Incarnation", p. 642.

[3] This sense of mystical conversion as a divine transformation occurs in much spiritual writing of the seventeenth century. Mystical conversion is seen not so much as a spiritual way but as a destination; not so much as the soul's *conforming* to God, but as being *transformed* into him: "Conversio Mystica est ad Deum & in Deum. Ad Deum converti animam eiusque potentias in Contemplatione ... conversio in Deum est Transmutatio ac Transformatio." No methods or appeals to the senses, imagination or understanding are envisaged since at this stage of spiritual experience the soul experiences God directly and is unified with him: "A formis & imaginibus, & rebus omnibus absoluat & expediat: Deum perpetuum essentiale obiectum habeat donec ipsum Deus in se trahat, rapiatque sic uniatur." M. Sandeus, *Pro theologia mystica clavis*, Köln (1640), reprinted: Heverlée-Louvain 1963, pp. 158, 159.

[4] The term *mystagogical* has been used to characterize the attempt of a spiritual writer to lead his reader towards mystical experience. See Haas, *Sermo mysticus*, p. 32.

spiritual conversion and the sanctification of souls. A few examples from these letters of spiritual guidance — addressed for the most part to close family members and Ursuline novices — should suffice to illustrate not only what she considered contemplative life to be, but also how she went about inveigling her reader to turn wholeheartedly to the path of spiritual perfection.[5]

Whereas the conversion of the Indians was a matter of "drawing them to the knowledge of [God's] name and holy law," and bringing them to obey his teaching as presented by the Church, the spiritual or "second" conversion which Marie envisaged, required an additional or deeper orientation within the faith towards God. This required an adherence not only to God's law or that which is precept, but also to those virtues and teachings which are "counsel", i.e., advisable but not strictly necessary. (C 88) Conversion in this sense means a total turning towards prayer and perfection for one already in possession of the grace of faith. The desired goal is not just salvation, but sanctity as well. Marie makes this distinction when she notes that while those who fear God try to avoid mortal sin and observe the commandments of God and the Church, those who set out to "live religiously" do not remain within the bounds of what is obligatory but rather attempt to avoid all imperfection and strive for that which is "most perfect." (C 369)

Indeed, Marie's advice with regard to spiritual self-improvement or the pursuit of sanctity sometimes reveals a sliding scale. Writing to one of her sisters, she explicitly states that high spiritual aspirations are not for all, and that "we must, each according to our state" prepare for the day of judgement. Noting the difference between their respective conditions — Marie was a nun, while her sister was a wife and mother — she counsels her sister to govern her family prudently and raise her children in the fear of God. (C 538) Elsewhere, however, inspired by "the desire ... for [her sister's] perfection," she includes personal tips as well as standard exhortations for "leading a perfect life." (C 369)[6] She recommends "interior mortifications" which "aim at the sanctification of the soul by the death of the passions and sensual appetites," and at the same time cautions that

<hr/>

[5] I am dealing specifically with Marie's practical application of her understanding of the spiritual life. Her spiritual doctrine *per se* is presented in F. Jetté's *The Spiritual Teaching of Mary of the Incarnation*, trans. Mother M. Herman, Montreal 1963. An excellent comprehensive study is M.-P. del Rosario Adriazola, *La Connaissance spirituelle chez Marie de l'Incarnation la "Thérèse du Nouveau-Monde"*, Paris 1989.

[6] Both letters are probably addressed to Marie's sister, Catherine. See Oury, *Marie de l'Incarnation (1599–1672). Corréspondance*, pp. 369, 539, 236.

exterior mortifications should be undertaken only on the advice of a spiritual director, who should likewise be her guide in times of doubt or difficulty. (C 369) She concludes:

> Continue then to perfect yourself on the path of virtue and sanctity; and never let up in your prayers, above all in mental prayer, in ejaculatory prayer and in the aspirations of your heart to God. (C 368–9)

In another letter, probably to this same sister, Marie draws on her own experience in the pursuit of virtue, appeals to their common childhood memories and couches her advice on sanctification in personal terms which draw on familiar concepts and motifs from their common store of Catholic devotion. She advises her sister to love, honour, and serve Joseph and Mary and "they will lead you to heaven" and recommends short fervent prayers rather than long ones; she recalls how their mother used to pray out loud during the course of the day, asking God for help in little matters, and urges her sister to do likewise since such prayers "enflame the heart and draw God into the soul." (C 236, 235)

While Marie felt that her sister should strive to improve herself and empty her "heart of the love of the vain things of this world," she did not encourage her to strive for spiritual experiences. (C 235) And yet on the upper end of the scale, she clearly believed that there are special souls which are not only disposed for the pursuit of sanctification, but which might also be blessed with divine illuminations. Writing to one of her favourite nieces, she assures her that spiritual purgation is part of God's plan "to make you more capable of his favours and holy impressions." (C 299) Also, in a letter to her son Claude she thanks God for "attracting [him] to the mystical life," and makes suggestions for his advancement while explicitly referring to the extraordinary graces which God had granted her. (C 515) Marie's letters to her son form the bulk of her correspondence on spiritual matters and many include a direct and detailed analysis of her mystical illuminations. In these same letters, however, there is often a cautionary note or self-effacing refrain which signals her distaste for the attempted description of experiences which, in her view, lie beyond the realm of human comprehension and which should not be set up as goals to strive for since they derive from God alone.[7]

Marie's reluctance to relate her own experience for fear of making it

---

[7] On the "dangers attending these favours," Poulain explains that "they are not to be desired. This would be to expose ourselves to all kinds of illusion." See *The Graces of Interior Prayer*, p. 458.

seem exemplary, and the general ambivalence which characterizes her treatment of things mystical, are also evident in her *Entretien spirituel sur l'Épouse des Cantiques*, a commentary on the *Song of Songs* which dates from the time when she was assistant novice mistress. The Ursuline community was made up of choir sisters and lay sisters; the former were trained for their function as religious educators, while the latter were responsible for the domestic upkeep of the convent. Marie had made her profession as a choir sister less than a year before she was appointed assistant mistress of novices.[8] Her task was to instruct the thirty odd novices under her charge in Christian doctrine in preparation for their future role as teachers. Such training was also conducted on an individual basis and spilled over into the nuns' personal prayer life, as Marie often helped the nuns to choose a scriptural passage as a subject for prayer or reflection and analyzed with them its spiritual message.

Marie's commentary on the *Song of Songs* is the only remaining sample of the numerous talks which she gave on this classic text, and was preserved by one of her disciples, Mère Angelique, who asked for a copy of the notes, which in turn made its way into the convent archives. This text illustrates Marie's concern for the nuns' spiritual welfare and is an excellent example of her attempt at conversion by imagery on a somewhat elevated level of instruction. Let us consider first of all *what* Marie says and then examine *how* she goes about impressing the message on her audience. For this mini-exegesis on the figure of the bride in the *Song of Songs* is not just a lesson in scriptural exegesis, but also an exercise aimed at converting the hearts and minds of her listeners.

Since religious practice was governed by the common rule of the Ursuline order, the nuns' personal devotions were carefully guided by their spiritual director. On a typical day the nuns would have a period in which they conducted spiritual exercises together — perhaps reciting the rosary or a litany — and read a devotional text in common, reflecting upon it as they sewed or embroidered some piece of handiwork. Given that Marie addresses her comments to novices who have already opted for the contemplative life, she is in effect preaching to the converted. And certainly, her commentary aims to explain to the novices how to live out the spiritual life which they had embraced. But apart from transmitting a message in collective terms, she is also concerned to involve the individual novices in a wholehearted and personal pursuit of sanctity. Because these young

[8] Despite her attraction for the choral office, Marie made a request, which was turned down, to opt for the more lowly function of lay sister. Oury, *Marie Guyart*, p. 147.

women had chosen to become Ursulines, whose spirituality is by definition of both a contemplative and active nature, she not only urges them to seek sanctification but also feels compelled to explain how best to fulfil their dual vocation. Her commentary on the Bride in the *Song of Songs* illustrates her own self-image as a spiritual guide of sorts, but also seems to indicate that these "great graces" are of two kinds, comprising those which help one on the way of sanctification, and those which in certain cases are granted to special souls which are singled out for mystical favours.

Again we encounter the idea that the nature of spiritual life and the exigencies of humility are such that one can strive only to advance in sanctity, not to attain mystical union which results from divine initiative alone. According to Marie, the Bride is the embodiment of the contemplative ideal to be espoused by an Ursuline. She presents the Bride as a guide on the subject of love in spiritual life. Commenting on the phrase "[My groom] has granted me entry into his wine cellar, and he has put in me the order of charity," Marie asks, "was her charity in disorder?," and explains that since one is supposed to love without order or measure, the Bride must mean here that "her Bridegroom gave her the love of her salvation before giving her the love of salvation of others," for "before working for the perfection of others, she should be perfect herself." (E I 409) Sanctification, in other words, is presented almost as a precondition for serving others.

The underlying theme of Marie's commentary, then, is the subordination of the active to the contemplative life.[9] In order to elucidate the pursuit of sanctity and prevent misunderstanding regarding the proper relationship between prayer and service, she uses the *Song* to exhort her listeners to seek sanctity in a progressive but moderate fashion. She explains that when the Bride demands that the Groom "kiss her with a kiss of his mouth," she is in fact teaching us that there is a progression in the demonstration of love, and that "it is necessary first to kiss the feet, by doing penance, then the hands by the practice of virtue, and then finally the mouth through a perfect love." (E I 405–6) The Bride, says Marie, is in effect asking that the Groom "pour his spirit into her, so that being fully transformed, she may cry: Here I have found him whom my soul loves; I have found him and I will not leave him." This, she explains, expresses the Bride's resolution to "remain inseparably attached to her Beloved," and in this "she invites us to imitate her." (E I 406)

Throughout Marie's commentary, however, one has the impression

---

[9] See Dom Jamet's introduction to the commentary, *Écrits* I, p. 401.

that this invitation to imitate the Bride, to turn to God and to "remain inseparably attached to Him" should be interpreted primarily as a call to spiritual self-improvement and not a reference to the extraordinary transformation which the Bride herself has experienced. She falls short of advocating total emulation of the Bride, avoiding altogether the topic of the latter's spiritual marriage with God. That is perhaps why she refers to the Bride as "attached" to God, and not as "united" with him. In the course of her commentary it becomes evident that she is teaching the novices about "love" in the sense of *agape*, not *eros*; the emphasis is on charity or service rather than on mystical union. Marie's opening comment is that the *Song of Songs*, which is a song of love, has an appropriate title, "since love is the virtue of virtues." The Bride serves as an ideal model insofar as she is the paragon of spiritual virtue and personifies the active pursuit of holiness, but not with regard to her role as a recipient of extraordinary mystical favours and as the bride of God. Marie teaches penance and virtue, but is reluctant to advocate the "perfect love" symbolized by the "kiss of the mouth" which the Bride demands of her Beloved. Hence the ambivalence regarding the Bride's exemplary value. On the one hand Marie calls the novices to be faithful and attentive "so that we may experience with [the Bride] the fruit of her fidelity," while on the other hand she takes care to make the point that whereas spiritual efforts give one the potential for spiritual marriage, they by no means earn one the right to be Christ's bride:

> We do not deserve to be the Brides of Jesus by practising these lofty works, but we can be [his brides] by embracing a perfect charity and by a close fidelity to all his wishes. (E I 412)

Thus, although Marie says "Let us follow her [the Bride] everywhere, and take her as a guide in the conduct of our loves," her account of how "this holy Bride" shows us how to "enrich ourselves like her" actually seems geared to distance the average nun from the mystical element of the Bride's experience. (E I 407, 408)

The implicit message of restraint or gradual progression in the pursuit of sanctity governs this commentary. Referring to the passage "We have a small sister, who as yet has no breasts. If she is a wall, let us build upon her a building of silver, and if she is a door, let us fortify her with cedar," she suggests that this "sister" represents the soul which is not yet able to give instruction to others, and who eventually does fill her bosom "in the repose of contemplation" and is then able to teach other souls by giving them "the milk of holy doctrine." (E I 410) The wall and the door represent the "two kinds of people who work for the salvation of others"; while the former refers to those who "preach the word of God," like the prophets of old who were like "mighty ramparts," staving off the torrent of human corruption, the latter stands for "those who guide souls" such as the pastors, prelates and monastic superiors, who like the apostles before them take the place of Christ and can "grant entry into the Church ... and even into heaven." (E I 410–11) Such souls must in any case be further edified or "built up" since even the most elevated souls "in whatever state, ... are always weak ... and need to be fortified." (E I 410) In the case of the preachers this is achieved by building "bastions of silver" — a metaphor for enriching oneself through "virtue and good works," becoming pure through innocent behaviour, and shining forth by preaching the word of God. The director of souls on the other hand must not only be impeccable or "incorruptible" as regards behaviour and teaching, but must also exude the odour of sanctity, of a holy and perfect life, which is symbolized by the "aromatic and incorruptible wood" of the cedar.

The ultimate message of these exegetical points is clear: Marie wishes the novices to see the Bride as a guide in the realm of spiritual efforts, but cautions them neither to strive for the special mystical favours enjoyed by the Bride, nor yet to aspire to too elevated a role in serving others. This is a subtle and ambivalent message and she manages to convey it by using the imagery and language as well as traditional interpretations of the *Song of Songs*.[10] Her interpretation of the figure of the Bride and its significance for the spiritual life appeals to the emotions, as well as to the collective imagination and memory of those listening.

She is addressing a specific audience, a group of religious novices, and in her endeavour to make the idea of spiritual conversion a personal goal for each, she draws on their shared tradition. She not only uses a well-known text, perhaps the *locus classicus* of mystical literature, but also invokes the authority of the "saints" in general, who teach that "there is progress in the demonstration of love." She also refers to one "saintly soul" in particular, Teresa of Avila, who teaches that the fruit which the Bride tastes derives from the tree of the cross. Furthermore, by highlighting the figure of the bride in the *Song of Songs*, she strengthens the self-image of the average nun or novice, who from time immemorial has seen the donning of the veil as an act of spiritual bonding with Christ.

---

[10] Dom Oury, while noting Marie's indebtedness to Saint Bernard's Sermons on the *Song of Songs* (particularly sermons 1,3,7,8,9), remarks that she also introduced concerns of her own into the commentary. *Marie Guyart*, p. 194.

Marie also takes for granted the idea of set roles, or an ecclesiastical division of labour, as a familiar and acceptable fact of religious life. This is reflected not only in her comments on the "wall" as preacher and the "door" as spiritual director, but especially in her recommendation that the novices strive only to be the "companions" of the Bride, not her equals. The virtues of penance, purity and prayer as means of advancing in perfection are enhanced by the sense images of which the *Song of Songs* is redolent and which she singles out for attention. Along with the aromatic cedar which symbolizes the odour of sanctity, or the silver bastions which symbolise the richness, purity and lustre of the Gospel sermons, she introduces the erotic image of the fruit "most sweet and most delicious to my taste" which she transposes to the suffering Jesus motif and interprets as the "sweet nectar which runs from the holy wounds" of Jesus. (E I 408)

In presenting "love" as the central theme of the commentary she is appealing to the novice's understanding and appreciation of love as both a religious principle and an emotional mechanism. In the case of converting the Indians, fear was often the operative element in the appeal to emotions and imagination; in the case of the novices who were being called to turn to a more perfect spiritual life, "love" was used as an effective motif in preparing the ground for the desired intensification of religious life. In both cases, Marie indicated her positive appreciation of conversion by imagery — whether by means of vivid pictorial representations or statues in the encounter with the Indians, or by means of literary images in the guidance of novices — as a method for effecting profound religious change.

She suggests, furthermore, that "love" serves as a kind of hermeneutic key to the "discourse of the Bride," who is so carried away that without any introduction, she begins her "song" by saying "let him kiss me with a kiss of his mouth! as if we knew, as well as she, who is this one who is the object of her passion." (E I 405) Marie explains that the purpose of the Bride's abrupt and empassioned opening cry is to indicate that in matters of spiritual love language serves a limited role, for "the soul which loves does not want so much discourse to explain the movements of its heart." (E I 405) An additional reason which she gives for the Bride's terseness of expression is the latter's assumption of a common understanding of the emotions, images and ideas associated with love, and which are conjured up by such an outburst: "By saying that she loves, she believes that she says all, and she figures that everyone understands her language." (E I 405)

What is missing in all of this is a direct and explicit treatment of the mystical element of the Bride's union with God and the pleasure which that entails. Marie stresses that when the Bride says "I have found him whom my soul loves," she is by no means indicating that she found her Beloved "through a sensual inclination," but by "a solid and deep love," and only through "special work and the corrections of those who govern me." (E I 407) The amorous embraces of the Groom, who "puts his left hand under my head, and ... embraces me with his right," are interpreted in conventional and rather practical terms of perseverance in suffering and grace; the "left hand" indicates the affliction of being baptized in "his baptism of suffering," and the "right hand" the consolation and reception of "the delights of his grace." Only in a somewhat muted fashion is the Bride presented as a "holy soul ... transformed into her Spouse." (E I 411, 409) The sublime metaphor of mystical delights, the "most sweet and most delicious" fruit mentioned by the Bride, is linked, as we saw, to the traditional image of blood flowing from Christ's holy wounds and by extension evokes the purgative principle. (E I 408)

Mystical discourse seeks to convey an ineffable reality by hiding it. In "making sense" of this traditional mystical text, Marie has opted for the language of explanation. In thus bringing the sublime discourse of the *Song of Songs* down to earth, and translating mystical images into ascetic messages or practical instructions for self-improvement, she seems to be saying that one cannot and should not aim to follow the Bride in her more sublime, celestial experiences. Having set up and so laboriously commented on the model of the Bride as spouse, preacher, director of souls etc., she proceeds to knock down the model, recommending only that the novices be the companions of this holy Bride, "whose loves, intentions and occupation we have described." She is directing the novices not so much to emulation of the bride as to imitation of the contemplative ideal represented by the Bride.[11]

The ostensible purpose of Marie's commentary is to exhort the novices to turn heart and soul to the contemplative life, and to explain what this means for an Ursuline. But perhaps a subsidiary purpose is to give them after all an inkling of the sublime experiences which characterize the highest stages of spiritual life. For this text includes enough hints and references regarding the mystical delights enjoyed by the Bride, that it seems as if Marie wants to fire them with the desire for such mystical favours nonetheless. In commenting on the Bride's exclamation that "his breasts, that is to say, his loves, are better than wine and more delicious than the most precious perfumes," she lets the images stand as they are

---

[11] See Dom Jamet, *Écrits* I, p. 400.

instead of reducing them to pat devotional principles. The Bride, she says, means "to say that his loves, having inebriated her more strongly than any wine could have done, and charmed her more strongly than the sweetest scents, she cannot bear to wait any longer, but all bold and completely beside herself, she says in all eagerness: Let him kiss me with a kiss of his mouth." (E I 406)

Throughout her commentary, as we have noted, Marie steadfastly avoids recommending the fruits of the spiritual life, and indicates that the nuns should neither strive for union with God, nor aspire to elevated religious tasks such as preaching or guiding souls, but simply embrace a perfect charity and close fidelity to God's will:

> In this way we shall follow the Bridegroom in aromatic places and on the mountain of perfumes which is none other than the mountain of the [New] Testament, the mountain of glory where we shall rest eternally on his breast. (E I 412)

In mentioning this spiritual *locus amoenus*, however, it is as if she wants to give them an idea of the splendour that not only awaits them in heaven, but can perhaps be glimpsed by mystical souls such as the Bride in the *Song of Songs*. By sprinkling her commentary with allusions to the sublime, and particularly in this reference to celestial glory, she is calling the novices to strive for greater sanctity by journeying in what, in Salesian terminology, is known as the "low valley" of spiritual life, but she is also giving them a hint of the mystical heights of contemplation.[12] Thus, although her commentary is allegorical for the most part, we see an anagogical element too, that is, an attempt to indicate something that lies beyond the ordinary bounds of textual interpretation or religious understanding.

Whether it is seen solely as an example of spiritual instruction or also as an implicit hint at extraordinary spiritual states, Marie's commentary on the *Song of Songs* suggests that if mystical experience cannot be presented as a concrete and conscious goal, it can perhaps effectively serve as a subconscious motif and tacit incentive in spiritual life. In either case, her use of words indicates her awareness of the emotional and cultural ground, in which she sought to root the spiritual conversion of the novices, who in their religious life had been nurtured from a common source of symbols, imagery and language and whose psychological as well as cultural make-up had been shaped by this shared tradition. This reckoning with the emo-

---

[12] François de Sales, *Introduction to the Devout Life*, p. 72.

tional and aesthetic components of religious consciousness reflects a view which in recent years has been increasingly espoused by cultural anthropologists, who argue that aesthetic factors should by no means be seen as "an unnecessary appendage to a theology of faith," but rather as an essential part of the "imaginative constructions embedded in the life of a religious tradition."[13] Drawing on the work of Clifford Geertz and others, for example, anthropologists like R.H. Bell highlight the importance of these "imaginative constructions" and of the "sensuous plane" of religious texts which "elicits a human emotional response," and helps link distant sensibilities.[14] In what follows I shall discuss how Marie employs this implicit aesthetic principle in recounting her ineffable mystical experiences in her spiritual autobiography.

In her *Relation de 1654*, Marie warns against the tendency of human nature to "seek by its own efforts to attain what is beyond its capacity," and makes an explicit distinction between the active and passive, or ascetic and mystical aspects of the spiritual life, between "the systematic knowledge necessary for leading a good life, for being suitably instructed in the path of virtue, and for avoiding error," for which one "should have recourse to spiritual fathers and to books"; and on the other hand "the graces and extraordinary lights wherein ... God leaves the soul satisfied." (A 77) With regard to these sublime instances of direct divine illumination, she recommends close consultation with one's spiritual director, since such guidance helps render

> the soul simple, draws down upon it God's grace and unites it to Him, a pure and simple Being who looks for souls which resemble Him (in simplicity) in order that He may communicate to them His holy impressions. (A 78)

Spiritual writing, as historians of spirituality are wont to reiterate, deals with both the ascetic and mystical elements of the spiritual life; it describes both ordinary human efforts in spiritual practice, and extraordinary experiences which derive from the divine realm; and for this reason, Marie's description of the spiritual landmarks in her life necessitated a dual mode of expression.[15] Her choice of imagery and mode of expression in describing her religious development was governed by her subjective

---

[13] See R.H. Bell, "The aesthetic factor in art and religion," *Religious Studies* 22 (1986), p. 186.

[14] Ibid., pp. 185, 186. See also E. Runggaldier, "Bericht: interdisziplinäres Seminar zur Anthropologie," *Zeitschrift für Katholische Theologie*, 109 (1987), p. 71.

[15] Knowles, *What is Mysticism?*, p. 22. See also pp. 36–37.

perception of these two aspects of her spiritual life. She is describing not just what *she* did to become more spiritually perfect, for instance in terms of prayer, sacramental life, ascetic exercises, but also what she felt *God* gave her in the form of mystical experiences. When describing the higher states of spiritual life and her increasingly sublime mystical favours, which brought with them a stilling of her senses, understanding and will, her choice of words suggests that the medium is the message. For she veers away from the familiar ground of religious imagery and expression, drawing on abstract formulations and paradoxical utterances to try and express the ineffable, while at the same time protesting that such experiences are beyond human comprehension and expression.

Her account also reflects the discrepancy she feels between her unworthiness as a sinner and her chosenness as a mystic. And while looking for words with which to try and convey the avowed ineffable quality of her mystical visions, humility compelled her to constantly repeat how unworthy she was for such favours. Both the stress on the ineffability of mystical experience and the humility-topos which run through the narrative and elevate the discourse to sublime heights, only to bring it back down to earth, not only reflect the literary and theological conventions which in general characterize this genre of spiritual writing, but also reveal the specific dilemma which she encountered in assessing her past experiences in light of her new spiritual identity.[16] Like St. Augustine's *Confessions*, Marie's *Relation de 1654* was written not only as a testimony of her sinful past and turn for the better, but as a monument to God's glory — the term "glory" signifying not only God's praiseworthiness, but also his inherent splendour, which Marie glimpsed in her extraordinary experiences.

Marie writes in her *Relation* that in the wake of her spiritual marriage her soul performed its "duties in order to seek His glory in and through all things, according to the lights He has given [it], and to promote His reign as absolute Master of all hearts." (A 59) The different aspects of her

---

[16] The avowed ineffability of mystical experience is a recurring theme among spiritual authors. The more profound the mystical experiences, "the less is it possible to give them expression in thoughts and words." Ibid., p. 22. The mystic's reticence with regard to the description of extraordinary experiences is also occasioned by humility. Teresa of Avila writes, "others will think I know about it through experience. This makes me extremely ashamed; for, knowing what I am, such a thought is a terrible thing." See *The Interior Castle*, p. 173. The religious career of the Theatine mystic, Benedetta Carlini (1590–1661), illustrates the degree to which spiritual hybris is seen to be incompatible with the claims of genuine mystical experience. See Brown, *Immodest Acts*.

endeavour to effect religious change in others can be summed up by the three terms "salvation of souls," "sanctity of souls" and "glory of God" which, in theological terms, indicate three different levels or contexts of the experience of divine grace. In its various forms, her conversion activity was conducted for the glory of God. If, in the final analysis, Marie's mysticism of service had the glory of God as its ultimate goal, the proximate goals, or means to this end, were the salvation and sanctification of souls.[17] Her missionary work was aimed at the salvation, i.e., the conversion and baptism of "pagan" souls, while her spiritual teaching stressed the "sanctity of souls", i.e., the conversion of believers to a more saintly life. In each instance, the immediate goal envisaged served the ultimate end of promoting the glory of God, by giving witness to his goodness and justice, and thereby bringing others to glorify him.[18]

But there is yet another meaning to the phrase "glory of God" which is worthy of closer scrutiny. In theological terms, one can speak of the "glory of God" as being extrinsic or intrinsic; while the former signifies the divine glory which is made manifest in creation and thus elicits the human response of rendering praise to God, the latter refers to the ineffable splendour that is intrinsic to God.[19] In introducing these terms it is not my aim to present the history of a theological concept, but rather to discuss Marie's conception of a theological idea — "glory" — which surfaces in her writing and reflects her awareness of its dual meaning — even if the specific adjectives "extrinsic" and "intrinsic" are not used. In the study of spiritual texts, as in the history of ideas in general, implicit conceptions as well as explicit words should be subjected to careful scrutiny.[20] The human capacity for experiencing essential glory — whether in the beatific state or in a mystical vision — has long been a point of debate in spiritual theology. Since Marie herself implies that she saw mystical experience as a foretaste of beatific glory, a few words by way of introduction to the issue will be both useful and appropriate.

---

[17] For a discussion of the relative meaning of each of these terms, see J. Aumann, *Spiritual Theology*, London 1980 p. 37 ff.

[18] Aumann notes that "God's extrinsic glory is at once something received from God and something returned to God," and regarding the human contribution to divine glory says that "sanctification and salvation are the most excellent and efficacious means of giving glory to the Trinity." Ibid., pp. 40, 39.

[19] Ibid., pp. 34–47. A survey of the scholastic and Tridentine interpretations of "glory of God" is found in "Gloire de Dieu", *Dictionnaire de Spiritualité*, vol. 6, pp. 463–487.

[20] See Q. Skinner, "Language and Social Change," in *Meaning in Context*, ed., J. Tooley, Princeton 1985, pp. 119–132.

Theologically speaking, the conversion, salvation or sanctification of souls both reflects and contributes to the glory of God.[21] Although God is the ultimate cause of all three, religious individuals can be seen to contribute to the process whereby this glory is made manifest, elicits praise, and is magnified, inasmuch as they are cooperative agents, who by free choice assent to the divine grace offered in each case. Marie was concerned to convert or turn others to the way of salvation and to the way of sanctity and to contribute thereby to the ultimate goal of furthering the glory of God. She was concerned, however, not only to raise up everything for the glory of God, but also to bring God's glory down to earth.

In the following discussion of her mystical writing, the focus will be not so much on God's manifest glory, i.e., his praiseworthy goodness and justice as reflected in his dealings with the world, but rather on his internal glory or that splendour which is promised in the after-life, but sometimes glimpsed by certain chosen souls in this life. In some instances — most notably when writing for the benefit of her son — Marie points the reader in the direction of the divine splendour which she herself had enjoyed in her mystical transformation. Thus her spiritual writing not only promotes the (extrinsic) glory of God, but also hints at the possibility of glimpsing his (intrinsic) glory. Her attempted description of mystical illumination points to the essential divine glory which she had experienced in fleeting fashion. Spiritual conversion is not just a way marked by a striving for perfection and offered to God to render him that "glory" (or praise) which is his due, but also a state or experience of extraordinary grace which confers upon chosen souls a special kind of divine illumination. The more sublime aspects of Marie's spiritual writing, then, emphasise not so much the task as the possible rewards of the spiritual life.

In stark contrast to her active role in the two ways of promoting conversion which were discussed earlier in this chapter, Marie's approach to mystical conversion was a cautious and limited one, and necessarily so. As a missionary she was involved in indoctrination, or the attempt to imprint a theological message in the souls of the Indians, and as a spiritual teacher her aim was to exercise souls already well-versed in doctrine. But as a mystic, trying to convey something of the ineffable illuminations she had enjoyed, she could only guide her reader towards the threshold of an experience which, by her own admission, is unattainable through human initiative. She could only hint at the idea of mystical transformation, not teach it. After briefly discussing in what way Marie's writing is mystagogi-

---

[21] On the connection between the glory of God and salvation, see "Gloire de Dieu", p. 471.

cal, i.e., aimed at leading others to apprehend something of the mystical glory which she herself had experienced, I shall comment on the nature of her mystical illumination relative to the beatific vision of divine splendour.

As in the case of other spiritual writers of her time such as Philip Neri in Italy or, closer to home, François de Sales and Pierre de Bérulle, Marie's caution with regard to mystical expression was due to her fear that those reading such material might entertain delusions of spiritual grandeur or become inflated by spiritual hybris in their eagerness for mystical illumination.[22] Furthermore, she shared with many of her contemporaries the view that mystical union or other extraordinary spiritual experiences are goals which, paradoxically, cannot be aimed for but only conferred by God. Such stages in the mystical life, then, are deemed to both lie beyond human endeavour and to defy human attempts at description.

In Marie's *Relation de 1654*, however, we see an exception to this rule of reticence in her literary attempt to approximate the mystical illuminations she had enjoyed. Reluctant from the outset to comply with her spiritual director's request that she compose an autobiographical "report" of all the graces she had received, she harboured grave reservations even after she had acceded to his wish. When fire swept the Ursuline convent one night in 1650, she in fact left the original draft to burn rather than throwing it from the window together with other documents she rescued. She used the excuse of this "*force majeure*," as her son puts it, to abandon these notes to the fire "for fear ... that they might fall into someone's hands." (C 426)[23]

Persuaded by both her son and her spiritual director that this providential accident by no means released her from her duty to commit her mystical experiences to paper, she resumed the task. She could at least reassure herself that this work was not intended for the spiritual beginner, but rather for her son and her spiritual director, both of whom were presumably advanced enough in matters of spiritual import as to be immune to the potential "dangers" of such a frank account of mystical delights. However, the main factor which helped her overcome her aversion to writing such a mystical account was her desire to guide her son in spiritual matters by sharing with him her own experiences. Claude Martin's use of emotional blackmail was effective, as his mother was persuaded that providing him with a full account of her mystical experiences was just

---

[22] Louis Lallemant was one of few who held the opposite view and felt that discouraging such mystical aspirations was "a great abuse." Quoted in Poulain, *The Graces of Interior Prayer*, p. 476.

[23] C. Martin, *Vie de la Vénérable Mère Marie de l'Incarnation*, p. xxi.

compensation for having left him to the care of others when she entered the convent in 1631.

After sending Claude an outline of the main points to be discussed in her autobiography, she asks him to guard

> the secrecy which you have promised me, for I do not want anyone but you to have sight of them. If you see any danger of that happening, burn them first, or even, so that my mind will be at rest, send them back to me. (C 549)

The resulting *Relation de 1654*, is not just a description of her mystical states and an elucidation of their spiritual meaning, but also an attempt to lead her son to glimpse the same reality. This text, then, is not only mystographic and mystological, but mystagogical as well, for though Marie does not actually advocate the pursuit of these mystical delights, she is nonetheless concerned to point her reader in that direction. It is in this sense that one commentator, while noting that her spiritual doctrine is generally expressed in a simple and direct fashion, also concedes the presence of a strong mystagogical tendency: "Marie de l'Incarnation does not teach a disciple the paths that she experiences, she leads the reader to the place to which she aspires."[24]

The final and compelling reason for "relating" her spiritual story was her conviction — born of an illumination she experienced in the spring of 1653 — that she should "undertake this task for God's honour and greater glory." (A 1) Marie was writing during a period in the Church's literary history when it was no longer felt that God should be left "to glorify himself," and her autobiography was one of many spiritual texts of the day written to inspire others to praise God.[25] Just as she saw her work among the colonists and Indians of New France as a contribution to building a "spiritual edifice for His own greater glory," she felt that through this written account of her spiritual experiences, God might be blessed and glorified. (A 106) In a letter to an Ursuline in Tours who offered up her prayers for the salvation of souls, Marie refers to her as "a mediator of the amplification of the glory of God." (C 355) However, while Marie's missionary work and spiritual teaching, which promoted the salvation of souls and sanctification of souls respectively, were aimed at the ultimate goal of enhancing God's glory by increasing his honour and praise, her mystical writing, or to be more precise, the mystagogical element in her

---

[24] Lonsagne, "Les écrits spirituels de Marie de l'Incarnation...", p. 182.

[25] H. Bremond, *Literary History of Religious Thought in France*, trans. K. Montgomery, London 1928–36, vol. 2, p. 4.

spiritual writing, not only contributed to God's extrinsic glory, but also aimed to convey something of his intrinsic glory to the reader.

This distinction between spiritual pedagogy and mystagogy is based on the assumption that both meanings of the phrase "glory of God" are discernible in Marie's mystical writing. Her stated intention to undertake the task of writing her mystical autobiography "for God's honour and greater glory" can thus be read in a dual sense.[26] The apposite terms "honour" and "glory," beyond their significance as synonyms, can be understood as two distinct motifs of her spiritual activity, one referring to God's extrinsic, the other to his intrinsic, glory. Let us pursue this line of thought for a moment. In her *Relation de 1654*, she mentions the importance of chanting the psalms and reflecting on their meaning: "The psalm *The heavens show forth the glory of God*, ... particularly touched my heart and transported my spirit." (A 82) She then adds "I would have wished that everyone had known and tasted the delights which my soul experienced in those testimonies." (A 82) The "delights" to which she refers signify not only the satisfaction derived from understanding or "knowing" Scripture or religious truths, but also the immediate presence of God which the mystics claim to enjoy in mystical experience. Central to this psalm that triggered her spiritual illumination or "transport" is the key motif, "the glory of God," which in her mind could equally mean God's manifest glory in the world and his intrinsic glory, which is commonly held to be inaccessible to human experience.

Thus when Marie announces that she would like everyone to share such "delights," she could be referring either to the satisfaction derived from spiritual life or to the extraordinary illumination which she herself had enjoyed.[27] As we saw in her commentary on the *Song of Songs*, she may well have desired that everyone know and taste the extraordinary delights which she herself had enjoyed, but in guiding the novices, her explicit instruction pertains only to the ordinary or accessible delights of the spiritual life. In her *Relation de 1654*, however, which was written primarily for the "spiritual advancement" of her son Claude, whom God was "calling to the mystical life," the spiritual guidance aims at something more than promoting her son's progress in sanctity. (C 527)

This assessment of Marie's motivation as a mystical writer hinges on the

---

[26] On the significance of the term "greater glory of God" see *Dictionnaire de Spiritualité*, vol. 6, pp. 487–494. See also above, chapter 3, n. 1.

[27] This distinction is similar to that of St. Teresa between spiritual consolations and spiritual delights. See *The Interior Castle*, p. 75.

assumption that the mystical illumination or "delights" to which she gives
witness in her autobiography are akin to the glory that is intrinsic to God.
To set this interpretation in its proper context, a few words are in order
about the theological connection — if any — between the mystical experience of the inner splendour of the divinity and the beatific vision in
which, it is promised, the blessed will see God face to face. The relative
significance of the mystical and beatific "visions" is an issue in spiritual
theology for which a thorough and unequivocal treatment is still outstand-
ing. In both the Latin and Orthodox traditions the exact nature, timing
and scope of the vision of God reserved for the Blessed in the after-life,
have been the focus of an extensive and long-standing debate.[28] However,
it is difficult to find a straightforward theological stance regarding the idea
of such a vision being possible in this life.

On the one hand, it has been suggested by writers like Evelyn Underhill
that in general terms the mystic often sees certain experiences of spiritual
union as "a foretaste of the Beatific Vision: an entrance here and now into
that absolute Life within the Divine Being"; the mystic has, she suggests,
"run ahead of human history: and attained a form of consciousness which
other men will only know when earthly life is past."[29] In strict theological
terms, on the other hand, most spiritual theologians tend to shy away from
this comparison of mystical illumination with the beatific vision, noting
that the mystical vision of God is in some way still veiled and therefore
"not beatific in the technical sense of the word." The Jesuit, Poulain,
typifies this position: "Theologians are almost unanimous in affirming
that mystic visions of the Divinity are not of the same kind as the beatific
vision. I am with them in holding this opinion."[30] Joseph Maréchal, whose
classic study on the psychology of mystics contains one of the most
rigorous discussions of the topic, shies away from an equation of the two
visions mentioned, but does concede that:

> The theory of an immediate but not strictly beatific vision of God has not
> yet found entirely satisfactory theological expression. Between this imper-
> fect, transitory vision and the true beatific vision it seems, as tradition
> would have it, that the difference should be something other than purely a

---

[28] V. Lossky, *The Vision of God*, London 1963, is the best study of the theological
controversy regarding the nature of this divine illumination in the Byzantine East and the
Latin West; it does not, however, examine at any length the issue of the proximity between
mystical experience and the beatific vision.

[29] Underhill, *Mysticism*, pp. 423–424.

[30] Poulain, *The Graces of Interior Prayer*, p. 568.

degree of intensity. But where should one look for this differentiating characteristic?[31]

The fact remains, however, that there is ample indication among spiritual writers and mystics themselves that such an association of the two visions is warranted, at least in qualitative if not in quantitative terms.[32] The theory which allows for the possibility of linking the mystical and beatific visions of divine splendour holds that

> the two kinds of vision would differ only in intensity, and therefore in clearness. In heaven there would be a plenitude of light and happiness; here below, the sole difference would be that the light would be faint and the happiness incomplete.[33]

The idea seems to be that while on earth, and governed by the physical limitations of the body, a human being could not possibly withstand the force of this vision for a sustained period. Hence the fleeting nature of the experience and the mystics' claim that they would expire if the vision did not pass.[34] The German mystic Henry Suso asks us to note that the blessed "are stripped of their personal initiative, and changed into another form, another glory, another power. ... And what is this other glory, if it be not to be illuminated and made shining in the Inaccessible light?"[35]

Closer to Marie's own time, Teresa of Avila, describing the heights of her mystical experience, writes: "I can say only that the Lord wishes to reveal for that moment, in a more sublime manner than through any spiritual vision or taste, the glory of heaven."[36] In the seventeenth century, writers such as Philip of the Trinity were even more forthright in their claim that mystical union and "the light of the higher order thus communicated to the mind, is a certain participation of the light of glory."[37] The argument is summed up as follows:

> In this way God is seen in Himself (in seipso), but not with the clearness and perfection of the state of glory, either the disposition of the subject, or the

---

[31] J. Maréchal, *Études sur la psychologie des mystiques*, Paris 1937, 2 vols., vol. 2, p. 47.

[32] St. Teresa and St. John of the Cross are two mystics who use the word glory "in a mystical sense, depicting a state where the soul 'tastes,' or experiences, something of the celestial glory of the beatitude of the blessed." See "Gloire de Dieu," p. 471.

[33] Poulain, *The Graces of Interior Prayer*, p. 569.

[34] "Gloire de Dieu," p. 472.

[35] Quoted in Underhill, *Mysticism*, p. 472.

[36] Teresa of Avila, *The Interior Castle*, p. 179.

[37] Quoted in Poulain, *The Graces of Interior Prayer*, p. 569.

restricted power of manifestation and elevation of this light being the cause of a deficiency. The resulting vision is then direct, as is the sight in heaven of God as seen in Himself, but is not so clear; and it is called vision in darkness.[38]

Interestingly enough, despite the rigour of doctrinal scrutiny in his day, Philip of the Trinity was not impugned by Church officials for holding this dissenting view.[39]

With regard to the nature and intensity of Marie's ongoing mystical transformation, her most celebrated commentator, Dom Oury, displays all the caution of a trained theologian. While noting that "she aspires to the stability of the blessed, captivated for eternity by the beauty of Him whom they wanted to contemplate and from whom it is no longer possible for them to turn away now that they see him face to face," he clearly states elsewhere that the mystic's

> face to face of the soul with the mystery of the divine Being is not that of the beatific vision which would set the soul forever in its state of eternity; but the mode approaches it for it seems to call up no reality of a psychological order, which tends to place a screen between the soul and God.[40]

Although aimed at making an absolute distinction between the two kinds of vision, his comment suggests that the main difference between them relates to duration and intensity, not necessarily to quality.

Marie herself perceived her mystical illumination to be not just an experience analogous to the beatific vision, but indeed a fleeting foretaste of that splendour. In praising the efforts of those who came to the Ursulines' assistance after fire demolished the convent, she says, "They will be recompensed a hundredfold in this life and then through glory in the next," thereby implying that such "glory" is something which can be enjoyed only in the after-life. (A 171) Yet in many other instances, though she does not say outright that her mystical states or visions are equal to the beatific vision, she does liken her experience to that of the blessed. On the one hand she affirms the overpowering quality of the vision of glory and states that the soul, even when it is already infused with divine love, "sees very clearly that he who is a searcher of the majesty of God shall be

---

[38] Ibid., p. 569.

[39] Ibid., p. 569.

[40] Oury, *Ce que croyait*, pp. 122, 150–1. Henri Cuzin stresses that Marie's sudden face-to-face with the Trinity is "of course one which is not that of the beatific vision." See *Du Christ à la Trinité*, p. 74.

overwhelmed by His glory." (A 46–7) On the other hand she indicates that it is precisely this transcendent realm to which the soul aspires on its mystical journey:

> The soul wishes to find the Beloved apart from any of the manifestations of His majesty which might render Him formidable, and this constrains it to say to Him: 'Flee, O my Beloved, betake Thyself to those things which smell of aromatic spices, go among the Cherubim, for they alone can bear Thy splendour. But come, O my Love, that I may pour myself out before Thee through a reciprocal love insofar as my lowliness makes it possible and Thou, O my Love, canst bear with it.' (A 49–50)

Marie echoes here the empassioned address of the Bride to her Beloved in the *Song of Songs*, and expresses the ambivalence of the mystic who concedes the unsuitability of the quest for celestial glory, but reaffirms its desirability.

Though it is difficult to establish the exact degree of affinity which she perceives between her mystical union in this life and the state of glory promised for the blessed in the after-life, it is clear that she closely associates the two. In characterizing the extraordinary experience of chosen souls to her son, she writes:

> just as in heaven, besides the essential glory, God lets the blessed taste the joys and felicity of his divine magnificence, so too in these chosen souls, where he makes his abode on earth, besides this deep possession which he gives them of himself, he lets them feel sometimes an outpouring of the joy which is like a foretaste of the state of the blessed. (C 765)

Marie, who considered herself to be among these chosen souls, is drawing on her personal experience of such celestial joy, which she refers to in her autobiography while explaining how God prepared her in a special way for each extraordinary grace which she received in her mystical life:

> This He did by means of a foretaste which, in the peace it begot, was like an experience of paradise. In view of the sublimity of the experience, I'm unable to express myself in any other way regarding it. (A 56)

Her descriptions of the elevated state of the soul and its union with God is reminiscent of the beatific vision:

> Although the soul knows that the Word is the great God, equal to the eternal Father, through whom all things have been made and subsist in being, still she embraces Him and speaks to Him face to face, knowing that she has been elevated to this dignity of having the Word for her Spouse and

of being His bride and hence in a position to say to Him: "Thou art my other self, Thou art all mine." (A 59)

Elsewhere, she states succinctly and unequivocally that "the sweet and loving union is already the beatitude begun in mortal flesh." (C 397)

Towards the end of her autobiography Marie sums up the nature and intensity of her own mystical experiences in terms which again suggest an intimate knowledge of the very splendour which is considered to lie beyond the common way of spiritual life. She refers to the mystical "impression" received by her soul as:

> something so elevated, so ravishing, so divine, so simple, and so far removed from what can be expressed in human language that all I can say is that during it I am in God, possessed by Him, and that He would soon consume me by the intensity and force of His love if I were not sustained by another impression which follows upon the former. This second impression doesn't cause the first to disappear but merely tempers its splendour, which is too great for one to bear in this present life. If it were not thus tempered by this second impression, which always has some reference to the adorable Word Incarnate, my Divine Spouse, I wouldn't be able to go on living ... (A 180–1)

In this passage she highlights three special features of her "elevated" mystical experience. She prefaces her description by stressing that this mystical state is indescribable, "far removed from what can be expressed in human language." She also claims that "the intensity and force" of God's love in this state render the experience impossible "for one to bear in this present life." It is in fact bearable only by virtue of the subsequent vision which "tempers" its splendour, and it is interesting to note that in contrast to the abstract, formless nature of the overwhelming vision, the additional or auxiliary vision does have symbolic import and is always related, Marie tells us, "to the adorable Word Incarnate, my Divine Spouse." What is significant here is that she is speaking not on a literary but rather on an experiential level. She suggests that familiar forms and traditional symbols are not just the basis for mystical expression of the ineffable experience but also for the experience itself. By her own admission it is the concrete vision of the spiritual *persona* of God as Word Incarnate or divine spouse, which makes it possible for her to enjoy the overwhelming splendour without expiring — a claim which recalls what we have already mentioned regarding the limitations inherent in the experience of celestial glory in this life.

The common thread in Marie's different attempts to describe her mystical encounter with God is her oft-repeated insistence on the ineffability of this state which "affords a divine nourishment which human language is unable to express, an intimacy and boldness, an inexplicable reciprocity of love between the Word and the soul." (A 63) Apologetically noting that "some might be inclined to think that I'm exaggerating," she insists that this experience is something "about which I can only stutter since it involves things which cannot be expressed." (A 66, 104) Trying to describe how her soul was denuded in the mystical state of victimhood, she says

> no doubt I speak obscurely; and yet I see it clearly myself, even though it is impossible to express the thousandth part of the impressions and operations which my Divine Spouse has produced in my soul. (A 172)

She also indicates the inadequacy of literary attempts to capture the essence of the soul's experience of union with God by stating that although nothing "better expresses what the soul feels" than the *Song of Songs*, this text is still only a faint approximation of mystical illumination, for the "natural experience" of this mystical state "begets an impression quite different from that begotten by merely listening to the words of that canticle." (A 63)

The question which immediately arises in view of Marie's insistence on the inability of human industry to describe, to attain, or to promote such a vision, is how she can convey something of this transcendent reality to her reader. How could she "lead" the reader to glimpse this splendour if such a mystical conversion lies beyond human endeavour and comprehension, and can be granted only through divine initiative? We saw that in her formative years Marie was drawn by the "beauty" of the human figure of Christ, and it was the powerful image of Christ's blood washing away her sins which occasioned her conversion at the age of twenty. But her subsequent experience of union with God was referred to in much more abstract terms, having, Marie insists, no relation to images. In her conversion activity she drew on the lessons of her own experience. While clearly acknowledging the usefulness of visual and literary images for teaching the Indians and for promoting spiritual conversion, she considered symbolic language and imagery inadequate, even irrelevant when it came to mystical expression. However, despite her frequent reiteration of the ineffability of such illuminations and her claim that the imagination plays no role in apprehending them, her account of these experiences does engage the reader's imagination in an effort to point beyond its limitations. Indeed, it is through use of paradoxical formulations and imagery that she attempts to convey something of the overwhelming transcendent quality of her experience.

In a letter written to her son around the time she composed her *Relation de 1654*, she explains that "symbolic things, or [things] which can be attached to some form or subject which derive from matter can be understood, but God has not led me by these paths." (C 533) In describing her "very elevated and pure" mystical union, she carefully adds: "though I speak of the sacred Word Incarnate I don't mean to imply that I have an imaginative image of Him." (A 179) This does not mean that in such experiences there could never be attendant images, but rather that the experience neither transpired in the imagination nor was it apprehended by any ordinary mode of understanding. The mystical vision of glory, which as we have seen is akin to the beatific vision, can neither be described nor promoted through images because, unlike the extrinsic or created glory which is encountered in religious life, it is non-iconic. Thus Marie writes in her *Relation*, "I pause to consider whether I might be able to find any suitable comparisons with things of this world, but I can find none which would help me to describe the embraces of the Word and the soul." (A 58–9)

In her autobiography Marie nonetheless makes an effort to express "those things which creatures are impotent to express." (A 45) She tells of "divine communications ... so intense, and so removed from one's perceptions that the soul seems to be absent from its Beloved, even though He is near." (A 51) In describing the impact of the soul's union with God she mentions "divine touches, so delicate but yet so crucifying," and states "the excess of His love in my soul was like a fire which stifled my breath." (A 51, 60) She notes the soul is

> entirely penetrated and possessed by Him. It is consumed by caresses and acts of love which cause it to expire in Him by suffering deaths the most sweet; moreover, these very deaths constitute the sweetness. (A 58)

By coupling the notions of love and death, and identifying spiritual pain with pleasure, she is following the well-trodden path of mystical writers who through the ages have sought to convey the paradoxical nature of an experience which can be grasped neither by the imagination nor the reasoning faculties.

Less than two years before she died, Marie, still elucidating points of her mystical states for her son, explains that in the most sublime stage of mystical life, "there is no place for the imagination, it flits hither and thither, trying to find something to feed upon ... not finding anything, it gradually ceases its activities," because in this state "none of the interior or exterior senses has any part to play, nor the discourse of reason." (C 897) She is again at pains to indicate that mystical union lies beyond the bounds of the imagination, senses and rational discourse. Elsewhere she refers to the mystical vision of the Trinity as "an impression without form or figure, yet more clear and intelligible than any light." (A 44) Although the experience could neither be explained nor understood, she insists it was "more intelligible than any light." By use of oxymora, contradiction and images of plenitude and excess she is in fact attempting to communicate something of the overpowering nature of *mors mystica* and *unio mystica*, and of the splendour in which the unitive experience is rooted, while at the same time reiterating their supra-rational or anti-imaginary nature.

The key to the mystagogical dilemma regarding the task of expressing the inexpressible lies in the view — which has been the backbone of traditional mystical theologies from the Church's earliest days, and which has been reiterated in more recent works on spirituality — that a self-negating discourse is the best vehicle for transmitting the super-positive, transcendent nature proper to God; where cataphatic theology affirms the goodness, justice and beauty of God in his immanence as manifest in the created world, apophatic theology can best indicate God's transcendent splendour which lies beyond attributes, words, images and rational concepts.[41] Implicit in mystical writing, however, is the assumption that negative or paradoxical formulations and even purportedly non-iconic expression can contribute positively to the reader's apprehension of the mystical reality being approximated, by virtue of their implicit relation to the very qualities or realities which they purport to surpass. It is as if this intrinsic divine splendour which transcends sense perceptions and images is nonetheless dependent on a tacit aesthetic principle.

Mystical writing is an attempt to give body to an absence, as De Certeau has aptly put it; it is an attempt to make a mystery visible, to give shape to what essentially lies beyond shape and form.[42] A mystical text that deals with an experience which is neither concrete nor empirically assessed presents the reader with an invitation to grapple with the reality which lies beyond accepted and normative forms of expression. The mystagogical approach is by definition a dialectical process or, as Alois Haas puts it, a

---

[41] This is one of the key premises elaborated by Hans Urs von Balthasar in the first volume of his major opus *The Glory of the Lord. A Theological Aesthetics*, vol. 1, "Seeing the Form," trans. E. Leiva-Merikakis, eds. J. Fessio and J. Riches, Edinburgh 1982.

[42] See De Certeau, *La Fable mystique*, pp. 12–22.

"dialogically-transmitted" kind of guidance.[43] The underlying principle is not unlike that found in classical rhetorics and in modern response theory in that it suggests that, though no overt message or concrete content is given, a meaning can nonetheless crystallize in the reader's mind as he comes to terms with the text.[44] Language and imagery have, as it were, an important but limited role to play in mystagogical writing, which aims not to effect but at least to hint at such experience and so to lead the reader as close as possible to the spiritual point where God alone can effect the ultimate transformation or mystical conversion. Hans Urs von Balthasar has most convincingly suggested that it is one of the striking characteristics of mystical experience, that while it is neither produced nor necessarily mediated by the imagination, it nonetheless stirs the recipient to an imaginative act, to an attempt to recapture and creatively render the reality he or she has glimpsed. Hence the striking convergence of the aesthetic and the mystical in the great works of mystical theology which, according to Balthasar, can be explained only "by affirming that what in God is formless and ineffable is offered as super-form which fascinates and transports man, eliciting from man and claiming for itself the answer of man's shaping powers."[45]

One of the striking features of Marie de l'Incarnation's writing is her use of language and imagery, both in interpreting her own religious transformation and in promoting such a change in others. Her approach to religious service centred on making something of God's essence accessible to others in a lasting and personal fashion. The "divine excesses" received in her spiritual life were perceived as "an inexhaustible fount constantly emptying itself into the soul, which is like a brook perpetually flowing back to its divine source, where it loses itself and seems to be one with her Beloved." (A 66) Once her mystical transformation had settled down into a pattern of life, Marie no longer saw her soul as a brook which is pumped with water that constantly circulates back to the source of its inflow, but rather as a reservoir which, once filled, spills over and seeps into the lives of others, thereby serving as a conduit for the divine favours which had been its own source. Marie's attempt to promote an interior change in others reflects one of the key principles of "theological aesthetics," which in recent years has offered a fresh appraisal of the nature of spiritual

---

[43] Haas, *Sermo mysticus*, p. 32.

[44] See S.E. Fish, *Self-Consuming Artifacts. The Experience of Seventeenth-Century Literature*, Berkeley 1972.

[45] von Balthasar, *The Glory of the Lord*, vol. 1, pp. 601–602.

theology and literature; for she grasped the importance — to quote von Balthasar — of "allowing God's Word, here and now, to make its own form prevail in those who hear it."[46]

As was the case in her missionary activity, Marie's spiritual teaching reveals her view that not just the content, but also the form and mood of religious experience are essential to making conversion an interior and lasting orientation. Though the two texts, *Entretien sur l'Épouse des Cantiques* and *La Relation de 1654*, have much in common and both deal with the experience of spiritual grace, they suggest a duality with regard to spiritual conversion, perceived on the one hand as the standard way of spiritual progress, and on the other, as a heightened experience of its rewards. The contrasting didactic thrust of the former text and the initiatory tone of the latter seem to indicate Marie's awareness of both her duty and her limitations as a writer dealing with, or trying to convey, the essence of spiritual transformation. In both kinds of writing she can be seen as guiding the reader to a certain kind of spiritual change; in the one instance she is clearly in the teaching role, but in the other she seems concerned to let God's pedagogy shine through.

As a missionary, spiritual guide and mystic, her special gift was her discernment of the important role of religious signs (rituals, gestures, processions, chants, images and other instruments of devotion) in bringing the individual to either an initial or intensified experience of God. As a mystic, trying to convey something of the transforming experience of divine splendour which lies beyond human signification, she understood a point which is central to von Balthasar's rehabilitation of mystical aesthetics, namely that "the beauty and glory which are proper to God may be inferred and 'read' off from God's epiphany and its incomprehensible glory"; by hinting at this epiphany, she aimed to lead others to a like experience.[47] With regard to the glimpse of this mystical glory, she could not cause the transforming conversion, any more than she could effect the primary conversion of the Indians, or the second conversion of her spiritual adepts. However, she was able to intimate something of God's glory and of the possibility for transformation in its light. In all her activities her task was to use those words, images and forms which were best suited to prod and push the prospective convert, whether listener or reader, believer or non-believer, to apprehend God's goodness or beauty as manifest in creation and in some instances even to move beyond this to an immediate

---

[46] Ibid., p. 593.
[47] Ibid., p. 124.

experience of God himself, who is in ultimate terms beyond form and words.

The theoretical, experiential and practical dimensions of conversion all played an important role in the life and work of Marie de l'Incarnation and shaped one another in a dynamic process. Her activities of conversion were influenced by traditional teaching and other formative influences, as well as by her own conversion experience. In so far as conversion is seen not just as a single event but also as an ongoing process, it is clear that her performative role as a missionary and spiritual guide not only complemented her personal spiritual transformation but also completed it. Thus, though her own conversion was initially shaped by her religious upbringing or formation, it was continually being enriched by her encounters with others and by her activity as missionary and spiritual guide. Finally, it should be noted that the formative ground or traditional context in which the conversion experience was rooted was, in turn, affected by the performative stage of Marie's conversion. For her spiritual and missionary writings — the literary side of her "conversion activity" — can be seen as a contribution to the body of devotional literature and mystical exposition, which together with Scripture and doctrine constitute that entity loosely known as Catholic tradition; and the latter, as we have seen, had been an essential formative ingredient of her own religious development.

This brief overview suggests that we have come full circle with the three stages or levels of conversion. Marie's formative context, or the grab-bag of scriptural images, theological concepts, popular devotions and traditional rites which she absorbed in her youth, contributed to her conversion in 1620 into a "new creature," whose transformation was to continue throughout the rest of her life. Both the formative and transformative stages of conversion shaped her conversion activity and all three stages are reflected in her writings. These texts have in turn been channelled into that ever-growing corpus of spiritual writing which forms part of the Church's literary tradition. Such writings, which are collected, sanctioned and passed on by the Church as *exempla* for the illumination of the faithful — to inform and reform, to instruct and inspire them to strive for a like transformation in their own lives — were the fruit of the formative seed which had taken root in Marie's childhood.

In this sense, then, conversion is a reciprocal operation deriving from, but ultimately also contributing to, the normative framework from which it issues. Marie's conversion of 1620, that central religious event described in her autobiographical *Relation de 1654* some thirty-four years after the fact, was not only a product of the normative theological and literary tradition in which she was embedded, it was also a formative force in its own right; for in its literary expression it gave new shape to the devotional model or structure of which it was an offshoot. The mediator in both cases was language — seen both as the closed system of theological and scriptural terms with specific referents which shaped her experience and perception of conversion, and as speech, or the creative act in which she functioned as mediator with the firm intention of expressing something.[48] For language is "neither structure nor event but the incessant conversion of one into the other in discourse."[49] In writing about her conversion and subsequent spiritual life, then, Marie crystallized her idea of conversion in all its dimensions and by so doing gave witness to the importance of both tradition and the individual's personal concerns and circumstances for the dynamics of religious experience.

[48] P. Ricoeur, "Structure, Word, Event," trans. R. Sweeney, in *The Conflict of Interpretations. Essays in Hermeneutics*, ed. D. Ihde, Evanston 1974, p. 85.
[49] Ibid., p. 89.

IMAGES OF THE OTHER AND MYSTICISM
IN THE NEW WORLD

In recent years considerable research has been done on the relation between spiritual sensibilities and religious activity in Puritan New England. It has been amply demonstrated that the religious life of those who settled in the New World was different from the European format not only in organizational and social terms but also in terms of basic religious perceptions.[1] Similar research on the significance of spiritual identity in Catholic New France is still a desideratum. The spiritual expression of the New France missionaries is usually treated only in reference to general devotional themes or trends in Europe at the time; Marie de l'Incarnation's mysticism, for example, has had a prominent place in studies on Catholic Reformation spirituality, but because she has been seen primarily as a typical representative of that spirituality, her mystical self-understanding — and specific contribution to the Christian mystical tradition — have not been adequately treated.

In the Christian spiritual tradition we can find precedents for Marie's characteristic brand of divine action deriving from mystical union, both in the spiritual thought of patristic authors for whom "contemplation and action [were] held together in Christian love," as well as in the writing of later mystics such as Jan Ruysbroeck or Richard of St. Victor, both of whom saw the special kind of service which issued from the transforming union as a higher kind of mystical experience.[2] For Ruysbroeck the summit of the inner life is a blend of absolute repose and absolute fecundity in the soul, for in mystical union God "breathes us out from Himself that we may love and do good works; and again he draws us into Himself, that we may rest in fruition."[3] Marie's combination of sublime repose in the divine image and the lowliness of spiritual service is also akin

---

[1] See introduction, note 4.

[2] Louth, *The Origins of the Christian Mystical Tradition*, p. 198.

[3] Quoted in Underhill, *Mysticism*, p. 434.

to the portrait of the elevated soul depicted in Richard of St. Victor's mystical treatise *The Four Degrees of Ardent Love*. In the fourth — and highest — degree of spiritual love, which represents the perfect coinherence of the "*frui* and *uti*" of mystical contemplation, the soul is not only "reborn, renewed and reformed to the image and similitude of God, but it now takes on the form of Christ's humility and servanthood, becoming all things to all men, seeking to bring others to spiritual maturity."[4] For Richard, then, the final mystical state is associated with a specific kind of spiritual action in service of others, namely, seeking their growth in sanctification.

Perhaps more than anyone else, Teresa of Avila springs to mind when we consider the resemblance of Marie de l'Incarnation's mystical thought to that of others in the spiritual canon. But apart from the fact that Marie, unlike Teresa, does not see spiritual marriage as the zenith of her mystical journey, there are other, more subtle differences between the two mystics — for example, with regard to the nature and source of the good works practised by the contemplative. For Teresa the saintly figures of Mary and Martha — who represent the passive contemplative and bustling activist respectively — must join together and serve God, even if "such service does not convert souls"; for conversion activity, as she explains, is perhaps not within everyone's ability.[5] The emphasis is therefore on exercising one's own will in applying the benefits of union, whereas in Marie's assessment of spiritual union, serving others is seen not as a possibility but rather as a necessity, almost as a mystical condition determined by the fact of her participation in the divine life. Marie also places much greater emphasis on the mystical nature and divine source of the action issuing from contemplation. And yet there is much that is similar in the accounts of these two mystics.

Marie de l'Incarnation's affinity with such mystics places her in good spiritual company, and those looking to slot her into an existing niche of tradition can do so easily. However, it must be remembered that her spiritual identity was shaped not only by her extraordinary interior experiences — which are akin to those described in traditional literature — but also by her interpretation and application of these experiences in the unique spiritual context of the New France mission. In this regard, she is

---

[4] See the introduction to Richard of St. Victor, *The Twelve Patriarchs, The Mystical Ark, Book Three of the Trinity*, trans. and intro. by G.A. Zinn, London 1979, p. 9.

[5] Teresa of Avila, *The Interior Castle*, p. 193.

in her own right "a spiritual master unbeknownst to herself."[6] This comment by Dom Oury reflects his traditional but not unequivocal appraisal of her mysticism, which affirms both its classic character and its originality. While claiming on the one hand that "her mystical itinerary is absolutely normal, even normative one might say," he also acknowledges that though "she isn't creating a school ... neither is she conforming to a [mystical] school."[7] The stress on victimhood, the recurring conversion motif and particular apostolic emphases which surface in Marie de l'Incarnation's mystical writing are certainly not peculiar to New France, but the fact that the New France context formed the prism for her assessment of her spiritual identity imbued her version of mystical ascent with new thematic emphases, if not wholly novel dimensions.

Attention has been drawn to the spiritual foundations of the French colony — i.e., the rich spiritual fibre of the missionaries and Church leaders in the colony — and due reference has been made to the formative influence of mystical trends in France at the time, but the differences between the French church and its colonial offshoot have not been sufficiently acknowledged. Dom Oury, whose numerous articles and monographs on religious life and personalities in New France have paved the way for research on various aspects of religious life in the colony, points to the *Spiritual Exercises* of Ignatius, as well as the confluence of the Berullian heritage and Cistercian and Carmelite mysticism, as key influences on early Canadian spirituality, but cautiously notes that much research remains to be done in the area of religious sentiment in seventeenth-century New France.[8] With regard to the religious life and organization of the colony, "the Church in New France was the creation of the metropolitan Church, but never became its creature."[9] In a similar vein, it must be said that the idea of a New France spirituality, with European roots but distinctive local features, warrants further study.[10]

Among the missionaries in New France the recurring redemption motif and specific prayers for obtaining application of the blood of the son of God to the souls of the natives were intertwined with the personal spiritual

---

[6] Guy-M. Oury, "Le sentiment religieux en Nouvelle-France au XVIIe siècle," *Société Canadienne d'Histoire de l'Église catholique*, Sessions d'étude 50 (1983), p. 267.

[7] Ibid., pp. 272, 265.

[8] Ibid., pp. 255–279.

[9] Jaenen, *The Role of the Church in New France*, p. viii.

[10] The numerous works published by Dom Guy-Marie Oury in the past two decades provide the raw material for such an enquiry. See also Boucher, *Le premier visage de l'Église du Canada*.

desire to be part of this process.[11] In the face of devastating rampages by warring tribes and horrifying cases of martyrdom, and in constant anticipation of renewed attacks, they found solace in their spiritual self-image as "victims consecrated to our Lord who must wait for his decision regarding the hour in which they would be offered up for his glory."[12] The most vivid example of this kind of spiritual self-definition is found in the *Vie de Catherine de St. Augustin*, a documentary biography based on the spiritual accounts of this Canadian saint, which was composed by the Jesuit Paul Ragueneau.[13] Up until the last years of her life Catherine enjoyed a devout girlhood and fairly "classic" mystical life.[14] During the last seven or eight years of her life, while a missionary in Québec, she endured a period of physical and spiritual torment, demonic temptations mingled with the burning desire to suffer for the sake of the souls of others. Nurturing a vivid sense of the ugliness of sin compared with the sanctity of God — an angry judge who must be appeased — she wished to be the "subject of his anger and offered [herself] to be the victim of his divine justice."[15]

The New World was the context for both her obsessive concern for the natives' salvation and her horror at the temptations which assailed her. The first attack of impure thoughts — experienced in the course of her nursing work which involved washing and dressing men in the colony's hospital — went hand in hand with the desire to return to France, a desire which she perceived as an evil temptation to spurn her Canadian vocation.[16] These thoughts were at the core of her spiritual development in "this little paradise of Québec," where she became convinced that her specific raison-d'être was to endure the intense suffering wrought by her battle with Satan, as penance for the sins of others.[17] In his rendering of her autobiographical accounts, Ragueneau highlights the New France setting as the crux of Catherine's spiritual self-image, and portrays it as the kingdom of Satan, which evokes God's wrath and requires a self-sacrificing victim to halt the rampage of sin and produce sanctity in the wilderness. Catherine's

---

[11] Pouliot, *Étude sur les Relations des Jésuites*, p. 212.

[12] Thwaites, *Jesuit Relations*, vol. 34, pp. 132–134. See also my "Strange Encounters: Missionary Activity and Mystical Thought in Seventeenth-Century New France," *History of European Ideas* 22/2 (1996), pp. 67–92.

[13] Paul Ragueneau, *La vie de la Mère Catherine de Saint-Augustin, religieuse hospitalière de la Miséricorde de Québec en la Nouvelle-France*, Paris 1671, new ed. Québec 1923.

[14] Oury, *L'itinéraire mystique de Catherine de Saint-Augustin*, p. 22.

[15] Ragueneau, *La vie de la Mère Catherine de Saint-Augustin*, p. 154.

[16] Oury, *L'itinéraire mystique de Catherine de Saint-Augustin*, p. 101.

[17] Ragueneau, *La vie de la Mère Catherine de Saint-Augustin*, p. 64.

mental world was peopled not just by the traditional saints, but by local figures, such as the Jesuit martyrs Isaac Jogues and Jean Brébeuf. The latter served as her invisible spiritual guide, and the former as a model of stability and inspiration in her battle with the temptation to abandon the New France mission. Jogues had in fact opened the door to the New World for Catherine, for her father had refused permission for her to go until he was powerfully moved by reading the account of Jogues' martyrdom.[18]

Similar motifs, concerns and Canadian content surface in the spiritual writing of Marguerite Bourgeoys, the founder of the first lay religious community in the colony.[19] The fulfilment of her whole spiritual life hinged on the Canadian turn which her life took. Like Marie de l'Incarnation she wavered between contemplative and active options of religious commitment. Having accepted the offer of Paul de Chomedey, the founder of Ville-Marie (present-day Montréal), to go to New France to work with a lay group devoted to rooting Christian faith in the settlement, she had doubts about abandoning her project of entering religious life. Reassured by a vision of the Virgin Mary telling her that she would accompany her on the journey, Marguerite went ahead with her plans only to have her commitment tested a second time by pressure from the Carmelites in Paris to accept their invitation to join their order. Again she had qualms, and again as the result of a spiritual illumination she received "great strength and great assurance" that she must go to Canada and do her bit to "gather the drops of Jesus' blood ... being wasted due to the ignorance of the peoples [there]."[20] For Marguerite Bourgeoys, as for Catherine de St. Augustin and Marie de l'Incarnation, spiritual fulfilment was inextricably bound up with active participation in the divine plan of saving souls, and found its expression in the sacred space of the Canadian wilderness.

It would require a separate study to investigate in what way the thought of Marie and other New France missionaries was indebted to certain aspects of Jesuit spirituality — not least of all because Jesuit writers of the day were themselves not in agreement over the precise relation between action and contemplation in spirituality. For one thing, although Jesuit spirituality in general views prayer life as a means to serve God better, and even sees the lofty form of infused contemplation as a means to this active

[18] Oury, *L'itinéraire mystique de Catherine de Saint-Augustin*, p. 104.

[19] See H. Bernier, *Marguerite Bourgeoys*, Collection classiques canadiens, no. 3, Montréal 1958; S. Poissant, *Marguerite Bourgeoys 1620–1700*, Montréal 1982.

[20] Quoted in Poissant, *Marguerite Bourgeoys*, pp. 23, 45.

end, not all Jesuit writers in the seventeenth century assessed the relation between action and contemplation in a like manner. There were those who saw infused contemplation as a special gift, one outside the ordinary path of sanctity, and others who saw it as the common goal to be aspired to in prayer life. In either case, whether it was considered an extraordinary experience bestowed by God upon a few chosen souls, or a desired feature of holy life, contemplation was seen as a means to the ultimate end of action for God.[21]

Certainly, those who were advanced in spiritual life were considered the best material for missionary work. Addressing those favoured with mystical illuminations, Jean Brébeuf stressed, "whoever you are, to whom God gives these feelings and illuminations, ... it is workers such as you whom we require here."[22] And such an appeal implies a functional assessment of spiritual life as a means to an end. This view was reflected in much spiritual literature and also adopted by those reading it. However, what is made clear by Marie de l'Incarnation and other missionaries is that not only was missionary work enhanced by a deep spirituality, but profound spiritual states were also enriched and nurtured by missionary work. For the latter was not just a complementary aspect of religious life, but rather, in the case of certain missionaries, an integral part of their mystical identity.

It is possible that the missionaries in New France were influenced by Louis Lallemant's doctrine, which was carried to New France by former students of his, who in their capacity as spiritual directors possibly transmitted his ideas to others in the colony. Many of the Jesuits in Canada had been instructed by Lallemant, who was director of third-year studies at Rouen and whose *Doctrine spirituelle* was adopted by them as a sort of spiritual manifesto.[23] Lallemant's stress on the primacy of infused contemplation for apostolic service led him to see this infused grace as a necessary prerequisite for the demanding apostolic vocation, so much so that he felt everything, including one's own initiative for active service, should be subordinated to the demands of interior prayer. However, perhaps more significant than the spiritual theories of the Jesuits were the spiritual ideals and experiences specific to the missionary venture of New France. In fact, Louis Lallemant himself expressed an ardent desire to travel to Canada to save souls, not only because he saw these souls as "images of God, adorned with the character of his resemblance and saved

[21] De Guibert, "Goûter Dieu, servir Dieu," pp. 337–353.
[22] Thwaites, *Jesuit Relations*, vol. 10, p. 98.
[23] See F. Roustang, *Jésuites de la Nouvelle France*, Paris 1961.

by the blood of his son," but also because of the hardship symbolized by the Canadian mission — one which was in his view "more fertile in labour and crosses" than others.[24] For Marie de l'Incarnation, as for others, the missionary call was a special form of service since, by bringing the Gospel message to distant lands, they were actively furthering the course of salvation history. This vocation was for some also the result of an interior illumination which meant release from spiritual turmoil.

Making a case for New World spirituality is not a simple task, given the subject matter. The past, as we know, is a foreign country; Amerindian tribal life, as we can imagine, is most certainly a foreign culture; and mysticism is, for most, a decidedly alien concept. Indeed, Paul Le Jeune's remark that "when a person first visits a country, he writes a great many things upon the words of others," neatly sums up the predicament of historians — including historians of spirituality — who must rely on the content and categories of earlier studies when making their own foray into the past. Fortunately, however, just as the original discovery of the New World taught European thinkers that old views must make way for new interpretations, the rediscovery of the New World in historical documents and travel literature has, in our own day, led scholars in all fields to be more innovative than ever in their approach to historical enquiry.[25] Certainly, the recent flurry of research activity on New World topics, inspired by the quincentenary of Columbus' arrival in the New World, has highlighted a very basic rule of thumb — namely that, like the explorers of yesteryear, today's modern travellers should not rely exclusively on the "words of others" as their tools of interpretation.

This is an obvious comment, but a pertinent one for students of mysticism, for although the history of spirituality has come of age in academe, it is a fledgling discipline of sorts, still groping for guidelines, if not definitions, as to its subject matter and methods.[26] Studies of mystical texts are heavily dependent on the existing, traditional secondary literature, which is very useful inasmuch as it provides background information and the

[24] L. Lallemant, *Doctrine spirituelle*, Paris 1959, p. 52.

[25] Michel De Certeau refers to travel narratives and missionary accounts as "interdisciplinary laboratories" which help us to investigate the relation between "systems of interpretation" and "their historical contexts." See "Travel Narratives of the French to Brazil: Sixteenth to Eighteenth Centuries," in *Representations* 33 (1991), pp. 221–222; Greenblatt, *Marvellous Possessions*; and T. Todorov, *The Conquest of America: The Question of the Other*, trans. R. Howard, New York 1984.

[26] See P. Sheldrake, *Spirituality and History. Questions of Interpretation and Method*, London 1991, pp. 5–6.

conceptual framework which enhance our understanding of the context of spiritual writing. But, as current research in the field of Jewish mysticism has made clear, many of the preconceptions engendered by earlier "classic" studies have clouded our perspective, and new approaches are required.[27] Most recently, Bernard McGinn has stressed the need for a more complete and critical knowledge of the history of Christian mysticism as the basis for an adequate theology of mysticism as a phenomenon. In the first volume of his planned four-volume history of Christian mysticism, he points to the impasse that still exists between empirical and transempirical assumptions in the reading of mystical texts, and welcomes new theological perspectives in Catholic studies on mysticism which challenge traditional views on spirituality. However, he acknowledges that the implications of these new theological directions for the interpretation of mysticism have yet to be spelt out, and though he himself suggests new terms of reference for discussing mysticism, he postpones his justification of the terminology to a later volume.[28]

The Catholic Reformation in all its manifestations marked a water-shed in the history of the Church, and it has been argued that spiritual trends in the sixteenth and seventeenth centuries are the key to understanding this period.[29] Traditional descriptive histories of spiritual literature and analytical spiritual theologies are plentiful and provide an essential starting point for a study of any spiritual text, but this material should be supplemented by a close consideration of the personal concerns expressed by spiritual writers. Since there is a common assumption that mystical writing in the Christian tradition adheres to and is to a certain extent prescribed by normative rules and patterns, interpretation has often meant comparing texts to well-known and well-established schemes, images and concepts from the existing literary tradition.[30] It is not surprising, then, that as a Catholic Reformation "contemplative in action," Marie has been referred to as the "Teresa of New France"; it is easy to see spiritual accounts such as her *Relation de 1654* as traditional, even predictable devotional material.[31]

Given the cultural embeddedness and religious horizons of a given mystic, traditional theological concepts and spiritual concerns obviously

---

[27] See M. Idel, *Kabbala: New Perspectives*, New Haven 1988, pp. xi–xx, 11–16; and Y. Libes, "Kivunnim hadashim ba'heker ha'kabbala" *Pa'amim* 50 (1992), pp. 150–170.

[28] B. McGinn, *The Foundations of Mysticism*. Vol. 1 of *The Presence of God: A History of Western Christian Mysticism*, London 1992, pp. xiii–xx, 267–291, 343.

[29] H.O. Evennett, *The Spirit of the Counter-Reformation*, Cambridge 1968.

[30] Katz, *Mysticism and Religious Traditions*, pp. 23, 35.

[31] Huijben, "La Thérèse de la Nouvelle-France," pp. 106–111.

constitute a large part of his or her self-image and, by extension, will surface in an interpretation of their writing. However, the primary purpose of Marie de l'Incarnation when composing her life story was not to represent tradition and pass on inherited patterns but rather to express the meaning which she herself gleaned from her experience in her given situation. Rather than being seen as holding up the mirror to tradition, then, such spiritual expression should be read for what it is: expression. Indeed, if we follow one of the basic assumptions of both language theory in general and the history of autobiography in particular, namely, that literary expression is constitutive of thought, then a spiritual text like Marie's *Relation* should not be seen as a static example of religious literature or a compilation of fine points of mystical theology, but first and foremost as an attempt to make manifest the specific meaning of her personal experience, as a widowed mother working in a transport company, as a contemplative nun living in a monastery, and as a Christian missionary in the New World.[32]

I have thus sought to understand the spiritual expression of Marie de l'Incarnation in terms of her own assessment and self-understanding and not exclusively in relation to traditional patterns of spiritual theology. Culture, especially religious culture, deals with the meanings which individuals confer on their experience. These meanings may have traditional roots, but they also express the moods and motivations of people living in specific situations in given times and places. Taking into account the particular circumstances or self-understanding of mystics, or trying to look at their religious life from their point of view is not incompatible with, and certainly does not entail the rejection of the substance of earlier studies whose methodology was different, more theoretical; but as Charles Cohen has noted with regard to the formation of spiritual identity in Puritan New England, traditional teaching had the first word, but not the last.[33] The study of spiritual literature, then, can be fruitfully pursued if spirituality is seen as part of a cultural system; as Clifford Geertz has defined it, this consists in a creative act of meaning-formation, in which individuals commonly use inherited conceptions or symbols to sustain their sense of human orientation, while at the same time imbuing these traditional patterns with new meanings gleaned from their specific milieu or personal experience.[34]

[32] See the introduction to C. Taylor, *Philosophy and the Human Sciences, Philosophical Papers*, 2 vols., vol. 2, Cambridge 1985, esp. pp. 3–5.

[33] Cohen, *God's Caress*, p. 21.

[34] Geertz, "Religion as a Cultural System," p. 89.

The simple claim that "no one returns unchanged from an encounter with the other" was a guiding principle of Michel De Certeau's work in his last years, and it can aptly be applied to the study of spiritual texts by missionaries such as Marie de l'Incarnation, whose encounter with the Amerindians affected their perceived encounter with God.[35] The particular features of her spirituality are closely linked with her shifting images of the "other" — that is, both God the sublime "other" experienced in mystical life, and the native Indian, the concrete "other" encountered in day-to-day life. Her writings not only shed light on the impact of the New World on attitudes to culture and religious experience, but insofar as they inject new substance into a long-standing spiritual tradition rather than merely reflecting its inherited patterns, they also suggest the need for a broader, more varied spectrum of typologies of mystical experience in the Christian tradition.

This study of Marie de l'Incarnation has dealt with two kinds of encounter: the first, the encounter between European missionaries and the natives of the New World, and the second — admittedly one of a less tangible nature — the encounter between religious individuals and God. What missionary writings from New France make clear is that in order to make sense of strange encounters it was becoming increasingly important for individuals to trust personal experience rather than relying exclusively on prevailing conceptions or traditional rules. Paul Le Jeune's rueful comment that if Christians were to execute "all their divine inspirations with as much care as our Savages carry out their dreams, no doubt they would very soon become great Saints," indicates that native culture gave the missionaries ample food for thought regarding both the harvest of souls and the sanctification of souls.[36] Indeed, Marie's portrayal of herself as a missionary and contemplative in New France suggests that at a time when the Catholic Church was busy delegating watch-dogs to monitor and regulate all spheres of Catholic life — from basic morals to complex theological points, from mystical claims of individuals to the collective enterprise of the overseas missions — there was still room for individuals to follow their own instincts and listen to their own dreams with regard to religious experience, be it in the conversion of others, or in their own ongoing spiritual conversion.

[35] L. Giard, "Michel De Certeau's Heterology and the New World," *Representations* 33 (1991), p. 216.
[36] Thwaites, *Jesuit Relations*, vol. 10, p. 169.

BIBLIOGRAPHY

A. WORKS BY MARIE DE L'INCARNATION

Jamet, A., ed. *Marie de l'Incarnation, Ursuline de Tours: Fondatrice des Ursulines de la Nouvelle-France, Écrits spirituels et historiques.* 2 vols. (Tours & Québec). (1929) Québec: Les Ursulines de Québec, 1985.

Mahoney, I., ed. *Marie of the Incarnation: Selected Writings.* New York: Paulist Press, 1985.

Marshall, J., trans. and ed. *Word from New France. The Selected Letters of Marie de l'Incarnation.* Toronto: Oxford University Press, 1967.

Martin, Claude. *La Vie de la Vénérable Mère Marie de l'Incarnation, Première Supérieure des Ursulines de la Nouvelle-France, tirée de ses lettres et ses écrits.* (1677) Repr. Solesmes-Paris: Jouve, 1982.

Oury, Guy-Marie, ed. *Marie de l'Incarnation, Ursuline (1599–1672), Corréspondance.* Solesmes: Abbaye Saint-Pierre, 1971.

Sullivan, J., trans. *The Autobiography of Venerable Marie of the Incarnation, O.S.U. Mystic and Missionary.* Chicago: Loyola University Press, 1964.

B. STUDIES ON MARIE DE L'INCARNATION

Adriazola, M.-P. del Rosario. *La connaissance spirituelle chez Marie de l'Incarnation, la "Thérèse du Nouveau-Monde."* Paris: Cerf, 1989.

Boucher, G. *Du Centre à la Croix. Marie de l'Incarnation (1599–1672). Symbolique spirituelle.* Montréal: Fides, 1976.

Bremond, Henri. *Histoire littéraire du sentiment religieux en France depuis la fin des guerres jusqu'à nos jours.* Vol. 6. La Conquête mystique, Marie de l'Incarnation, pp. 3–176. Paris: Bloud et Gay, 1923.

Chabot, M.-E. *Marie de l'Incarnation d'après ses lettres.* Ottawa: Éditions de l'Université d'Ottawa, 1946.

Cuzin, Henri. *Du Christ à la Trinité d'après l'expérience mystique de Marie de l'Incarnation, Ursuline de Tours et de Québec.* Lyon: Librairie du Sacré-Coeur, 1936.

Deslandres, D. "L'éducation des Amérindiennes d'après la corréspondance de Marie Guyart de l'Incarnation." *Sciences Religieuses,* 16/1 (1987), 91–110.

Ganay, M.C. De. "Une femme missionnaire au Canada: la Vénérable Mère Marie de l'Incarnation, ursuline." *La Vie spirituelle,* 7 (1922), 207–231, 309–328.

Huijben, J. "La Thérèse de la Nouvelle-France." *Supplément à la Vie spirituelle,* 22 (1930), 97–128.

Jetté, F. "L'Itinéraire spirituel de Marie de l'Incarnation. Vocation apostolique et mariage mystique." *La Vie spirituelle,* 92 (1955), 618–643.

—— "L'oraison apostolique de Marie de l'Incarnation." *Spiritus*, 6 (1965), 55–66.
—— *The Spiritual Teaching of Mary of the Incarnation*. Trans. Mother M. Herman. Montréal: Palm, 1963.
Klein, J. *L'Itinéraire mystique de la Vénérable Mère Marie de l'Incarnation, Ursuline de Tours et de Québec, 1599–1672*. Paris: Dillen, 1938.
Labelle, S. *L'Esprit apostolique d'après Marie de l'Incarnation*. Ottawa: Éditions de l'Université d'Ottawa, 1968.
Lonsagne, J. "Les écrits spirituels de Marie de l'Incarnation. Le problème des textes." *Revue d'Ascétique et de Mystique*, 44 (1968), 161–182.
Lubac, Henri De. "Marie de l'Incarnation et la Sainte Vierge." In *Maria, études sur la Sainte Vierge, sous la direction d'Hubert Du Maunoir*. Vol. 3. Paris: Beauchesne, 1954, pp. 3–60.
Michel, R. *Vivre dans l'Esprit: Marie de l'Incarnation*. Montréal: Bellarmin, 1975.
Oury, Guy-Marie. "Action et contemplation chez Marie de l'Incarnation." *Église et Théologie*, 3 (1984), 203–216.
—— *Ce que croyait Marie de l'Incarnation et comment elle vivait de sa foi*. Paris: Mame, 1972.
—— "Jeanne Mance, Marie de l'Incarnation et Mme. de la Peltrie." *Bulletin de la Société historique et archéologique de Langres*, 14 (1968), 322–337.
—— Marie de l'Incarnation (1599–1672). Sablé-sur-Sarthe: Abbaye Saint-Pierre, 1973.
—— "Marie de l'Incarnation et la bibliothèque du noviciat des Ursulines de Québec." *Revue d'Ascétique et de Mystique*, 46 (1970), 397–410.
—— "Pour une meilleure connaissance de la formation spirituelle de Marie de l'Incarnation; le mouvement de restauration catholique en Touraine, 1599–1639." *Église et Théologie*, 1 (1970), 39–59, 171–204.
Pénido, M.T.-L. "Marie de l'Incarnation. Aperçus psychologiques sur son mysticisme." *Nova et vetera*, 10 (1935), 397–430.
Rayez, A. "Marie de l'Incarnation et le climat spirituel de la Nouvelle-France." *Revue d'Histoire de l'Amérique française*, 16 (1962), 3–36.
Renaudin, P. *Une grande mystique française au XVIIe siècle. Marie de l'Incarnation, Ursuline de Tours et de Québec. Essai de psychologie religieuse*. Paris: Bloud et Gay, 1935.
Rétif, A. "Marie de l'Incarnation et la Mission." *La Vie spirituelle*, 91 (1954), 175–192.
—— Marie de l'Incarnation et la mission. Tours: Mame, 1964.
Thiry, A. *Marie de l'Incarnation. Itinéraire spirituel*. Paris: Beauchesne, 1973.

C. SECONDARY LITERATURE

d'Acreigne, C. *Récit véritable de la deffaite des trouppes de Mr. le prince par Mr. le duc de Guise, le septiesme de ce mois. Ensemble le départ du roy pour venir à Tours*. Paris: S. Lescuyer, 1616.
Ariès, P. *Centuries of Childhood*. Trans. R. Baldick. London: Jonathan Cape, 1962.
Armstrong, C.J.R. *Evelyn Underhill (1875–1941)*. London: Mowbray, 1975.
Aubin, P. *Le problème de la conversion*. Paris: Beauchesne, 1963.

Augustine. *The Confessions of St. Augustine*. Trans. R. Warner. New York: Mentor, 1963.

Aumann, J. *Spiritual Theology*. London: Sheed & Ward, 1980.

Axtell, J. *After Columbus: Essays in the Ethnohistory of Colonial North America*. Oxford: Oxford University Press, 1988.

—— *Beyond 1492: Encounters in Colonial North America*. Oxford: Oxford University Press, 1992.

—— *The Invasion Within: The Contest of Cultures in Colonial North America*. Oxford: Oxford University Press, 1985.

—— "Were Indian Conversions Bona Fide?" In *After Columbus: Essays in the Ethnohistory of Colonial North America*. Oxford: Oxford University Press, 1988, pp. 100–121.

Balthasar, Hans U. von. *The Glory of the Lord. A Theological Aesthetics*. Vol. 3. Seeing the Form. Trans. E. Leiva-Merikakis. Eds. J. Fessio and J. Riches. Edinburgh: T. & T. Clark, 1982.

Beckford, J. "Accounting for Conversion." *British Journal of Sociology*, 29/2 (1978), 249–260.

Bell, R. H. "The aesthetic factor in art and religion." *Religious Studies*, 22 (1986), pp. 181–192.

Bernard, C.-A. *Traité de théologie spirituelle*. Paris: Cerf, 1986.

Bernier, H. *Marguerite Bourgeoys*. Montréal: Collections classiques canadiens, no. 3, 1958.

Bollème, G. *La Bibliothèque bleue. Anthologie d'une littérature "populaire."* Paris: Flammarion, 1973.

Bossy, J. "The Counter-Reformation and the People of Catholic Europe." *Past and Present*, 47 (1970), 51–70.

Boucher, G. *Le premier visage de l'église du Canada. Profil d'une église naissante. La Nouvelle-France 1608–1688*. Montréal: Bellarmin, 1986.

Bouyer, L. *The Spirit and Forms of Protestantism*. Trans. A.V. Littledale. London: Harvill, 1956.

Bremond, Henri. *Histoire littéraire du sentiment religieux en France depuis la fin des guerres de religion jusqu'à nos jours*. 12 vols. Paris: Bloud et Gay, 1924–1936.

—— *Literary History of Religious Thought in France*. 3 vols. Trans. K. Montgomery. London: SPCK, 1928–1936.

Briggs, R. *Communities of Belief. Cultural and Social Tensions in Early Modern France*. Oxford: Oxford University Press, 1989.

—— *Early Modern France 1560–1715*. Oxford: Oxford University Press, 1977.

—— "*Idées* and *Mentalités*; the case of the Catholic reform movement in France." *History of European Ideas*, 7 (1986), 9–19.

Brown, J. *Immodest Acts. The Life of a Lesbian Nun in Renaissance Italy*. Oxford: Oxford University Press, 1986.

Brown, P. *Augustine of Hippo. A Biography*. London: Faber, 1967.

—— "A Dark-Age Crisis: Aspects of the Iconoclastic Controversy." *English Historical Review*, 88 (1973), 1–34.

Bruss, E.W. *Autobiographical Acts: The Changing Situation of a Literary Genre*. Baltimore: 1976.

Campeau, L. *Les Cent-Associés et le peuplement de la Nouvelle-France (1633–1663)*. Montréal: Bellarmin, 1974.
—ed. *Monumenta Novae Franciae*. 5 vols. Roma: Apud "Monumenta Hist. Soc. Jesu," 1967–
Carrithers, M., S. Collins, and S. Lukes. eds. *The Category of the Person. Anthropology, Philosophy, History*. Cambridge: Cambridge University Press, 1985.
Certeau, Michel De. *La Fable Mystique. XVIe–XVIIe siècle*. Paris: Gallimard, 1982.
—"Travel Narratives of the French to Brazil — 16th to 18th Centuries." *Representations*, 33 (1991), 221–226.
Chadwick, O. *The Reformation*. Harmondsworth: Penguin, rev. ed. 1973.
Chartier, R. *The Cultural Uses of Print in Early Modern France*. Trans. L. Cochrane. Princeton: Princeton University Press, 1987.
Chartier, R., D. Julia, and M. Compère. *L'éducation en France du XVIe au XVIIe siècle*. Paris: SEDES, 1976.
Chemnitz, Martin. *Examination of the Council of Trent*. (1565) 2 vols. Trans. F. Kramer. St. Louis: Concordia Publishing House, 1971.
Clark, M.T. "The Trinity in Latin Christianity." In *Christian Spirituality: Origins to the Twelfth Century*. Eds. B. McGinn & J. Meyendorff. New York: Crossroad, 1985, 276–290.
Cognet, L. *Crépuscule des mystiques. Le Conflit Fénelon-Bossuet*. Tournai: Desclée, 1958.
Cohen, C. *God's Caress. The Psychology of Puritan Religious Experience*. Oxford: Oxford University Press, 1986.
La Conversion au XVIIe Siècle. Actes du XIIe Colloque de Marseille, C.M.R. 17, 1983.
Courcelle, P. *Les Confessions de Saint Augustin dans la tradition littéraire. Antécédents et Postérité*. Paris: Études Augustiniens, 1963.
Dagens, J. *Bibliographie chronologique de la littérature de spiritualité et de ses sources, 1501–1610*. Paris: Bruges, 1953.
Davis, N.Z. *Society and Change in Early Modern France*. Stanford: Stanford University Press, 1975.
Delumeau, J. *Catholicism between Luther and Voltaire: a new view of the Counter-Reformation*. Trans. J. Moiser. London: Burns & Oates, 1977.
— *Le catholicisme entre Luther et Voltaire*. Paris: P.U.P., 1971.
— "Missions de l'intérieur au XVIIe siècle." In *Un chemin d'histoire. Chrétienté et christianisation*. Paris: 1981, 154–187.
Dickason, O. *The Myth of the Savage and the Beginnings of French Colonialism in the Americas*. Edmonton: University of Alberta Press, 1984.
Dicken, E. W. Trueman. "Teresa of Jesus and John of the Cross." In *The Study of Spirituality*. Eds. C. Jones et al. London: SPCK, 1986. 363–376.
Dickens, A.G. *The Counter-Reformation*. New York: Norton, 1979.
Dilthey, W. *Gesammelte Schriften*. Vol. 7. *Der Aufbau der geistlichen Welt in den Geisteswissenschaften*. Göttingen: Vandenhoeck & Ruprecht, 1979.
XVIIe siècle. 41 (1958).
Dompnier, B. "Le débat sur les images dans la France du XVIIe siècle." *History of European Ideas*, 9 (1988), 423–441.

Egan, H. *What are They Saying About Mysticism?* New York: Paulist Press, 1982.

Elliott, J.H. *The Old World and the New. 1492–1650.* Cambridge: Cambridge University Press, (1970), new ed. 1992.

Evennett, H.O. *The Spirit of the Counter-Reformation.* Cambridge: Cambridge University Press, 1968.

Febvre, L. *Life in Renaissance France.* Ed. and trans. M. Rothstein. Cambridge, Mass.: Harvard University Press, 1977.

Fish, S.E. *Self-consuming Artifacts. The Experience of Seventeenth-Century Literature.* Berkeley: University of California Press, 1972.

François de Sales. *Introduction to the Devout Life.* Trans. J. Ryan. New York: Harper & Row, 1966.

Fredriksen, P. "Paul and Augustine: Conversion narratives, orthodox traditions and the retrospective self." *Journal of Theological Studies,* N.S. 37 pt. 1 (1986), 3–34.

Gagnon, F.-M. *La conversion par l'image. Un aspect de la mission des jésuites auprès des Indiens du Canada au XVIIe siècle.* Montréal: Bellarmin, 1975.

Gagnon, F.-M. and N. Cloutier. *Premiers Peintres de la Nouvelle-France.* Vol. 1. Québec: Ministère des affaires culturelles, repr. 1982.

Geertz, C. "Religion as a Cultural System." In *The Interpretation of Cultures. Selected Essays.* New York: Basic Books, 1973, pp. 87–125.

Giard, L. "Michel De Certeau's Heterology and the New World." *Representations,* 33 (1991), 212–221.

Gimello, R. "Mysticism in its Contexts." In *Mysticism and Religious Traditions.* Ed. S. Katz. Oxford: Oxford University Press, 1983, pp. 61–88.

Ginzburg, C. "High and Low: The Theme of Forbidden Knowledge in the Sixteenth and Seventeenth Centuries." *Past and Present,* 73 (1970), 28–41.

"Gloire de Dieu." *Dictionnaire de Spiritualité.* vol. 6, pp. 421–487.

Graham, V.E. and W. McAllister Johnson. *The Paris Entrées of Charles IX and Elisabeth of Austria, 1571.* Toronto: University of Toronto Press, 1954.

Grant, J. *Moon of Wintertime: Missionaries and the Indians of Canada in Encounter since 1534.* Toronto: University of Toronto Press, 1984.

Greenblatt, S. *Marvellous Possessions. The Wonder of the New World.* Oxford: Oxford University Press, 1992.

Gueudré, M. de Chantal. *Histoire de l'Ordre des Ursulines en France.* 2 vols. Paris: 1957–1960.

Guibert, J. De. "Goûter Dieu, servir Dieu." *Revue d'Ascétique et de Mystique,* 7 (1926), 337–353.

—— *The Jesuits. Their Spiritual Doctrine and Practice.* Trans. W. Young. Ed. G. Ganss. 3rd Printing. St. Louis: Institute of Jesuit Sources, 1986.

—— "'Mystique'." *Revue d'Ascétique et de Mystique,* 7 (1926), 3–16.

—— *The Theology of the Spiritual Life.* Trans. P. Barret. London: Sheed & Ward, 1954.

Haas, Alois. *Sermo mysticus. Studien zu Theologie und Sprache der deutschen Mystik.* Freiburg: Universitätsverlag, 1979.

Hallowell, A.T. *The Role of Conjuring in Saulteaux Society.* Philadelphia: University of Pennsylvania Press, 1942.

Happold, F.C. *Mysticism. A Study and Anthology.* Harmondsworth: Penguin, repr. 1971.

Hay, D. *Annalists and Historians: Western Historiography from the Eighth to the Eighteenth Centuries.* London: Methuen, 1977.

Hazard, P. *The European Mind.* Trans. J. Lewis May. Harmondsworth: Penguin, 1973.

Heirich, M. "Change of Heart." *American Journal of Sociology,* 83 (1977), 653–680.

Hodgen, M. *Early Anthropology in the Sixteenth and Seventeenth Centuries.* Philadelphia: University of Pennsylvania Press, 1964.

Idel, M. *Kabbala: New Perspectives.* New Haven: Yale University Press, 1988.

Ignatius Loyola. *The Spiritual Exercises of St. Ignatius based on Studies in the Language of the Autograph.* Trans. L. Puhl. Chicago: Loyola University Press, 1950.

Jaeger, W. *Early Christianity and Greek Paideia.* London: Oxford University Press, 1962.

Johnston, W. *The Mysticism of the Cloud of Unknowing.* New York: Desclée, 1967.

Jones, C. et al., eds. *The Study of Spirituality.* London: SPCK, 1986.

Katz, S. "The 'Conservative' Character of Mysticism." In *Mysticism and Religious Traditions.* Oxford: Oxford University Press, 1983, pp. 3–60.

—— Ed. *Mysticism and Religious Traditions.* Oxford: Oxford University Press, 1983.

Knowles, D. *What is Mysticism?* London: Burnes & Oates, 1967.

Kolakowski, L. *Religion.* London: Fontana, 1982.

Krailsheimer, A.J. *Conversion.* London: SCM, 1980.

Ladner, G.B. *The Idea of Reform: Its Impact on Christian Thought and Action in the Age of the Fathers.* Cambridge, Mass.: Harvard University Press, 1959.

Lafontaine, J.S. "Person and individual: some anthropological reflections." In *The Category of the Person. Anthropology, Philosophy, History.* Eds. M. Carrithers, S. Collins, and S. Lukes. Cambridge: Cambridge University Press, 1985, pp. 123–140.

Latourette, K. S. *A History of the Expansion of Christianity.* Vol. 3. Three Centuries of Advance. A.D. 1500–A.D. 1800. New York: Harper, 1939.

Latreille, A., E. Delaruelle, and J.-R. Palanque. *Histoire du catholicisme en France sous les rois très chrétiens.* 3 vols. Paris: Spes, 1957.

Leclercq, J. "La royauté du Christ dans la spiritualité français du XVIIe siècle." *La Vie spirituelle,* Supplément I (1947), 216–229, 291–307.

—— Intro. to *The Roots of the Modern Christian Tradition.* Ed. E.R. Elder. Kalamazoo: Cistercian Publications, 1984, pp. x–xi.

Lescarbot, M. *The History of New France.* Trans. W.L. Grant. Toronto: The Champlain Society, 1807–1814.

Leeuw, G. van der. *Religion in Essence & Manifestation. A Study in Phenomenology...* Trans. J.E. Turner. London: G. Allen & Unwin, 1938.

Libes, Y. "Kivvunim hadashim ba'heker ha'kabbala." *Pa'amim* 50 (1992), 150–170.

Lofland, J. and R. Stark. "Becoming a World Saver: A Theory of Conversion to a Deviant Perspective." *American Sociological Review,* 30 (1965), 862–875.

Longridge, W.H. intro. *The Spiritual Exercises of Saint Ignatius Loyola.* 4th ed. London: Mowbray, 1950.

Lossky, V. *The Vision of God.* London: Faith Press, 1963.

Louth, A. *Discerning the Mystery. An Essay on the Nature of Theology.* Oxford: Clarendon Press, 1983.

—— *The Origins of the Christian Mystical Tradition. From Plato to Denys.* Oxford: Clarendon Press, 1983.

Lovejoy, D. *Religious Enthusiasm in the New World: Heresy to Revolution.* Cambridge: Harvard University Press, 1985.

Luther, M. *Reformation Writings.* Trans. B.L. Woolf. London: Lutterworth, 1937.

Mali, A. "Patterns of Conversion in Christianity." *Studies in Spirituality.* 2 (1992), 209–222.

—— "Strange Encounters: Missionary Activity and Mystical Thought in Seventeenth-Century New France." *History of European Ideas.* 22/2 (1996), pp. 67–92.

Maréchal, J. *Études sur la psychologie des mystiques.* 2 vols., Paris: Desclée de Brouwer, 1937.

Marquis, T.G. *The Jesuit Missions. A Chronicle of the Cross in the Wilderness.* Toronto: University of Toronto Press, repr. 1964.

McGinn, B. *The Presence of God: A History of Western Christian Mysticism.* Vol. 1. The Foundations of Mysticism. New York: Crossroad, 1992.

McGinn, B. and J. Meyendorff, eds. *Christian Spirituality: Origins to the Twelfth Century.* New York: Crossroad, 1985.

Ménard, M. *Une Histoire des mentalités religieuses au XVIIe siècle. Mille retables de l'ancien diocèse du Mans.* Paris: Beauchesne, 1980.

Michel, A. *Les décrets du Concile de Trente.* Paris: Letouzey et Ané, 1938.

Moussé, Ch. *Le Culte de Notre Dame en Touraine.* Tours: Mame, 1915.

Mullett, M. *The Counter-Reformation and the Catholic Reformation in Early Modern Europe.* London: Methuen, 1984.

Neill, S. *A History of the Christian Missions.* London: Penguin, 2nd ed. 1986.

Nock, A.D. *Conversion. The Old and the New in Religion from Alexander the Great to Augustine of Hippo.* Oxford: Oxford University Press, 1960.

Oberman, H. *The Dawn of the Reformation. Essays in Late Medieval and Early Reformation Thought.* Edinburgh: T. & T. Clark, 1986.

—— "*Quo Vadis, Petre?* Tradition from Irenaeus to *Humani Generis.*" In *The Dawn of the Reformation. Essays in Late Medieval and Early Reformation Thought.* Edinburgh: T. & T. Clark, 1986, 269–296.

O'Brien, E. *Varieties of Mystic Experience. An Anthology and Interpretation.* Toronto: Mentor, 1965.

Ohly, F. *Grundzüge einer Geschichte der Hoheliedauslegung des Abendlandes bis um 1200.* Wiesbaden: Steiner, 1958.

Ong, W. "'A.M.D.G.': Dedication or Directive?" *Review for Religious,* 11 (1952), 257–264.

Oury, G.-M. "Le sentiment religieux en Nouvelle-France au XVIIe siècle." *Société Canadienne d'Histoire de l'Église catholique,* Sessions d'étude, 50 (1983).

—— *L'itinéraire mystique de Catherine de Saint-Augustin.* Chambray: C.L.D., 1985.

Pagden, A. "'The Impact of the New World on the Old': The History of an Idea." *Renaissance and Modern Studies.* 30 (1986), 1–11.

Parker, T.M. "The Papacy, Catholic Reform, and Christian Missions." In *The New Cambridge Modern History*. Vol. 3.

Patout-Burns, J. "Grace: The Augustinian Foundation." In *Christian Spirituality: Origins to the Twelfth Century*. Eds. B. McGinn and J. Meyendorff. New York: Crossroad, 1985, pp. 331–348.

Poissant, S. *Marguerite Bourgeoys 1620–1700*. Montréal: 1982.

Poulain, A. *The Graces of Interior Prayer. A Mystical Treatise*. 6th ed. Trans. L. Smith. London: Kegan Paul, Trench, Trubner, 1928.

Pouliot, L. *Études sur les "Relations" des Jésuites de la Nouvelle-France (1632–1672)*. Paris: Desclée, 1940.

—— *Le Père Paul Le Jeune S.J. (1591–1664). Textes choisis et présentés par Léon Pouliot*. Paris: 1957.

Rambo, L. "Current Research on Religious Conversion." *Religious Studies Review*, 8 (1982), 146–159.

—— "Conversion." *Encyclopedia of Religion*. Vol. XVI, pp. 73–79.

Reardon, B. *Religious Thought in the Reformation*. London: Longman, 1980.

Rees, D. et al. *Consider your Call. A Theology of Monastic Life Today*. London: SPCK, 1978.

Richard of St. Victor. *The Twelve Patriarchs. The Mystical Ark. Book Three of the Trinity*. Trans. and intro. G.A. Zinn. London: SPCK, 1979.

Richeome, L. *Trois discours pour la religion catholique: des Miracles; des Saincts; & des Images*. Paris: Jamet et Metayer, 1602.

Ricoeur, P. "Structure, Word, Event." Trans. R. Sweeney. In *The Conflict of Interpretations. Essays in Hermeneutics*. Ed. D. Ihde. Evanston: Northwestern University Press, 1974, pp. 79–96.

Riehle, W. *The Middle English Mystics*. London: Routledge & Kegan Paul, 1981.

Roustang, F. *Jésuites de la Nouvelle France*. Paris: 1961.

Roy, P.-G. *A travers l'histoire des Ursulines de Québec*. Lévis: 1939.

Runggaldier, E. "Bericht: interdisziplinäres Seminar zur Anthropologie." *Zeitschrift für Katholische Theologie*, 109 (1987).

"Sacred Heart." *A Dictionary of Christian Spirituality*. Ed. G. Wakefield. London: SCM, 1983, pp. 347–348.

Sandeus, M. *Pro theologica mystica clavis*. Köln (1640) repr. Heverlee-Louvain: Ed. de la Bibliothèque SJ, 1963.

Sanctis. S. De. *Religious Conversion: a bio-psychological study*. Trans. H. Augur. New York: Harcourt, Brace & Co., 1927.

Scholem, G. *Major Trends in Jewish Mysticism*. New York: Schocken, 1941.

Sheldrake, P. *Spirituality and History. Questions of Interpretation and Method*. New York: Crossroad, 1991.

Skinner, Q. "Language and Social Change." In *Meaning in Context*, ed. J. Tooley. Princeton: Princeton University Press, 1985.

Spence, J.D. *The Memory Palace of Matteo Ricci*. New York: Viking, 1984.

Spitz, L.W. "Reformation." *Dictionary of the History of Ideas*. Vol. IV, pp. 60–69.

Taylor, C. "The Person." In *The Category of the Person. Anthropology, Philosophy, History*. Eds. M. Carrithers, S. Collins, and S. Lukes. Cambridge: Cambridge University Press, 1985, pp. 257–281.

—— "Self-Interpreting Animals." In *Human Agency and Language. Philosophical Papers*. 2 vols. Vol. 1. Cambridge: Cambridge University Press, 1985, pp. 45–76.

Teresa of Avila. *The Interior Castle*. Trans. K. Kavanaugh and O. Rodriguez. New York: Paulist Press, 1979.

—— *The Life of Saint Teresa by Herself*. Trans. J.M. Cohen. Harmondsworth: Penguin, reiss. 1987.

Thwaites, R.G. ed. *The Jesuit Relations and Allied Documents*. 73 vols. Cleveland: Burrows Bros., 1876–1901.

Todorov, T. *The Conquest of America: The Question of the Other*. Trans. R. Howard, New York: 1984.

Trigger, B.G. *The Children of Aataentsic: A History of the Huron People to 1660*. 2 vols. Montreal: McGill-Queen's University Press, 1976.

—— *Natives and Newcomers: Canada's "Heroic Age" Reconsidered*. Montreal: McGill-Queen's University Press, 1986.

Trudel, Marcel. *The Beginnings of New France, 1524–1663*. Toronto: McClelland & Stewart, 1973.

Underhill, E. *Mysticism. A Study in the Nature and Development of Man's Spiritual Consciousness*. (1955) New York: Meridian, repr. 1974.

Underwood, A.C. *Conversion Christian and non-Christian, a comparative and psychological study*. New York: Macmillan, 1925.

Warner, M. *Alone of All Her Sex. The Myth and the Cult of the Virgin Mary*. London: Quartet, 1978.

Vovelle, M. "La conversion par l'image: Des vanités aux fins dernières en passant par le macabre dans l'Iconographie du XVIIe siècle." In *La Conversion au XVIIe Siècle. Actes du XIIe Colloque de Marseille*. C.M.R. 17: 1983, pp. 297–310.

Ware, T. *The Orthodox Church*. Harmondsworth: Penguin, 1963.

Weintraub, K. *The Value of the Individual. Self and Circumstance in Autobiography*. Chicago: University of Chicago Press, 1978.

Wilenski, R.H. *French Painting*. London: The Medici Society, 1931.

Wright, M. "François de Sales: Gentleness and Civility." In *The Roots of the Modern Christian Tradition*. Ed. E.R. Elder. Kalamazoo: Cistercian Publications, 1984, pp. 124–144.

Wynne, J. *The Jesuit Martyrs of North America*. New York: Universal Knowledge Foundation, 1935.

Zakai, Avihu. *Exile and Kingdom: History and Apocalypse in the Puritan Migration to America*. Cambridge: Cambridge University Press, 1992.

INDEX OF NAMES

Acadia, 111
d'Acreigne, C., 16n.
Adriazola, M.-P. del Rosario, 136n.
Ariès, P., 18, 19
Armstrong, C.J.R., 58n.
Arnauld, A., 50
Aubin, P., 36n.
Augustine, 39, 47, 53, 59n., 60, 85, 146
Aumann, J., 147n.
Axtell, J., 111n., 123n., 127n., 131, 132n.

Babous de la Bourdaisière, 13
Balthasar, H.U. von, 159n., 160, 161,
Beaumont-les-Tours, 40
Bell, R.H., 145
Bernard, C.-A., 2n.
Bernard of Clairvaux, 141n.
Bernier, H., 168n.
Bérulle, P. de, 22, 149, 166
Bossuet, 19
Bossy, J., 5n., 6n., 8n., 14n., 20n.
Boucher, G., 119n., 122n., 166n.
Bourgeoys, M., 168
Bouyer, L., 6n.
Brébeuf, J. de, 115, 168, 169
Bremond, H., xvi, 19n., 38n., 50n., 62-3n., 69n., 150n.
Briggs, R., 5n., 7, 16n., 49n.
Brown, J., 59, 146n.
Brown, P., 4, 10n., 50n., 53, 114
Bruss, E., 60n.
Bruyas, J., 105-6

Campeau, L., 101n., 110n.
Canada, 73-4, 91, 93, 105, 119
Carlini, B., 146n.
Cartier, J., 111

Catherine de St. Augustin, 167-8
Catherine of Siena, 40, 67n.
Certeau, M. De, 38n., 159, 170n., 173
Chadwick, O., 10, 12
Champlain, S. de, 111
Chantal, C.-B. de, 50
Chantal, J. de, 50
Chartier, R., 2n., 6n., 18n.
Chartier, R. et al., 37n.
Chemnitz, M., 9–10
Chomedey, P. de, 168
Clark, M.T., 81n., 83n., 85n.
Cognet, L., 38n.
Cohen, C., xivn., 172
Colombe, M., 13
Columbus, 170
Courcelle, P., 39n.
Cousins, E., 58n.
Cuzin, H., 62n., 63n., 84, 154n.

Dagens, J., 38n.
Davis, N.Z., 6n., 11
Delumeau, J., 12n., 30n., 37n.
Deslandres, D., 122n.
Dickason, O., xivn., 112n.
Dicken, E.W. Trueman, 47n., 66n.
Dickens, A.G., 5n.
Dilthey, W., 62n.
Dinet, J., 50
Dompnier, B., 10n.

Egan, H., 58n.
Elliott, J.H., 104n.
Evennett, H.O., 171n.

Febvre, L., 10–11
Fish, S.E., 160n.
Francis de Paola, 14

François de Sales, 50, 144n., 149
Fredriksen, P., 59n.

Gagnon, F.-M., 128–9n.
Gagnon, F.-M. and N. Cloutier, 129n.
Garnier, C., 129n.
Geertz, C., 33n., 123, 145, 172
Gertrude of Helfta, 40
Giard, L., 173n.
Gimello, R., 69n.
Ginzburg, C., 5n.
Graham, V.E. and W. McAllister
    Johnson, 16n.
Greenblatt, S., 102, 170n.
Gueudré, M. de C., 95n.
Guibert, J. De, 47n., 56n., 76n., 94n.,
    169n.
Guyart, F., 13
Guyart, M., 13. See also Marie de
    l'Incarnation

Haas, A., 48n., 135n., 159–60
Happold, F.C., 58n.
Hay, D., 36n.
Haye, G. de la, 96
Hazard, P., 2n., 39n.
Heirich, M., 33n.
Hodgen, M., 109n.
Huijben, Dom J., 22, 45n., 54n., 99n.,
    171n.

Idel, M., 171n.
Ignatius Loyola, 55, 166

Jaeger, W., 3, 4, 79
Jaenen, C., 111n., 166n.
Jamet, Dom A., xvi–xviin., 46, 48n.,
    50n., 58n., 78n., 139n., 143n.
Jetté, F., 62n., 97n., 99n., 135n., 136n.
Jogues, I., 168
John of the Cross, 73n., 153n.

Katz, S., xvn., 53n., 69n., 86n., 171n.
Knowles, D., 86n., 94n., 145n.
Kolakowski, L., 33n.
Krailsheimer, A.J., 45n., 46n.

Labelle, S., 134n.
Ladner, G.B., 4n.
Lafontaine, J.S., 1n.
Lalemant, J., 115
Lallemant, L., 46, 149n., 169–70
La Peltrie, M.-M. de Chauvigny de,
    74, 101, 113
Latourette, K. Scott, 108n., 113n.
Latreille, A. et al., 12n., 16n.
Leclercq, J., 4, 16n.
Leeuw, G. van der, 34n.
Leibniz, 2n.
Le Jeune, P., 101, 105, 110, 111, 114,
    121, 122, 124–5, 131, 170
Libes, Y., 171n.
Lonsagne, J., 52n., 150n.
Lossky, V., 152n.
Louis XI, 16
Louis XIII, 15
Louth, A., 3n., 4n., 22–3, 82n., 83n.,
    164n.
Lovejoy, D., xivn.
Lubac, H. De, 28
Luther, M., 8

Maréchal, J., 152
Marie de l'Incarnation,
    active-contemplative identity, xvii,
        62, 71, 73, 89, 91, 94–101, 134,
        139, 162–3
    Amerindians, view of, 103, 74
    apostolic spirit, 73–4, 90
    Catholic upbringing, 1–2, 4,
        17–23
    conversion in her life and writing,
        xvii, 35–55, 62, 63, 78, 103,
        113–19, 125, 133–6, 157, 161–
        3
    glory of God, 146–55, 158
    imitation of Christ, 62, 79, 80, 85
    missionary activity, xvii, 54, 81,
        84, 88, 91, 97–107, 134
    missionary vocation, 73, 90, 97,
        101, 134
    mystical experiences, 27, 41, 48,
        57, 63–76, 90–1, 134
    New France, xiv–xvi, 74, 90–3,

97, 101–7, 150
poverty of spirit, 66, 75, 85
purification, 49, 63–4, 66, 75, 80
revolt of passions, 75
sacraments, 14, 23, 25, 29, 45
salvation of souls, concern for, 91, 97–9, 102–3, 121, 134, 139
Scripture, 22–4
sermons, 22, 24–5, 40
Song of Songs, commentary on, 138–44
spirit of Jesus, 63, 66, 75 80–81, 86, 91
spiritual direction, importance of, 56–7, 60–1, 66, 89, 92, 93, 137, 141–2, 145
spiritual marriage, 67, 68, 84, 87, 88, 95, 140
spiritual states (*états d'oraison*), 57–8, 62, 63–76, 78, 79, 88
spiritual teaching, xvii, 135–146, 148, 151, 160–1
tradition, view of, 1–2, 12–17, 22–5, 27, 45–5, 53, 89
Trinity, 67–9, 72, 81–4, 96
union with God, 54, 58–9, 64, 65, 69, 71, 79, 81, 84–5, 87, 96, 98, 100, 134–5, 142, 155, 158
Ursulines, 71, 95, 98, 138
victimhood, xvi, 66n.,75, 76, 77, 84, 88, 157, 166, 167
Virgin Mary, 28, 30, 75, 90
Writings: correspondence, xvi, 15, 28, 47, 85, 100, 106, 111, 113, 114, 116, 117–33, 135–7, 149–51, 155–6, 158, 159; *Entretien spirituel sur l'Épouse des Cantiques*, 138–144, 161; *La Relation de 1633*, 51; *La Relation de 1654*, 15–16n., 21, 52, 53, 56–89, 91, 99, 107, 145, 149, 151, 158, 161, 162, 171, 172; *Supplément à la Relation de 1654*, 98
Marquis, T.G. 111n.
Marshall, J., 27n.
Martène, Dom E., 14

Martin, C., the elder, 40, 41, 42, 43
Martin, C., the younger, 19, 29n., 42, 47, 50–2, 85, 106, 137, 149–50, 151
Mason, M.G.., 61n.
McGinn, B., 171
Ménard, M., 11
Michel, A., 9n.
Michel, R., 48n.
Michelet, J., 13
Montaigne, M. de, 125
Moussé, Ch., 28n.
Mullett, M., 6n.

Neill, S., 108n., 109n., 110.
Neri, P., 149
New England, xiv, 127, 164, 172
New France, xiv–xvii, 73–4, 88, 90, 93, 101–7, 110–14, 119, 121, 125, 127, 150, 164, 165, 167
Nock, A.D., 32, 35–6, 42n.

Oberman, H., 5n., 8–9n.
O'Brien, E., 57n., 78n., 84n.
Ohly, F., 70
Ong, W., 56n.
Oury, Dom G.-M., xvi–xvii, 13n., 14n., 15, 18, 20, 22–3, 24n., 26n., 29n., 30, 40, 41, 48, 52n., 54n., 67n., 80, 84n., 113n., 136n., 141n., 154, 166, 167n., 168n.

Pagden, A., xiii
Pascal, J., 19
Paul, 39, 55, 73, 77
Pénido, M.T.-L., 63n., 80n.
Philip of the Trinity, 153-4
Pierron, J., 129
Poissant, S., 168n.
Poulain, A., 57n., 58n., 66n., 67n., 68n., 71n., 83n., 84n., 86, 94n., 96n., 137n., 138n., 152, 153n., 154n.
Pouliot, L., 102n., 105n., 114n., 125n., 167n.
Pseudo-Dionysius, 38

Québec, xviii, 111. *See also* New
   France
Quimby, G. Irving, 131n.

Ragueneau, P., 167
Raymond de St. Bernard, 92, 96
Reardon, B., 8n.
Renaudin, P., 97n.
Rétif, A., 99n., 134n.
Richard of St. Victor, 164, 165
Ricoeur, P., 163n.
Riehle, W., 78n., 79n., 81n.
Rouen, 169
Roustang, F., 169n.
Roy, P.-G., 95n.
Runggaldier, E., 145n.
Ruysbroeck, J., 164

St. Jure, Jean Baptiste de, 63n.
Sandeus, M., 135n.
Scholem, G., xv
Sheldrake, P., 170n.
Skinner, Q., 147n.
Spitz, L.W., 3n., 78n.
Sullivan, J., 57n., 63n., 66n.
Suso, H., 153

Taylor, C., 1n., 2n, 34n, 172n.
Teresa of Avila, xv, 21–2, 29, 38, 53,

60, 65n., 68n., 72n., 73n., 86, 87,
   141, 146n., 151n., 153, 165
Thiry, A., 48n., 64n., 80n.
Thomas Aquinas, 100n.
Thwaites, R.G., xiiin., 101n., 104n.,
   105n., 106n., 110n., 112n., 114n.,
   115n., 121n., 122n., 125n., 126n.,
   127n., 128n., 129n., 131n., 132n.,
   167n., 169n., 173n.
Todorov, T., 170n.
Tours, xviii, 13, 14–17, 24, 98, 103,
   119, 150
Trigger, B., 101n., 111., 116, 117n.,
   121n., 122n., 131, 132n.
Trois Rivières, 116

Underhill, E., xvn., 57n., 58n., 62n.,
   70n.

Vimont, B., 122
Virgin Mary, 28, 30, 74–5, 90, 130,
   131, 137, 168
Vovelle, M., 39n.

Warner, M., 10n.
Weintraub, K., 1n., 59n., 60n., 61n.,
Wilenski, R.H., 15n.
Wynne, J., 111n.

Zakai, A., xivn.

INDEX OF SUBJECTS

accommodation, Jesuit policy of, 109, 110, 131

action and contemplation, xv, 86, 93–4, 139, 165, 168–9, 171

Algonkins, 114

A.M.D.G. (Ad Majorem Dei Gloriam), 56

Amerindians, 61, 73, 74, 89, 103, 110–33, 148, 170, 173
 culture, xiv, xvii, 106, 109, 123–8, 132–3
 Marie's views on, 103–4, 123–31

Augustinians, 112–13

autobiography, 59–62, 77, 89
 Marie's spiritual autobiography, 52, 56–7, 60–2, 63–89, 77, 103, 106–7, 125, 150, 152, 156, 162

baptism, 14
 of Amerindians, 114–18, 127–8, 147

beatific vision, 147, 149, 152–6

capacitas Dei, 24

Capuchins, 24

Carmelites, 16, 95, 166

Catholic Reformation, xiv, xvi, xviii, 4–13, 5–6n., 36–7, 51, 73, 108–112, 164, 171

Church,
 early church, 105, 119
 in France, 13–16, 166
 in Middle Ages, 4–5
 in New France, xiv–xv, 166
 in Reformation, 4–5, 173

Cistercians, 166

cognitio Dei experimentalis, 69

Company of New France (Company of the One Hundred Associates), 110

contemplation, 86, 93–4
 infused as opposed to acquired, 46–7, 94, 98, 99, 138
 contemplative ideal, 96, 139, 143–4

conversion,
 in Christian tradition, 36–7, 42, 54–5
 in 17th century, 32–40, 54–5, 106–7, 135, 157
 Marie's views and experience of, 35–55, 62–3, 74, 78–9, 80, 83, 95, 103, 106–7, 113–19, 125, 133, 135, 157, 161–3
 missionary approach to, 37–9, 103, 110, 112–33
 mystical conversion, 135, 148, 157
 second conversion, 46–7, 161
 social and psychological theories of, 32–6
 spiritual conversion, 1, 37–8, 136, 148, 161

Council of Trent, 6, 9, 12

counter-reformation, 5. *See also* Catholic Reformation

creatio ex nihilo, 3n.

cultural anthropology, 34, 145

Dominicans, 16, 108

Edict of Nantes, 13

Estates General, 16

Feuillants, 24, 95, 96

formation, idea of, 2–4, 132–3

francisation, missionary policy of, 122

Franciscans, 108

glory of God, 56, 106–7, 110, 146–8,
150–4, 156, 161

Hurons, 76, 97, 114, 126

image of God, 3n., 78–9, 81, 83,
169–70
images,
Marie's use of, 157–9, 160, 161
missionary use of, 128–32, 138
mystical images, 143, 145–6
reform controversy over religious
use of, 10, 142
imitation of Christ, 62, 79–81, 105
Iroquois, 74, 76, 114, 116, 118, 120–1,
131

Jesuits (Society of Jesus), xiii–xiv, 46,
50, 56n, 60, 105, 108–15, 119,
121–32, 168–9

martyrdom, 29, 168
Minims, 14
missionary activity,
and Amerindian culture, xiv, 109,
111, 112, 122–33
in the Americas, 97, 109, 111
in Canada (New France), xiii, 74,
91–3, 97, 101, 102–7, 110–32
in China, 109
in Far East, 109
in India, 109
in the Indies, 109
in Mexico, 110
in Peru, 110
inner mission as opposed to overseas, 37
in sixteenth and seventeenth centuries, 108–11
of Jesuits, xiii, xiv, 108–15
mysticism,
Christian tradition of, xv–xvi, 38,
79, 86–7, 162, 164, 170–1
conservative element in, 53
French school, xvi,
in seventeenth century, xiv, xvi
literary expression, 158–62, 171–2

mors mystica, 104, 159
mystagogy, 148–9, 150, 151, 159–60
mystical union, 58–9, 69, 80–7, 96,
98–100, 140, 143–4, 155, 156, 158,
159, 164, 165

New World, 39, 88, 89, 90, 92–3, 102,
104, 110, 112, 164
idea of, xiii–xiv, xvi
spiritual identity in, 164–73
Marie's encounter with, 90, 93,
106–7

Oratorians, 22

paideia, 3–4
Port-Royal, 50
Protestant reform, 2, 5–13, 18–20, 37,
127
Puritans, xiv, 127, 164, 172

Quietism, 76n., 86

Recollets, 111, 123
réductions, 111
Relations, Jesuit, xiiin., 101, 104n.,
105n., 106n., 110n., 112n., 113,
114n., 115n., 121n., 122n., 125n.,
126n., 127n., 128n., 129n., 131,
132n., 167n., 169n., 173n.
retables, 11

sacraments, 13–14
Sacred Heart of Jesus, 67
saints, 14–15, 20, 39
salvation of souls, 108, 110, 116–17,
118
scientific revolution, xiii
sola scriptura, 8
Song of Songs, 24, 70, 86, 87, 138
Marie's commentary on, 138–44,
151, 157
Spirit of Jesus, 81, 90–1, 97
spiritual direction, 137, 141, 144, 149,
151
spirituality
active-passive aspects, 86–7

history of xv, 37–8, 88, 145, 164, 170–1
in Catholic Reformation, xviii, 73, 164, 171
in New World, xiv, 105, 106, 164, 166
spiritual literature, 145, 162, 172–3
spiritual marriage, xvi, 58, 68, 81, 87, 88, 140, 164
spiritual theology, xiv, 58, 83–6, 147–8, 152, 159, 160, 171, 172

threefold pattern of mystical ascent, 55
tradition
    Amerindian, 121–33
    Christian, 61, 93, 128–32
    Marie's view of, 1–2, 12–17, 22–5,

27, 45–6, 53, 89
Protestant and Catholic views of, 8–12
role in conversion, 43, 53, 54–5, 162–3
travel literature, xiii, 113, 170
Trinity, 27, 67–72, 78, 81–6, 96, 100, 134, 159

Ursulines, xiv, 71, 74, 95, 97, 98, 112–13, 119, 120, 134, 138–9, 149, 150, 154

via illuminativa, 58, 67, 78, 79, 86
via purgativa, 58, 64, 74, 79, 86
via unitiva, 58, 63, 66, 78, 81, 86
Visitation, Order of the, 50
vita activa and *vita contemplativa*, 101

Studies in the History
of Christian Thought

EDITED BY HEIKO A. OBERMAN

Recent volumes in this series:

55. NELLEN, H. J. M. and RABBIE, E. (eds.). *Hugo Grotius – Theologian*. Essays in Honour of G. H. M. Posthumus Meyjes. 1994
56. TRIGG, J. D. *Baptism in the Theology of Martin Luther*. 1994
57. JANSE, W. *Albert Hardenberg als Theologe*. Profil eines Bucer-Schülers. 1994
59. SCHOOR, R.J.M. VAN DE. *The Irenical Theology of Théophile Brachet de La Milletière (1588-1665)*. 1995
60. STREHLE, S. *The Catholic Roots of the Protestant Gospel*. Encounter between the Middle Ages and the Reformation. 1995
61. BROWN, M.L. *Donne and the Politics of Conscience in Early Modern England*. 1995
62. SCREECH, M.A. (ed.). *Richard Mocket, Warden of All Souls College, Oxford, Doctrina et Politia Ecclesiae Anglicanae*. An Anglican Summa. Facsimile with Variants of the Text of 1617. Edited with an Introduction. 1995
63. SNOEK, G.J.C. *Medieval Piety from Relics to the Eucharist*. A Process of Mutual Interaction. 1995
64. PIXTON, P.B. *The German Episcopacy and the Implementation of the Decrees of the Fourth Lateran Council, 1216-1245*. Watchmen on the Tower. 1995
65. DOLNIKOWSKI, E.W. *Thomas Bradwardine: A View of Time and a Vision of Eternity in Fourteenth-Century Thought*. 1995
66. RABBIE, E. (ed.). *Hugo Grotius, Ordinum Hollandiae ac Westfrisiae Pietas (1613)*. Critical Edition with Translation and Commentary. 1995
67. HIRSH, J.C. *The Boundaries of Faith*. The Development and Transmission of Medieval Spirituality. 1996
68. BURNETT, S.G. *From Christian Hebraism to Jewish Studies*. Johannes Buxtorf (1564-1629) and Hebrew Learning in the Seventeenth Century. 1996
69. BOLAND O.P., V. *Ideas in God according to Saint Thomas Aquinas*. Sources and Synthesis. 1996
70. LANGE, M.E. *Telling Tears in the English Renaissance*. 1996
71. CHRISTIANSON, G. and T.M. IZBICKI (eds.). *Nicholas of Cusa on Christ and the Church*. Essays in Memory of Chandler McCuskey Brooks for the American Cusanus Society. 1996
72. MALI, A. *Mystic in the New World*. Marie de l'Incarnation (1599-1672). 1996
73. VISSER, D. *Apocalypse as Utopian Expectation (800-1500)*. The Apocalypse Commentary of Berengaudus of Ferrières and the Relationship between Exegesis, Liturgy and Iconography. 1996

Prospectus available on request

E. J. BRILL — P.O.B. 9000 — 2300 PA LEIDEN — THE NETHERLANDS